5926

291

CONFRONTING

THE NEW

**HOW TO
RESIST
A GROWING
RELIGIOUS
MOVEMENT**

AGE

DOUGLAS R. GROOTHUIS

foreword by Walter Martin

INTERVARSITY PRESS
DOWNERS GROVE, ILLINOIS 60515

InterVarsity Press is the book-publishing division of InterVarsity Christian Fellowship, a student movement active on campus at hundreds of universities, colleges and schools of nursing. For information about local and regional activities, write Public Relations Dept., InterVarsity Christian Fellowship, 6400 Schroeder Rd., P.O. Box 7895, Madison, WI 53707-7895.

Distributed in Canada through InterVarsity Press, 860 Denison St., Unit 3, Markham, Ontario L3R 4H1, Canada.

All Scripture quotations, unless otherwise indicated, are from the Holy Bible, New International Version. Copyright © 1973, 1978, International Bible Society. Used by permission of Zondervan Bible Publishers.

Cover illustration: Roberta Polfus

ISBN 0-8308-1223-7

Printed in the United States of America

Library of Congress Cataloging in Publication Data

Groothuis, Douglas R., 1957-
    Confronting the new age.

    Bibliography: p.
    Includes index.
        1. New Age movement—Controversial literature.
2. Witness bearing (Christianity)   3. Apologetics—
20th century.   I. Title.
BP605.N48G76   1988   299'.93   88-13016
ISBN 0-8308-1223-7

17   16   15   14   13   12   11   10   9   8   7   6   5   4   3   2   1
99   98   97   96   95   94   93   92   91   90   89   88

To Lillian C. Groothuis, my mother, for her unfailing love,
devotion and concern.
To Paul and Jean Merrill, for their powerful prayers, abiding love
and boundless enthusiasm.
To Becky Merrill Groothuis, my partner in ministry.
And to the Giver of all these good gifts.

Foreword

In his first book, *Unmasking the New Age,* Douglas Groothuis demonstrated an excellent grasp of the Hindu-based philosophy of the New Age movement and its theological incompatibility with the Judeo-Christian religion of the Bible. It provided a much needed balance to the religious paranoia and conspiracy theory alarmism espoused by other less informed and theologically limited authors. In this companion volume he continues his mature and readable analysis of the New Age, concentrating primarily on the practical aspects of sharing the gospel with those trapped in the movement's tentacles.

After outlining New Age religion and pointing out its nature as a counterfeit faith, Groothuis proceeds to describe steps to confront people in the New Age movement and gives some helpful hints about a proper Christian approach.

What interested me, and in fact is worth the price of the entire volume, is his three chapters on witnessing to New Agers and the guidelines he succinctly sets forth. Groothuis covers such topics as the Bible, reincarnation, the doctrine of God, Christ and Christian morality. His chapter on education for a New Age underlies a sobering fact that "the Aquarian Conspirators" are "more involved in education than any other single category of work." Here he puts his finger on the festering ulcer of the penetration of New Age thinking into the American educational system.

Throughout the book Groothuis maintains a balanced approach and sees New Agers as objects of evangelism, souls for whom the Lord Jesus Christ died. The book is very strong in its defense of Christianity. His philosophical insights and theological discernment make it a provocative exposé of the world of the occult from an orthodox Christian perspective.

When he deals with the future of the New Age movement he is

quite correct: "The New Age intoxication with a mystically endowed evolutionary process is inferred from insufficient data. The many problems with macro-evolutionary theory—such as the dearth of fossil evidence for transitional forms, the stasis (relative unchange-ableness) of species, and the radical discontinuity between humans and animals (concerning abstract thought, speech and cultural infor-mation) is conveniently ignored in favor of evolution as the engine of enlightenment, with an impersonal God somehow at the helm."

The New Ager stands at the end of the assembly line of the evo-lutionary hypothesis and blindly proclaims that the process designed and created the finished product. This is akin to standing at the end of the assembly line at the General Motors plant in Detroit and pro-claiming that the Cadillac rolling off the assembly line was created and designed by the machinery! The engineering department which designed the Cadillac demonstrated organized thought, mathemat-ical precision and, above all, efficiency of design. Life on earth surely deserves equal consideration with the assembly of an automobile! Both are the product of superior intelligence of a personal nature; the assembly lines are the means to that end, *not* the end itself.

In Groothuis's appendix he speaks of "event-specific evangelism" which is "street evangelism"—in his own words, "where the Christian brings the gospel directly to the non-Christian in a public manner." Such an appendix is a very usable tool.

This is an important book, the first of its kind written by a dedi-cated, philosophically oriented Christian scholar and apologist. It is notable for its fidelity to the Scriptures and for its sophisticated theo-logical viewpoint.

It is my conviction that it will have a wide distribution and con-structive effect in both the proclamation and defense of the gospel.

Dr. Walter Martin
Founder and Director of Christian Research Institute
May 1988

Preface

These days demand spiritual discernment. My previous book, *Unmasking the New Age,* attempted to explain the rise, extent and nature of the New Age movement and to subject it to a Christian critique. *Confronting the New Age* attempts to build on that foundation by developing strategies for reaching New Agers and confronting New Age cultural advances with the truth of Christianity.

Although there is some similarity between chapter one and the first chapter of *Unmasking, Confronting* is not a rehashing of old material but rather a further development of many of the ideas addressed in the first book. I have also tried to stay abreast of recent trends within the New Age movement not elaborated in *Unmasking,* such as channeling and New Age music. Nevertheless, one need not read *Unmasking* to understand this book—although together they form a fairly comprehensive treatment of the subject.

Having just spent two days rechecking my footnotes, I hope my readers will avail themselves of them! Often I cite classic pieces of Christian literature by Calvin, Augustine, Pascal or others well worth investigating. I also sometimes cite authors I largely disagree with— such as Hans Küng—if they are making a particularly good point. As an evangelical Christian I feel free to utilize truth wherever found.

Although this book is written primarily for Christians, I hope and pray that those sympathetic with the New Age movement will read it also, particularly chapters one, four, five and six which defend the Christian message against the New Age challenge. Nothing I have written should be interpreted as advocating the restriction of New Agers' religious freedom. I seek to persuade, not coerce.

I want to thank James Sire, Gordon Lewis and Eric Pement for their helpful comments on the entire manuscript and Richard Watring for his suggestions on "New Age Business." My editor, Michael Maudlin, has been a great help throughout the editing process.

My greatest debt of gratitude, though, goes to Becky Merrill Groothuis, my wife, who crucially contributed to the structure, content and style of _Confronting_. Without her intellectual and spiritual assistance, this book would not have been written.

Laying the
Foundation

I

The Challenge of the New Age Counterfeit

1

Back ground

T WENTY CHRISTIANS KNELT IN PRAYER THE NIGHT BEFORE NEW YEAR'S EVE.
They came from different churches scattered throughout the greater
Seattle area to meet at the office of a campus ministry. Many of them
had not met before, and probably would not meet again; yet they
were one in purpose. They would get little sleep that night. It would
be spiritual warfare; something had to be done.

Their aim was to confront the New Age movement with the gospel.
Their target was the Seattle Kingdome, which from midnight until five
in the morning would house the "World Peace Event," sponsored by
a host of New Age groups in the Seattle area. Similar events were
being held worldwide with the hope of bringing peace through
collective meditation. The idea was that if enough people would simultaneously harmonize their positive energy—at twelve noon,
Greenwich mean time—this would create a "critical mass" of con-

sciousness which would in turn paranormally galvanize and tranquil-
ize the consciousness of the entire planet and catapult us into a New
Age. —

Controversy over the apparently harmless event—who could be
against world peace?—had been stirred up in the previous days as
informed Christians seeded the media with little-known facts. Although it was hailed as ecumenical and interfaith, the "Peace Event"
was inspired by John Randolph Price, a New Age writer who teaches
that everyone should affirm, "I and the Father are one, and all the
Father has is mine. In truth I am the Christ of God."[1] He also tars as
"anti-Christ" those under-evolved, ignorant ones who deny "the divinity of all men" (pantheism).[2]

The public was also apprised of the fact that Mr. Price was on good
terms with an "awakened one" (spirit-guide) named "Asher" who
informed him that "Nature will soon enter her cleansing cycle" in
which individuals with "lower vibratory rates" (monotheists like Jews,
Christians and Muslims) will be "removed from the planet during the
next two decades."[3]

These metaphysical musings were reiterated on five thousand leaflets distributed by the twenty Christian volunteers in the chilly morning air to those entering the Kingdome. The leaflet also highlighted
Christ's message of true peace for those who come to him in faith.[4]

A few minutes before the "hour of peace" was to commence, the
last of the five thousand leaflets were handed out. Four of the Christians decided to attend the event and made their way into the sta-
dium to observe and pray for those involved. They heard a Science
of Mind minister prepare for the "hour of peace" by delivering a New
Age homily. He concluded his talk with a quotation from Emerson to
the effect that prayer was reflecting on the facts of life from the
highest point. Some in the audience adjusted their postures for yoga;
some chanted; many visualized world peace, convinced that their
mental act could help harness positive energy worldwide.

The hour began with twenty minutes of highly repetitive "New Age music" (which we will analyze in a later chapter) followed by ten minutes of silence; more music followed until, near 5:00 A.M., a chorus led the seven thousand pilgrims in a droning song written for the event, called "We Are One Love." At the end of the song, the faithful throng lifted their hands over their heads . . . and it was over.

At the risk of being labeled antipeace, antilove and, of course, intolerant, these Christians took a stand. That's what this book is all about: taking an informed, compassionate stand for the gospel by confronting the spiritual deception of the New Age movement.

But just what is the New Age movement? And how has it affected our culture? To stand against something, we need to understand what it is we oppose and why. The following outline of New Age thought should help explain its world view and also, through examples, show how it is penetrating our world.

An Old/New Counterfeit

In 1930, G. K. Chesterton observed that "We hear much about new religions; many of them based on the very latest novelties of Buddha and Pythagoras."[5] The *New* Age movement is not new; it is the most recent repeat of the second oldest religion, the spirituality of the serpent. Its impulse is foreign to none of us. The appeal is ancient indeed; its rudiments were seductively sold to our first parents in the garden. Human pride was tickled, and it jumped.

The offer was to forsake God's way of life and to believe the serpent's promise that in rebelling against God they could "be as gods" and would not die. In essence, they could gain power and knowledge apart from God, and suffer no ill effect. Satan lied; Adam and Eve complied; and we all died.[6]

Most all New Age prophets, politicians, educators, business people, scientists and entertainers try to sell us on the idea that we can "be as gods." Either directly or indirectly they reject as a malignant mythology the Genesis account of our descent into sin. Yet they echo the deception of the serpent by teaching that we can save ourselves, that we need not cry out to God above and that we can heal the planet.

﹏ *The New Age movement* is an umbrella term referring to a variety of people, organizations, events, practices and ideas. Sociologically speaking, it is not a centrally organized movement with one human leader. Although it includes cults, sects and even denominations, it is not restricted to any one of these. Rather it is a constellation of like-minded people and groups all desiring a spiritual and social change that will usher in a New Age of self-actualization. Usually this scenario entails that we throw off both traditional monotheism (Judaism, Christianity, Islam) and secular humanism (rationalism, atheism, skepticism). Scores of New Age groups—whether they concern holistic health, politics, science, religious cults or psychology—loosely coordinate their efforts through "networking," making contacts through any available media. The Seattle "Peace Event" was a clear example of such networking.[7]

﹏ People identifying with the New Age Movement have different levels of involvement and commitment. Some dabble with astrology or occult visualization but have yet to commit themselves wholeheartedly to any organization. Others commit themselves to various groups in various degrees, whether they be holistic health associations, New Age dating services, cult groups or religious denominations such as Unity or Religious Science. Even in some Christian denominations, there are those who have embraced—knowingly or unknowingly—New Age viewpoints and practices. ﹏

﹏ The ideas and practices of the New Age also cover a broad range of plausibility. Some New Agers claim their ideas are supported by august disciplines such as quantum physics,[8] while others embrace exotic beliefs—of the *National Enquirer* variety—with little concern for intellectual respectability. ﹏

Although the history of serpentile religion is as old as it is varied—captivating poets, philosophers, politicians and pedestrians on every continent in every century—its resurgence can be traced most recently in the West to the counterculture of the 1960s in America and Europe.[9]

At that time ideas and practices traditionally held at bay by a Christian consensus (or the memory of one) began to burst on the scene. Youth overthrew as much of Western civilization as possible (stereos excepted). The West welcomed the East and tasted its mysteries as a flood of gurus, yogis and swamis swarmed society. Mind-altering drugs—hawked by intellectual apologists such as Aldous Huxley, Alan Watts and Timothy Leary—were hailed as liberating. Sexual morality was first up for grabs, and then down for the count. Besides introducing a score of new religious movements, the counterculture also fanned the embers of various Eastern, mystical and occult ideas which had made their way westward since the eighteenth century, and which had been propagated by Transcendentalism, Theosophy, Anthroposophy, Unity, Religious Science and others.

The hippies may be gone, but the effect of the counterculture remains. The age of exotic, Eastern "guruism" may be waning, but the gurus' teachings are not. What was once on the esoteric periphery has moved into the spotlight. Much of what used to be underground is seeping—if not rushing—into the mainstream, as a plethora of New Age teachers, practices and events contend for our souls.

This multifaceted phenomenon poses a tremendous challenge to Christians. The New Age is more than a passing fad—although it is not without faddishness; it is a deep cultural trend attracting scores of people from all walks of life. It claims to offer spiritual reality, fulfillment and world harmony. Yet its promises spring from what turns out to be a spiritual counterfeit.

Scripture repeatedly speaks of spiritual counterfeits, warning of counterfeit Christs (Mt 24:5; Acts 5:36-37), counterfeit prophets (Deut 13:1-4; Mt 7:15; 24:11), counterfeit miracles (Ex 7:8-13), counterfeit angels (2 Cor 11:14), counterfeit gods (Gal 4:8), counterfeit good works (Mt 7:15-23), counterfeit godliness (2 Tim 3:5), counterfeit converts (1 Jn 2:19; 2 Cor 11:26), counterfeit spirits (1 Jn 4:1-3), counterfeit doctrine (1 Tim 4:1-3) and counterfeit gospels (Gal 1:6-10). ⌐

To sort the genuine from the counterfeit requires biblical discernment, not just the identification of New Age buzz words like *holistic* and *global.* A rich knowledge of the genuine article—biblical Christianity—throws the counterfeit into clear relief.

Despite the diversity within the New Age movement, several of its unifying ideas can be distilled into its basic world view, which are summarized below into nine beliefs or doctrines. After describing each concept we will compare it with the biblical world view. As we will see, the New Ager and the Christian scan the world through very different lenses. Thus they answer life's ultimate questions of purpose, value, significance and meaning quite differently.

1. Evolutionary Optimism: A Counterfeit Kingdom

The New Age movement teaches that we are poised on the edge of a quantum leap in consciousness as evolution surges upward. We face a great time of both planetary crisis and opportunity. Some New Agers sound apocalyptic tones, warning that without a massive raising of consciousness, the planet will face severe catastrophes that will "cleanse" it from error. (Exactly what is meant by *cleansing* varies. Some think in terms of a peaceful transition; others believe that non-New Agers must be somehow disposed of. See chapter ten for more on this.)

Yet there remains a general optimism that we are moving into a New Age of spiritual discovery—called the Aquarian Age in astrological lore. We must wake up to "the divine within" in order to usher in the millennium. New Age utopians envision a New World Order— sometimes described as involving a one-world government, global socialism or New Age religion—wherein self-realized righteousness dwells. Some individuals and groups expect a world leader, sometimes (falsely) called "the Christ," to show us the way to the New Age. Others emphasize personal direction and shun any outside guidance.

Christians have traditionally confessed the Creator God as Lord over history. He is making the reality of his kingdom known. We turn to him and his Word for social righteousness as well as for personal salvation and holiness. Christians should reject any mystical utopianism (counterfeit kingdom) as ignorant at best and deadly at worst. Hitler, Stalin and Mao were utopians, but they were ruthless in instituting their particular brand of a "New Age." Thirsting for heaven on earth, they delivered hell instead. This may not be true of all utopians, but we should be wary of all attempts of humanity to create its own heaven. Christians live in the anticipation that history will culminate in a literal, physical and visible return of Jesus Christ in power and glory, and not in a New Age brought about by some immanent evolutionary process.

2. Monism: A Counterfeit Cosmos

All is one. One is all. The musical refrain for the "World Peace Event" mentioned earlier was "we are one love; we are one." The event was geared toward this "realization"—there is no separation; there are no ultimate boundaries; we are but waves in one cosmic ocean. Annette Hollander writes that "the more we can experience our interconnectedness [oneness], the less willing we will be to destroy each other and the world."[10] She suggests that this realization should be the focus of developing our children's spirituality. (This will be taken up in chapter seven.)

The idea that all is one—monism—is contrary to the biblical view of God's creation as a wondrous diversity of created things not reducible to a mystical oneness. Genesis 1:2 records that at the onset of God's creation "the earth was formless and empty." He spoke the word, and plurality burst forth in trees, animals, clouds, humans and a million things more. "God saw all [plural] that he had made, and it was very good" (Gen 1:31). The New Age viewpoint, in a sense, seeks to return to the formless and empty primeval soup and sinks therein. It must dismiss the diversity of creation—which we must presuppose in order to perform philosophical tasks such as counting (above one) and kissing (someone else)—as somehow unreal.[11]

All things have a common Creator and are sustained by Christ (Heb 1:3). In this sense we live in a *uni*verse, not a *multi*verse. God unifies history according to his will. But the unity of God's plan does not destroy the real differences in his creation. Likewise, Jesus taught the unity of his followers as the body of Christ (Jn 17), as did Paul (1 Cor 12:12-31), and yet this unity is not the undifferentiated oneness taught by the New Age. All people will one day stand before their Maker as individuals. None will have their case dismissed by dissolving into the great ocean of Being.

3. Pantheism: A Counterfeit God and Humanity

The great Oneness of Being is thought to be "God." All that is, at metaphysical root, is God.[12] Robert Ellwood observed during the early seventies that the new religious movements shared "the common metaphysical characteristic" of an impersonal view of God, in which "the absolute itself is not the personal Judeo-Christian God, but some more abstract entity, usually capitalized, like 'Infinite Intelligence,' 'Principle,' etc."[13] We could add to this list "the Force," "Consciousness," "Energy" and so on. The New Age "God" is not a moral Being worshiped as supreme. Such a God is an impersonal and amoral it, not a he (or she, for that matter—all the "earth goddess" language notwithstanding). Furthermore, the Deity is democratized: We are all God.

Shirley MacLaine's concluding credo from her best-selling book *Dancing in the Light* hits the pantheistic nail on the head: "I *know* that I exist, therefore I AM. I know the God-source exists. Therefore IT IS. Since I am part of that force, then I AM that I AM."[14]

The biblical Deity is a moral Being as Isaiah declared, "For the LORD is our judge, the LORD is our lawgiver" (Is 33:22). God the Creator revealed to Moses through the burning bush that "I AM WHO I AM" was his divine name (Ex 3:14). This uniquely designated him as personal, uncreated and self-existent. Jesus Christ, God the Son, owned that name when he proclaimed to a stunned Jewish audience, "Before Abraham was born born, I am!" (Jn 8:58). Since they did not recognize Jesus as the Messiah, their reaction was swift and telling: they lunged for rocks with which to stone him for blasphemy (see Lev 24:16). Yet today a self-deifying Ms. MacLaine dodges no angry projectiles. She is safe dancing in the spotlight. People hurl praises and money.

Self-deification is now as popular as it is unbiblical and unrealistic. The New Age takes the truth that we are made in God's image and warps it to mean we are all gods. The same "impossible dream" was at the heart of the serpent's temptation, as Hexam and Poewe make clear: "At the heart of the fall is the desire for sudden and total freedom and power, unrestricted by the limits of the human condition. . . . The Bible presents the fall as an act of unrestricted self-indulgence based on the impossible desire to be like God. Instead of leading to freedom, it results in bondage."[15]

4. Transformation of Consciousness: Counterfeit Conversion

It is not enough merely to believe New Age teachings. They must be experienced. New Agers are often encouraged to be initiated, not just interested. Many mystical means serve the same exotic end, whether they be non-Christian meditation techniques, drugs, yoga, martial arts, the use of crystals or spontaneous experiences such as near-death encounters. The end is a feeling of oneness with everything that is, and the realization of one's own divinity, sometimes called the "Higher Self."

The lure of such transcendental experiences is their supposed superiority to conventional "old age" religion and "ordinary consciousness"—the state of mind while doing the dishes or mowing the lawn, for instance. The resulting state of awareness has many names such as "at-one-ment" (biblical *atonement* redefined), self-realization or God-realization (the two are interchangeable), enlightenment and attunement.

Rather than preaching repentance from sin, the New Age pushes reawakening to self. The New Age counterfeit replaces prayer (communication with a personal God) with meditation (the journey within the self). It exalts experience of self above faith in Christ, and thus is a counterfeit of genuine Christian conversion. Instead of teaching the necessity of being born again from above, it teaches the rediscovery of the true, inner and divine self.

5. Create Your Own Reality: Counterfeit Morality

The phrase "create your own reality" is often intoned in New Age circles as a basic premise. The idea is that we are not under any objective moral law. Rather, we all have different ways to realize our divine potential. And since "all is one" (monism), we can't slice up life into categories like good versus evil. That is too dualistic; we must move "beyond good and evil" in order to realize our full potential. A supposed spirit-guide named Ramtha teaches that God—of which we are all a part—is neither good nor bad. God does not judge. No one sins, and there is no need for forgiveness. Ramtha continues: "Every vile and wretched thing you do broadens your understanding. . . . If you want to do any one thing *regardless* of what it is, it would not be wise to go against that feeling; for there is an experience awaiting you and a grand adventure that will make your life sweeter."[16]

Not all New Age teaching is this extreme, but New Age ethics is largely unrooted in any objective moral order. If New Agers assert moral absolutes, they usually do so more instinctively than reflectively. Some may speak of the law of karma as regulating moral rewards and punishments in reincarnation, but the notion of morality is usually relativized or jettisoned entirely.

Biblical morality is anchored in the unchanging moral character and will of a personal God, who has issued the Ten Commandments, not the ten suggestions. Christians become more spiritual in thought, character and deed by obeying the will of their Lord, not by pretending to create their own rules as they go along.

6. Unlimited Human Potential: Counterfeit Miracles

If we are all God it is thought that the prerogatives of the Deity pulsate within. We arc cndowed beyond measure. We are miracles waiting to happen. Untethered from such old-age fables as human finitude, depravity and original sin, we are free to explore the luminous horizons of godhood. Ignorance is our only problem. In *Dancing in the Light* Shirley MacLaine insisted to an underachieving friend, *"You are unlimited. You just don't realize it."*[17]

The unlimited ones yearn for mastery of self and cosmos (if such a distinction is even permitted). Knowledge of "the God within" results in power over all. A host of subliminal tapes are now hitting the market promising to transform us through reprogramming the subconscious to do whatever we want. In essence, the subconscious is deified. An inaudible voice track mixed below the music level tells us we will lose weight, have a better self-image or even be open to our Higher Self and psychic potential.[18] Whether it be through subliminal tapes or a hundred other means, a panorama of the paranormal promises power—ESP, telepathy, clairvoyance, precognition (predicting future events), remembrance of supposed past lives (reincarnation), psychic healing, out-of-body experiences, divination, even psychokinesis or PK (affecting objects through sheer mind power). Consciousness is key. We are not fettered by an external and objective reality (whether spiritual or physical); rather we "create our own reality."

A Dallas newspaper covered a conference attended by a hundred and fifty Seth devotees who practiced the principle that "we literally create our reality through the beliefs we hold, so by changing those beliefs, we can change reality."[19] Sethian conferees thus put on a "spoon bending party" during which they were told that they could make silverware as soft as putty simply through nonphysical mind power. The news report claims that one-third of the spiritual spoon benders were successful, including a confirmed skeptic who predicted that "PK (psychokinesis) parties are going to become like the Pet

Rock and the Hula Hoop."[20] Whether anything paranormal occurred is debatable, yet the fact remains that people are enticed by such reports to further investigate New Age claims.

Paranormal possibilities have even interested the legal profession. A lead story in *The National Law Journal* reported that "Defense lawyers in two celebrated murder cases—the trial of Jean Harris for the shooting of Scarsdale Diet author Dr. Herman Tarnower, and the prosecution of Joan Little for stabbing a North Carolina guard—consulted psychics to help pick the juries."[21] The legitimacy of psychic testimony is still a matter of intense debate, with most courts being reluctant to admit it. "Nonetheless, more lawyers these days are consulting psychics for personal and professional reasons."[22] This includes the prestigious tort lawyer Melvin M. Belli who claims to have profitably used psychics "a couple of times in picking a jury." One Los Angeles-based legal research group, the Mobius Society, assigns seven to eleven psychics to each criminal case.[23] Some police departments are also consulting psychics for leads on crimes.[24]

Whatever may be the accuracy and frequency of this psychic detection, such an interface between the established field of law and the purportedly paranormal socially reinforces the notion of innate psychic abilities.

Although many of these paranormal reports may be fraud or misinterpretation, the Bible warns of the reality of counterfeit miracles malevolently engineered by the Enemy. A supernatural Creator can and does miraculously intervene in his creation for the purpose of demonstrating his reality; yet counterfeits abound for the purpose of deceiving the world. (See chapter two for further discussion.)

7. Spirit Contact: Counterfeit Revelations

Seth, the philosopher behind the silverware stretching, is a discarnate entity who communicated twenty books worth of revelations through the late Jane Roberts. Seth is but one of a galaxy of masters, entities, spirits, extraterrestrials and other talkative types who communicate (via either automatic writing or vocalization) through mediums—who are more recently called "channelers" (an apt title for the television age). Channeling has always been tied up with the New Age, but is now gaining more popularity as channelers address large audiences and engage in extensive private consultations. Earlier channelers influential in the West included H. P. Blavatsky, Edgar Cayce and Alice A. Bailey.

In 1888, H. P. Blavatsky, cofounder of the influential Theosophical Society in 1875, claimed to have received the two-volume *The Secret Doctrine* from the higher planes.

Edgar Cayce (1877-1945), known as the "sleeping prophet," was also a New Age precursor for channeling, and is still quite popular through the work of the Association for Research and Enlightenment (ARE). Cayce's revelations on the so-called lost years of Jesus, reincarnation, Atlantis and other occult topics were supposedly derived from our collective consciousness and were not channeled from a particular spirit. Yet Cayce's readings were given by a voice not his own (often in languages he had never learned), concerned subjects he knew little or nothing about and directly contradicted the Bible—three good reasons to consider demonic involvement.[25]

The idea of channeled material also gained popularity through the voluminous writings of Alice A. Bailey who claimed to be in contact with the Tibetan teacher Djwhal Khul (or DK). Between 1919 and her death in 1949 she "wrote two dozen books on occult philosophy, most of which claimed to be his teachings" which "present a comprehensive system of esoteric science and occult philosophy, cognizant of contemporary social and political developments."[26] Bailey's writings help make up one of the roots from which the New Age movement has sprung.[27]

New Age channeling adds a "higher" dimension to the older spiritualism movement of a century ago which was often content to summon the departed spirit of a relative for a few post-mortem comments concerning accommodations in the afterlife. According to

New Age writer Brad Steiger, "this new kind of channeling" concerns messages which seem to come from "a higher source, and here I mean a more abstract source, a source that deals with universal principles or laws."[28] The "new kind of channeling" thus becomes more of a counterfeit of biblical prophecy because the true prophets in the Bible were sent by God to proclaim his universal truth, not just particular bits of information.[29] Prominent New Age teacher and writer David Spangler has claimed contact with several entities, one of whom bears the expansive name "Limitless Love and Truth."[30]

An entity of some repute is one "Ramtha," a thirty-five-thousand-year-old warrior who channels through J. Z. Knight, a rural Washington housewife who first met him in 1977 after experimenting with crystal pyramids. Since then, Ramtha has put on the metaphysical ritz in appearances on the "Merv Griffin Show" and satellite TV, public speeches and expensive private consultations. As recorded in *Dancing in the Light,* Ramtha was one of Shirley MacLaine's favorite spirit guides. MacLaine claims that Ramtha was one of two spirit guides who entered and energized her body during one of her Broadway performances when she was too physically drained to perform adequately alone.[31]

Ms. Knight claims to lose normal consciousness when channeling Ramtha. Her countenance becomes masculine and authoritative as Ramtha preaches that we are all God, that we have infinite potential, that we "create our own reality," that we are bound by no moral absolutes and (naturally) that we will not be judged by God. Among other things, Ramtha claims to be infinite.

Ramtha's slick, high-profile image has been lampooned even in New Age circles.[32] But the social impact is real, as is the influence of other channelers such as Kevin Ryerson, a friend of Shirley MacLaine's who claims to have channeled entities on MacLaine's nationally televised autobiographical miniseries, *Out on a Limb.* Ryerson believes the revelations are important: "Entities or spirit beings . . . have important implications to us as human beings . . . because of the insight and factual information that has come through."[33]

Predictably, the doctrines espoused by the entities are less than biblical. Some channelers supposedly give vent to biblical characters and some even claim to channel Christ himself, whom they have saying some particularly unchristian things such as, "The sayings in the Epistles and in the Gospels and in Revelation to the effect that my blood saves from sin are erroneous."[34] The supposedly channeled material—by "Jesus" again—of the three-volume *A Course in Miracles* has gained a large following, with 160,000 of the expensive sets published since 1975 and over 300 American groups organized around its New Age teachings which use Christian phrases but deny all cardinal Christian doctrines.[35]

Such "revelations" cause us to remember the apostle Paul's stern warning that "even if we or an angel from heaven should preach a gospel other than the one we preached to you, let him be eternally condemned!" (Gal 1:8). The channeled "gospel" is one of self-deification, relativism and reincarnation.

Whether any particular channeler is involved in actual demonic activity (where deceiving spirits impersonate various characters), is mentally unbalanced or is engaged in New Age histrionics or forgery, the message conveyed—and often believed—is the New Age gospel, which is based on counterfeit revelations imitating the revelation of Christ and the Bible.

8. Masters from Above: Counterfeit Angels

In much of New Age thought the distinction between the extraterrestrial and the spiritual is blurred when UFO sightings and even encounters ("of the third kind") become mystical experiences. UFOs (and their passengers) are sometimes claimed to exhibit paranormal phenomena. Hynek and Valle comment,

> If UFOs are indeed somebody else's "nuts and bolts hardware," then we must still explain how such tangible hardware can change shape before our eyes, vanish in a Cheshire cat manner (not even

leaving a grin), seemingly melt away in front of us, or apparently "materialize" mysteriously before us without apparent detection by persons nearby or in neighboring towns. We must wonder too, where UFOs are "hiding" when not manifesting themselves to human eyes.[36]

Those supposedly contacted by the UFOs often display traits common in other kinds of occult phenomena such as a trance state, automatic writing, peering into crystals, the poltergeist effect, levitation, psychic control, psychic healing and out-of-body experiences.[37]

A shift in science-fiction writing in the mid-1960s prepared the public to view extraterrestrials more mystically. The futuristic scientific scenarios of writers such as Isaac Asimov were challenged by New Age authors such as Ursula LeGuin who "offer us a world inhabited by spirit beings motivated by magical spells rather than Martians, spaceships, and ray guns."[38]

In Shirley MacLaine's *Out on a Limb* she claims that an extraterrestrial named "the Mayan" instructed one of MacLaine's spiritual counselors to lead MacLaine into the New Age.[39] They are supposedly servants from the stars.

Some groups claim that the more evolved "Space Brothers" have much to teach us so that we might avoid a planetary catastrophe; and you can guess the message is not biblical. David Spangler notes that many groups have tuned in to the Space Brothers' frequency. The message is that earth will experience tremendous changes before the New Age fully arrives. A "cleansing" must take place; but, on the positive side, he says that much of the material received from "on high" was "uplifting, speaking of the Divinity within all life which would most surely triumph over the difficulties of the moment."[40]

Spangler later records the cosmic comments of an entity named "John" who says that "some of the space Beings . . . are actually *very high hierarchal Beings and Masters* [spirit guides] who adopt planetary garb simply because there are some people who will accept their teachings only in that way. . . . There has been a good deal of beneficent masquerading going on."[41] Christians should reinterpret the situation as very possibly the malevolent masquerading of some very low demonic beings and monsters.

9. Religious Syncretism: Counterfeit Religion

New Age spirituality is a rather eclectic grab bag of Eastern mysticism, Western occultism, neopaganism and human potential psychology. But New Age spokespeople tend to view the true essence of all religion to be one. For example, Elizabeth Burroughs, a "Christian mystic" in the Northwest, divides religious expression into the "literal" and the "deeper." She claims that the "deeper teachings of Christian philosophy" are "in harmony with all other religions."[42] If externals appear different—say, between Hindu pantheism and Christian theism—an appeal is made to a supposedly mystical core that unites all religions: All is one, all is God, we are God, we have infinite potential, we can bring in the New Age.

This mystical method rides roughshod over the express teachings of the nonpantheistic religions, but the New Age claims that the supposedly "esoteric" elements in these religions have been suppressed. The New Age confidently (but groundlessly) affirms, for instance, that reincarnation was extracted from the Bible in the sixth century by power-hungry clerics because, according to Ruth Montgomery, "it was so much easier for the church to control the masses if they thought they had only one lifetime to do it right. . . . If people thought they could come back again and again, they might not be nearly as supportive of the church."[43] (Her contention will be disputed in chapter five.)

To make their case, New Age teachers sometimes enlist the testimony of assorted Jewish, Muslim and Christian heretics who claim to be one with God. In so doing, they mistake the deviant for the normative. They embrace a counterfeit instead of the genuine.

Christians reject syncretism on at least three counts. First, it disregards the historical differences between religions. Second, it distorts Christianity by making it fit onto a pantheistic Procrustean bed. Third, it demotes Jesus Christ to merely one of many masters enshrined in the pantheistic pantheon, a position he expressly denied by claiming to be "the way and the truth and the life" (Jn 14:6).[44]

Rather than being a mere fad, the New Age movement is a substantial cultural trend that is not destined quickly to blow away in the wind. It offers Christians a deep challenge to unmask and lovingly confront a very potent spiritual counterfeit. In the following chapters we will lay a foundation for confronting the New Age, discuss specific areas of New Age evangelism and apologetics, deal with the rise of New Age concepts in business and education, consider important issues in discernment and ponder the future of the New Age movement.

Before proceeding, a challenge from Martin Luther is in order: "If I profess with the loudest voice and the clearest exposition every portion of the truth of God except precisely that little point which the world and the devil are at that moment attacking, I am not confessing Christ, however boldly I may be professing Christ."

Notes

[1]John Randolph Price, *The Planetary Commission* (Austin, Tex.: Quartus Foundation, 1984), p. 157.

[2]Ibid., p. 163.

[3]John Randolph Price, *Practical Spirituality* (Austin, Tex.: Quartus Foundation, 1985), pp. 18-19.

[4]The leaflet is reprinted in the appendix.

[5]G. K. Chesterton, *The Thing: Why I Am a Catholic* (New York: Dodd, Mead, 1930), p. 174.

[6]For a perceptive explanation of the Fall, see Augustine *City of God* 14.13.

[7]On the New Age conspiracies see Douglas Groothuis, *Unmasking the New Age* (Downers Grove, Ill.: InterVarsity Press, 1986), pp. 33-36; and Spirtual Counterfeits Project Staff, "The Final Threat: Cosmic Conspiracy and End Times Speculation," in Karen Hoyt, ed., *The New Age Rage* (Old Tappan, N.J.: Revell, 1987), pp. 185-201.

[8]See Groothuis, *Unmasking,* pp. 93-109, for the dissenting view.

[9]The best Christian critique of the counterculture is by Os Guinness in *The Dust of Death* (Downers Grove, Ill.: InterVarsity Press, 1975).

[10]Annette Hollander, *How to Help Your Child Have a Spiritual Life* (Bantam: New York, 1980), p. 12. ·

11For a variety of criticisms of monism see C. E. M. Joad, *The Recovery of Belief* (London: Faber and Faber, n.d.), pp. 164–76.

12On the varieties of pantheism see Normal Geisler, *Christian Apologetics* (Grand Rapids, Mich.: Baker, 1981), pp. 173–92.

13Robert S. Ellwood, *Religious and Spiritual Groups in Modern America* (Englewood Cliffs, N.J.: Prentice-Hall, 1973), p. 29.

14Shirley MacLaine, *Dancing in the Light* (New York: Bantam, 1985), p. 420.

15Irving Hexam and Karla Poewe, *Understanding Cults and New Religions* (Grand Rapids, Mich.: Eerdmans, 1986), p. 86.

16Quoted in Martin Gardner, "Issness Is Her Business," *New York Review*, April 9, 1987, p. 18.

17MacLaine, *Dancing in the Light*, p. 133.

18For a somewhat skeptical look at this trend see Art Levine, "The Great Subliminal Self-Help Hoax," *New Age Journal* (February 1986), pp. 48ff.

19Jennifer Beoth Donovan, "Seth Followers Spoon Up Fun in Their Goal to Enjoy Living," *The Dallas Morning News*, July 1, 1986.

20Ibid.

21Mary Ann Galante, "Psychics: Lawyers Using Seers to Help Select Juries, Find Missing Children," *National Law Journal* (January 27, 1986), p. 1.

22Ibid., p. 2.

23Ibid.

24See Ron MacRae, *Mind Wars* (New York: St. Martin's Press, 1985), pp. 8–14.

25For a thorough treatment of Cayce see Gary North, *Unholy Spirits* (Tyler, Tex.: Dominion Press, 1986), pp. 193–225.

26Bruce F. Campbell, *Ancient Wisdom Revived* (Berkeley: University of California Press, 1980), pp. 151–52.

27See Groothuis, *Unmasking*, pp. 119–20; and Campbell, *Ancient Wisdom Revived*, pp. 150–55.

28Brad Steiger, *Revelation: The Divine Fire* (Englewood Cliffs, N.J.: Prentice-Hall, 1973), pp. 42–43.

29See Abraham Heschel, *The Prophets* (U.S.A.: Jewish Publication Society of America, 1962), p. 472.

30See David Spangler, *Revelation: Birth of a New Age* (Scotland: Findhorn, 1976).

31MacLaine, *Dancing in the Light*, pp. 128–31.

32See Schuyler Ingle, "Heeere's Ramtha!" *New Age Journal* (June 1986), p. 12.

33Mark Vaz, "The Many Faces of Kevin Ryerson," *Yoga Journal* (July/August 1986), pp. 26–27.

34Steiger, *Revelation*, p. 52.

35See Dean C. Halverson, "A Course in Miracles: Seeing Yourself as Sinless," *Spiritual Counterfeits Project Journal* Vol. 7, no. 1 (1987), pp. 18–29.

36J. Allen Hynek and Jaques Valle, *The Edge of Reality: A Progress Report on Unidentified Flying Objects* (Chicago: Regnery, 1975), pp. xii–xiii, quoted in North, *Unholy Spirits*, p. 300.

37Jacques Valle, *Messengers of Deception* (New York: Bantam, 1980), pp. 33, 224–25.

38Hexam and Poewe, *Understanding Cults*, p. 30.

39For a Christian critique of UFOs see North, *Unholy Spirits*, pp. 288–328; also, Ellwood,

Religious and Spiritual Groups, pp. 131–56, gives sociological observations.
[40]David Spangler, *Links with Space* (Marina Del Ray, Calif.: Devorss, 1978), pp. 10–11.
[41]Ibid., p. 34; emphasis mine.
[42]Quoted in Krysta Gibson, "Christian Mystic to Debate Christian Attorney at Seattle Center," *Seattle Times,* January 10, 1987.
[43]Quoted in Florence Graves, "Searching for the Truth," *New Age Journal* (January/February 1987), p. 28.
[44]Groothuis, *Unmasking,* pp. 146–57.

Spiritual
Warfare

2

An ATTRACTIVE AND SOFT-SPOKEN FORTY-YEAR-OLD WOMAN CONVERSED with two spunky hosts on an afternoon television program before a live audience. She seemed quite average and a bit ill at ease. Why was she being interviewed? What had the large audience come to see? The woman wasn't a Hollywood actress, a politician, a noted intellectual, a comedienne or—in herself—very special.

Then the program cut to a film clip where J. Z. Knight, the woman being interviewed, enters a trance in order for the entity Ramtha to be channeled through her. We see her on a stage seated in a luxurious chair, surrounded by flowers and Ramtha's followers. Mrs. Knight becomes very still and begins to breath deeply. She then contorts, and her head is tossed about for a few seconds. Strange growling sounds accompany the transformation. Her face seems changed in appearance. Then she stands erect in jerky, almost marionette-like motions.

Ramtha has arrived. He speaks in a masculine tone with a nondescript accent (possibly lower Atlantian). Ramtha's followers hang on every occult oracle.

The program cuts back to J. Z. The hosts are not skeptical. They want to know where J. Z. is when Ramtha holds forth.

Angels and Demons

In this television program, spiritual poison was liberally dispensed over the airwaves and into the souls of thousands. Whether or not Mrs. Knight was actually demonized, the occult was made to look very appealing. Those watching might develop further interest by reading Ramtha's books or by attending seminars not far from where the program was aired.

A Christian foundation for confronting the New Age must be rooted in an awareness of spiritual warfare. Both Christianity and the New Age movement enthusiastically affirm the reality of the spiritual world. But their topographies differ greatly.

The New Age strives to achieve an altered state of consciousness that triggers unlimited potential. Spirit guides may be there to help us evolve.

For Christians, the Bible, properly interpreted (see chapter five), serves as our foundation for discerning spiritual realities (Ps 119; Acts 17:11; 2 Tim 3:15-17). There we learn that the spirit world is populated by both good (angelic) and bad (demonic) spirits.

Angels are the "messengers" of God sent to do his will, usually behind the scenes. The Bible never tells Christians to cultivate conscious relationships with angels, although they do visibly appear throughout both the Old and New Testaments. After the great revelation to the apostle John, John says, "I fell down to worship at the feet of the angel who had been showing [the visions] to me. But he said to me, 'Do not do it! I am a fellow servant with you and with your brothers the prophets and of all who keep the words of this book. Worship God!' " (Rev 22:8-9; see also Col 2:18). Angels are unfallen, spiritual beings obedient in consciously implementing God's will. They're on the side of God and his redeemed people. "For he will command his angels concerning you to guard you in all your ways" (Ps 91:11; see also 34:7). Elisha discovered the protection of the angelic host when the angry king of Aram sent a strong force of horses and chariots to wipe out the prophet. In consoling his frightened servant, Elisha said, "Those who are with us are more than those who are with them." This truth was soon evident to the servant whose eyes were opened to see "the hills full of horses and chariots of fire all around Elisha" (2 Kings 6:16-17).[1]

Demons are fallen spiritual beings (2 Pet 2:4; Jude 6) disobedient to the declared will of God, under the direction of the devil (Mt 25:41). They are not impersonal influences, but personal agents of the Adversary. Michael Green notes that the Bible credits them with "at least four of the criteria we should want to apply to personality": they have knowledge (Mk 1:24; Acts 19:15); they have emotion (Mk 1:24: Jas 2:19); they speak (Acts 19:15); and they have will power (Mt 12:44).[2]

Popular opinion to the contrary, demons are very much involved in the common—and not so common—affairs of everyday life. In tribal cultures they hold entire populations in bondage through animism, the belief that everything has a spirit that must be placated through ritual magic.[3] But demons—and their director—are also being welcomed by increasing numbers of "civilized Westerners" through numerous occult practices, including divination (tarot cards, I Ching, runes, psychic readings), trance channeling (mediumship), non-Christian meditation or other potentially demon-inducing or demon-inspired activities, all expressly forbidden and called "detestable" by Scripture (Deut 18:9-14; see also Is 8:19-20; 47:8-14; Gal 5:19-20: Rev 22:15). Although detestable to God, delightful to the devil, unhealthy for humans and impotent to save (Is 47:12-15), the occult draws adherents like metal to a magnet because "it gives rein to the religious instinct deep within a person but does not make upon him any claims for love, holiness, or service to others."[4]

The Father of Lies

Christians should know their "enemy the devil" (1 Pet 5:8), but only well enough to discern, disarm and denounce him. Christians should carefully ration their knowledge of the occult, always careful to avoid becoming experts in "Satan's so-called deep secrets" (Rev 2:24). The occult may be fascinating, but it is not edifying; it should only be studied by those who put themselves under Christ's protection and who are called to bring the victory of Jesus to bear on individuals and cultures spiritually oppressed by Satan.[5] And despite whatever good intentions New Agers may have, it is Satan, the spiritual counterfeiter himself, who ultimately inspires all false religion.

Jesus called Satan "the evil one" (Mt 5:37; 6:13; 13:19), stressing his malevolent, immoral motivation. His evil emanates from his unyielding opposition to a good God. Jesus describes him as "a murderer from the beginning, not holding to the truth, for there is no truth in him. When he lies, he speaks his native language, for he is a liar and the father of lies" (Jn 8:44).

But he is not a stupid liar, casually tipping his hellish hand. Rather, he is "the tempter" (Mt 4:3; 1 Cor 7:5; 1 Thess 3:5) who mixes just enough truth with falsehood to make the falsehood seem true—and intensely appealing. When tempting Jesus, he quoted Scripture, though radically out of context and with wrong intent. The devil tempts by deception. Paul tells us that in the garden, Eve was "deceived by the serpent's cunning" (2 Cor 11:3). He is a crafty liar. Paul says that "Satan himself masquerades as an angel of light" and his servants masquerade as "servants of righteousness" (2 Cor 11:14).

The New Age offers "light"; it twists the Bible; it tempts our pride by offering us godhood; it takes the truth that we are made in God's image (Gen 1:26) and inflates it to the falsehood that we are God. Irenaeus, Bishop of Lyons in the second century, knew the reality of the devil's deceptions. In responding to the Gnostic heresies of his day he declared, "Error, indeed, is never set forth in its naked deformity, lest, being thus exposed it should at once be detected. But it is craftily decked out in attractive dress, so as, by its outward form, to make it appear to the inexperienced more true than the truth itself."[6]

The devil's influence is wide but not total. His jurisdiction is limited and he has no tenure. God alone owns the earth and is sovereign over creation (Ps 24:1-2). Satan is called "the god of this age" because he has "blinded the minds of unbelievers, so that they cannot see the light of the gospel of the glory of Christ" (2 Cor 4:4; see also Eph 2:2). As a supernatural being he and his minions can exert supernatural influence on the natural world through "counterfeit miracles, signs and wonders" (2 Thess 2:9; see also Ex 7—8; Rev 13:13; 16:14)[7] and full-fledged demonization, as many of the Gospel accounts reveal. Satan is the "ape of God." He is not creative, but rather a spiritual counterfeiter; he issues, endorses and engineers illicit imitations of good for evil purposes.

The Bible urges us "to resist the devil" (Jas 4:7) because we are in combat conditions, with no demilitarized zones available this side of heaven. C. S. Lewis warned us that "there is no neutral ground in the universe: every square inch, every split second, is claimed by God and counterclaimed by Satan."[8] As Calvin declared, we are involved in kingdom warfare: "If we are animated with proper zeal to maintain the kingdom of Christ, we must wage irreconcilable war with him who conspires its ruin."[9] James Kallas says:

> A war is going on! Cosmic war! Jesus is the divine invader sent by God to shatter the strengths of Satan. In that light, the whole ministry of Jesus unrolls. Jesus has one purpose—to defeat Satan. He takes seriously the strengths of the enemy.[10]

Defeating the Devil

Jesus has indeed defeated Satan! John declares that "the reason the Son of God appeared was to destroy the devil's work" (1 Jn 3:8). Christ triumphed over sin, death and the devil by his crucifixion and resurrection (Heb 2:14; Col 2:14-15). It is in his power that Christians wage their spiritual war as loyal soldiers of the risen King. Any other allegiance is to no avail. Paul should inspire us in this. When opposed by false teachers seducing the Corinthian church, Paul said,

For though we live in the world, we do not wage war as the world does. The weapons we fight with are not the weapons of the world. On the contrary, they have *divine power* to demolish strongholds. We demolish arguments and every pretention that sets itself up against the knowledge of God, and we take captive every thought to make it obedient to Christ. (2 Cor 10:3-5; emphasis added)

Paul takes on false teaching, not in his own strength, but by wielding God's weaponry. He is on the offensive. Confrontation with New Age forces requires the same empowerment.

Because of Christ's victory over Satan, James can say to Christians, "Submit yourselves, then, to God. Resist the devil, and he will flee from you. Come near to God and he will come near to you" (Jas 4:7-8). As we submit to Christ's lordship we are given authority to scuttle Satan. Christians are no longer under "the dominion of darkness" (Col 1:13). God alone has ultimate cosmic authority, and he teaches citizens of his kingdom to pray that his "kingdom [may] come . . . on earth as it is in heaven" (Mt 6:10). After his resurrection, Jesus charged the disciples to "make disciples of all nations" because he had "all authority in heaven and on earth" to make it happen (Mt 28:18-20). He still does.[11]

Jesus is Victor, but the victory is being progressively executed through his people. The outcome is sure, but the battle rages on. The German theologian Oscar Cullman likened Jesus' crucifixion-resurrection victory to D-Day, the turning point of World War II when the victory of the Allied forces was assured. Yet from this decisive point until the actual end of the war in Europe (called V-E Day) the combat continued. The soldiers still fought, but with a renewed vision for victory. Such is the Christian's position: all will be completed at Judgment Day, and so we should fight the good fight of faith today.[12]

Paul gives us the essentials for Christian combat in Ephesians 6.

He reiterates that "our struggle is not against flesh and blood, but . . . against the powers of this dark world and against the spiritual forces of evil in the heavenly realms" (v. 12). Therefore, he urges us to "stand [our] ground" by putting on "the full armor of God," which includes (1) "the belt of truth"—a deep knowledge of God's character and will as applied to our lives; (2) "the breastplate of righteousness"—a godly character; (3) "feet fitted with the readiness that comes from the gospel of peace"—a willingness to proclaim the gospel; (4) "the shield of faith"—the protection of complete trust in the Commander-in-Chief that "extinguish[es] all the flaming arrows of the evil one"; (5) "the helmet of salvation"—the assurance of a right relationship with God through faith in Christ; (6) "the sword of the Spirit, which is the word of God"—the offensive weapon of scriptural truth applied to all situations. Paul also adds that we should "pray in the Spirit" that our spiritual suit of armor might not slip off due to lack of closeness to God.[13]

Psalm 91 also offers rich assurance of the protection of the believer in the "shelter of the Most High" and in the "shadow of the Almighty" (v. 1). The psalmist later declares the believer's power over evil: "You will tread upon the lion and the cobra; you will trample the great lion and the serpent" (v. 13; see also Rom 16:20).

Power Encounters

The armored Christian is ready for encounters with the enemy, and there will be encounters any time the gospel is brought to bear on a Satanic stronghold such as the New Age movement. Many involved in the New Age may not believe in Satan or may not consciously contact spirit guides or may have no overtly ill intentions, but inasmuch as they reject the gospel of Christ for a counterfeit gospel they are of their "father the devil" (Jn 8:44). They believe the lie the serpent used in the garden; they want "to be as gods."[14]

Acts 13:6-12 gives us an example of a confrontation between opposing spiritual powers, which might be called a "power encounter."

We see Paul confront an occult deceiver, "a sorcerer and false prophet" known as Bar-Jesus or Elymas. We should remember that at that time the gospel was spreading like wildfire over the known world, as Jesus' resurrected power was being unleashed in preaching, healing, signs and wonders. The kingdom of darkness was being displaced by the kingdom of God. Conflict necessarily ensued.

Paul and Barnabas had come to Cyprus to preach the gospel. At Paphos they met a sorcerer who was "an attendant of the proconsul, Sergius Paulus" (v. 6). It was then common for political leaders to enlist occult assistance; and this was part of the demonic design that Jesus came to destroy. The proconsul sent for Paul and Barnabas because he was interested in the Word of God. But Elymas the sorcerer "opposed them and tried to turn the proconsul from the faith" (v. 8). Perhaps he figured that if his superior were converted he would be out of a job. Paul, filled with the Spirit, sprang into spiritual action. Staring down the official "secretary of sorcery," he condemned him as a "child of the devil" hell-bent on "perverting the right ways of the Lord" (v. 10). Paul then pronounced that he would be shut up by being blinded for a time. And he was. At this, the proconsul "believed, for he was amazed at the teaching about the Lord" (v. 12).

This power encounter manifests several critical points. First, the gospel was opposed by the sorcerer; spiritual warfare erupted. Second, Paul rose to the occasion, not by an outburst of human anger, but as he was "filled with the Holy Spirit." Then, and only then, did he have the authority to bind the evil attacker. Third, both the message and the miracle convinced Sergius Paulus, and he was converted. God's power through God's minister overcame the power of the enemy.[15]

As Christians do battle with New Age influences throughout Western culture they dare not forget that they are dealing with power encounters, not just interacting with ideas, individuals and events. We triumph "not by might nor by power, but by my Spirit, says the LORD Almighty" (Zech 4:6).

Signs and Wonders

The New Age tantalizes with its appeal to the paranormal, and according to a poll by sociologist Andrew Greeley and colleagues at the University of Chicago's National Opinion Research Council (NORC), more Americans are claiming to have experienced the paranormal in one form or another. In 1973, 27% of those polled claimed contact with the dead; in 1984, 42% did. In 1973, 58% claimed they had experienced ESP (extra sensory perception); in 1984, 67% did. In 1973, 24% claimed to experience clairvoyance; in 1984, 31% did. In 1973, 58% claimed to experience *deja vu;* in 1984, 67% did. Greeley notes that those who have "tasted the paranormal" are not "religious nuts or psychiatric cases. They are, for the most part, ordinary Americans, somewhat above the norm in education and intelligence and somewhat less than average in religious involvement."[16]

Greeley concludes his article by saying that whether the number of people claiming to have such experiences "is growing or they're just now ready to tell about it, that many people capable of trust can have a lasting effect on the country."[17] The New Age claim that we have unlimited access to the paranormal and the occult by virtue of our innate divinity is readily received.

Here again, spiritual discernment is crucial. We need to see that some paranormal activity is initiated by Satan, not by God. Satan and his demons have some room to influence the natural order for the sake of deception and spiritual bondage. The following chart makes clear the counterfeiting dynamic of demonic influences. As Kurt Koch notes, occult phenomena is in contradistinction to the biblical reality of *charismatic* (divinely inspired) phenomena.

- ☐ Messages from God (Lk 1:26) vs. spiritism
- ☐ Prophecy vs. clairvoyance
- ☐ Divine promises (Lk 1:76) vs. divination
- ☐ Testing the spirits (1 Jn 4:1) vs. mediumistic abilities
- ☐ The prayer of faith (Jas 5:14) vs. magic
- ☐ Healing by faith in God (Mt 16:17) vs. conjuring and psychic

healing

☐ Outpouring of the Holy Spirit (Acts 2) vs. psychokinesis/tele-kinesis

☐ Devoted surrender to Christ (Lk 5:28) vs. obsession with the occult

☐ Assurance of God's protection (Mt 28:20) vs. superstition (crystals, amulets, astrology and so on)

☐ Service of heavenly messengers (angels) (Acts 12:6–10) vs. spirit guides (demons)

☐ Anchoring of the soul in Christ (Heb 6:19) vs. out-of-body experiences.[18]

Any purported paranormal event should be interpreted according to the Word of God by those filled with the Holy Spirit, if true discernment is desired. As Koch comments, "The sign is in itself no indicator of the origin which inspires it. It requires the word of God as its interpreter and formal principle."[19] If someone is healed of cancer through the laying on of hands by biblically discerning Christians, this is a sign of the kingdom of God. Yet if a psychic healer heals a person of cancer (which is rare) by occult means, this is not from God, although the result—at least in the short run—is similar. As Deuteronomy 13 makes clear, even the appearance of the paranormal is not sufficient evidence to embrace false teaching:

If a prophet, or one who foretells by dreams, appears among you and announces to you a miraculous sign or wonder, and if the sign or wonder of which he has spoken takes place, and he says, "Let us follow other gods" (gods you have not known) "and let us worship them," you must not listen to the words of that prophet or dreamer. The LORD your God is testing you to find out whether you love him with all your heart and with all your soul. (Deut 13:1–3)

The principle is straightforward: Even the miraculous is not a sure sign of spiritual legitimacy. Test the spirits! (1 Jn 4:1–4). Just as trained agents test counterfeit money against the real thing—which they know by heart—so should Christians test everything against the real

Word of God (see Acts 17:11).

Furthermore, many miraculous claims may be merely that, claims. A good deal of outright fakery and self-delusion exists in New Age circles concerning the miraculous. A psychic, for instance, who appears to read her client's mind may have really consciously or unconsciously mastered "cold reading." This technique makes the unwary think their minds are being read when in fact the reader has learned to make general comments about the client which elicit specific information which she incorporates and expands on in her comments. Professional magicians often employ this trick with no supernatural assistance whatsoever.[20]

Whether paranormal phenomena are demonically induced or simply misunderstood natural occurrences, the result is often tragically the same: people are deceived into thinking they possess divine power.

Christian discernment, then, demands a realistic appraisal of any given miraculous claim that both realizes the reality of the supernatural and refuses to promiscuously invoke it.

Notes

[1]On angels and demons see John Calvin *Institutes* 1.14.3–19.

[2]Michael Green, *I Believe in Satan's Downfall* (Grand Rapids, Mich.: Eerdmans, 1981), p. 126.

[3]On the destructive effects on cultures of pantheism/animism, see North, *Unholy Spirits*, pp. 273–87.

[4]Green, *I Believe in Satan's Downfall*, p. 125.

[5]See North, *Unholy Spirits*, pp. 2–3, 18, 399; and Kurt Koch, *Occult ABC* (Grand Rapids, Mich.: Literature Mission Aglasterhausen, 1983), pp. 3–4.

[6]*The Writings of Irenaeus*, Vol. 1 (Edinburgh: T. & T. Clark, 1868), p. 2; quoted in Mark Albrecht, *Reincarnation: A Christian Appraisal* (Downers Grove, Ill.: InterVarsity Press, 1982), p. 105.

[7]Some argue that Satan and demons cannot perform miracles but only imitate them. I find this contrary to Scripture and other testimony. See Mark Albrecht and Brooks Alexander, "Biblical Discernment and Parapsychology," *Spiritual Counterfeits Journal* 4, no. 2 (Winter 1980-81), pp. 17–26.

[8]C. S. Lewis, *Christian Reflections* (Grand Rapids, Mich.: Eerdmans, 1978), p. 33.

[9]Calvin *Institutes* 1.14.15.

[10]James Kallas, *The Real Satan* (Minneapolis, Minn.: Augsburg, 1975), p. 60; quoted in

John Wimber with Kevin Springer, Power Evangelism (San Francisco, Calif.: Harper and Row, 1986), p. 13.

[11]On dealing with the demonic—especially in relation to healing—see John Wimber with Kevin Springer, Power Healing (San Francisco, Calif.: Harper and Row, 1987), pp. 97-125.

[12]Oscar Cullmann, Christ and Time (Philadelphia: Westminster, 1964).

[13]See Mark Bubeck, Overcoming the Adversary (Chicago, Ill.: Moody, 1984), pp. 64-137.

[14]On the Fall see Carl F. H. Henry, God, Revelation, and Authority, Vol. 6 (Waco, Tex.: Word, 1976), pp. 244-50.

[15]See also the power encounters between Elijah and the prophets of Baal (1 Kings 18:16-46), Moses and the magicians (Ex 7—8) and those described in Wimber with Springer, Power Evangelism, pp. 15-31.

[16]Andrew Greeley, "Mysticism Goes Mainstream," American Health (January/February, 1987), p. 48.

[17]Ibid., p. 49.

[18]Adapted from Kurt Koch, Christian Counseling and Occultism (Grand Rapids, Mich.: Kregel, 1981), p. 273. On classifying the paranormal see also Andrew Neher, The Psychology of Transcendence (Englewood Cliffs, N.J.: Prentice Hall, 1980), p. 137.

[19]Koch, Christian Counseling, p. 272.

[20]On the issue of faking the supernatural see Danny Korem, The Fakers (Grand Rapids, Mich.: Baker, 1980.)

Converting
a Culture

3

J UST AS SPIRITUAL COMBAT SKILLS ARE REQUIRED FOR EFFECTIVE MINISTRY, SO a renewed mind is a vital weapon in the arsenal for confronting the New Age. Strictly speaking, no real separation can be made between spiritual insight and renewed thinking. The two fit hand in glove.

Paul views intellectual renewal as a spiritual process. Our sanctification demands cognitive reformation. He urges us to be no longer conformed to this world but rather transformed through the renewing of our minds that we might know the will of God in every area of life (Rom 12:1-2). Although God may sometimes grant supernatural information, wisdom or insight, the ordinary way for us to know God's will is through the sanctification of our critical faculties, not through the "RPM method" (revelations per minute).

Richard Lovelace points out that "in our quest for the fullness of the Spirit, we have sometimes forgotten that a Spirit-filled intelligence is one of the powerful weapons for pulling down satanic strongholds." At the other extreme is an arid rationalism that trusts only in "inherent brain power, forgetting that only the Holy Spirit can effectively guide us in wielding the sword of the Spirit."[1]

An often neglected intellectual aspect of the New Age challenge is the question of the Christian's relationship to the culture in which he or she lives. Yet this will greatly influence just how Christians confront the New Age—or if they will confront it at all. The New Age movement is wielding considerable cultural clout, as we have noted. One area of culture after another is being touched—if not consumed—by a New Age orientation. The New Age agenda is to transform our society and the world. If Christians are to meet this challange effectively, we must have a biblical understanding of how we are to relate to culture.

What is _culture?_ Essentially, culture describes our way of life—how we interact with ourselves, our environment and God. It includes manners, morals, habits and artifacts. Culture differs from nature in that it is humanly engineered. People use the God-given material of the creation and give it the unmistakable human touch—of paintings, ceremonies, cooking, gardens and gulags. The creation gives us chunks of gold; humans—creatively endowed by virtue of being created in the Creator's image—create gold rings, necklaces, tooth fillings, crosses and Buddha figurines. Culture comes as people cultivate what God has created.

Cultures spring from the world views of the culture-formers. Henry Van Til puts it succinctly by saying, "culture is religion externalized."[2] Our social world results, to a significant degree, from our world view. Francis Schaeffer observed that "people are unique" in that the "results of their thought-world flow through their fingers or from their tongues into the external world. This is true of Michelangelo's chisel, and it is true of a dictator's sword."[3] Yet it is just as true that world views are influenced by a person's surrounding culture. Clearly, the biblical injunction is to base our thinking on God's transcultural truths and seek to apply them to our particular culture. But how should this be done in relation to the New Age's cultural impact?

There are at least three scriptural themes addressing a Christian's interaction with culture. They all contribute needed building materials for laying a foundation to confront the New Age.

Separation

All Christians should know enough to separate themselves from such New Age practices as "trance channeling," since the Old Testament strictly condemns mediumship (Deut 18:9-14). The Scripture makes plain that God's people are to have nothing to do with this "detestable practice" which calls forth God's judgment on cultures that practice it. There is absolutely no way to sanitize it or Christianize it. Christians are to be separate from it.

The idea of *separation* is central throughout Scripture. God chose the children of Israel to be a nation "set apart" from the surrounding paganism. When Israelites assimilated into the pagan culture instead of separating themselves, they were judged by God for their spiritual adultery. A good God gives principles of separation so that his people can maneuver through this fallen world without making any more trouble for themselves than is required in service to God. Being separate from sinful cultural patterns and separate unto God glorifies God, who himself is separate from all sin, being morally perfect. We are to be holy (or separate) because God is holy.

Psalm 1 teaches the wisdom of separation, warning us not to "walk in the counsel of the wicked, or stand in the way of sinners, or sit in the seat of mockers" (v. 1), lest we lose the blessing of separating ourselves unto God. The apostle John underscores this when he tells us not to love "the world or anything in the world," because it is all passing away (1 Jn 2:15, 17). John here does not mean to shun the entire world (creation) or avoid all of human culture, but rather to shun the worldly "cravings of sinful man, the lust of his eyes and the boasting of what he has and does" (v. 16).

James also teaches that "friendship with the world is hatred toward God" (Jas 4:4). Paul exhorts us not to be "conformed to this world" (Rom 12:2). Jesus repeatedly taught that total obedience to him means separation from evil in every form. "You cannot serve both God and Money," he said (Mt 6:24). Although Jesus socialized with outcasts and open sinners, he did not adopt their sinful ways. He was passionately involved, but without succumbing to cultural sin of any stripe.

Separation is crucial for confronting the New Age. The New Age perspective is antithetical to biblical Christianity. God is either personal or impersonal, not both; God is either moral or amoral, not both; people are either nondivine or divine, not both; there is either resurrection or reincarnation, not both; and so on. You cannot serve both God and the New Age. To be "New Age" is to build your house on sand and to be out of God's will, pure and simple. In a pluralistic culture where many perspectives are given equal respect, it is considered impolite to dispute the *truth* of another's beliefs. But the Christian must cry, "No! I cannot agree with pantheism, monism, relativism, spiritism and the rest. I will have no part. These beliefs are both false and dangerous."

If Christians hope to confront effectively, they cannot let themselves become prisoners of what they are confronting! Wherever culture is becoming New Age—or unbiblical in any form—we must be separate. If, for example, Christian parents find that the public school their son attends is teaching Eastern meditation (disguised as "centering" or "focusing"), they must not let their son take part. He must be separate, lest he become polluted by the world. (See chapter seven for specific strategies.)

Yet if *separation* is not complemented and balanced by *transformation* and *conservation* (discussed below), Christians may view themselves as "more separate than thou" and unwisely separate themselves to the extreme of retreating from legitimate cultural involvement.

Those who ignore the separation theme risk falling prey to the New Age by refusing to distinguish between the kingdom of God and the kingdom of darkness. They underestimate the potency and prevalence of error and thus condone it with silence. For example, a father may choose not to discuss his children's school life, only to find later that yoga was required in a physical-education class.[4]

Transformation

Christians believe that Jesus Christ is their Redeemer. He came to restore our fellowship with the Father through his atoning death on the cross and to restore our works that they might honor God (Eph 2:8-9). This necessitates our transformation. Paul says that if anyone is in Christ he or she is a "new creation" (2 Cor 5:17), and he exhorts us to "be transformed through the renewing" of our minds (Rom 12:2).

James Orr underscores the need for the renewed mind to develop a Christian world view:

He who with his whole heart believes in Jesus as the Son of God is thereby committed to much else besides. He is committed to a view of God, to a view of man, to a view of sin, to a view of Redemption, to a view of the purpose of God in creation and history, to a view of human destiny, found only in Christianity. This forms a "Weltanschauung," or "Christian view of the world" and stands in marked contrast with [other] theories.[5]

Separation cautions us to avoid the sinful patterns of fallen human culture. *Transformation* inspires us to apply our faith and Christian world view to the world for the glory of God (1 Cor 10:31; Col 3:17). From the beginning, God charged Adam and Eve to "have dominion" over (or to transform) the earth for his glory (Gen 1:26-28). We are called, notes Calvin Seerveld, "to exercise dominion over the whole earth, subdue it, make the world serviceable, turn all creation into a footstool that doubles its native praise of the Lord. God elected man . . . to rule the world and make the name of Yahweh reverberate from one end of the cosmos to the other."[6] That calling has not been revoked. Resisting evil is not enough. We must also march ahead to recapture territory—New Age or otherwise—too long held by Satan, the usurper.

Hans Rookmaaker makes this clear:

> The fact that Jesus Christ died to take upon Himself the sin of mankind is not just something for the "soul." The whole cosmos is to be redeemed, to be "brought back," for all things are under the curse of sin and evil. His saving grace, His offer of new life in all its fullness, for He is the Way, the Truth, and the Life, excludes no aspect of human reality.[7]

Although Christianity proclaims a world to come and does not see this world as the final frame of reference, it is passionately concerned with this world as the theater of redemption and the beginning of restoration. We pray "your kingdom come, your will be done *on earth* as it is in heaven" (Mt 6:10; emphasis mine). The kingdom of God has both a present and future reality. We pray and labor that the realities of God's kingdom may be manifest in all of life. John Stott forcefully states this:

> For the Kingdom of God is God's dynamic rule, breaking into human history through Jesus, confronting, combating, and overcoming evil, spreading the wholeness of personal and communal well-being, taking possession of his people in total blessing and total demand.[8]

The kingdom of God is expansive and aggressive.[9] Kingdom workers should not be content to divide "the sacred" (prayer, Bible reading, church attendance) from "the secular" (work, education, politics), but rather they should see everything in relation to the lordship of Jesus Christ. As Francis Schaeffer proclaimed, "True spirituality covers all of reality. . . . The Lordship of Christ covers *all* of life and *all* of life equally."[10]

If we only separate from and condemn evil, we may become merely reactionary—anti–New Age rather than pro-Christ. Our demonology becomes more developed than our Christology. Our constructive values—inasmuch as we develop them at all—take a back seat to our critical evaluations. Instead of seeking first the kingdom of God, we seek first to expose the kingdom of evil. We think more of hell than of heaven, and in so doing we surrender more cultural ground to the hordes of hell who are well disposed to advance where we retreat.

The kingdom of evil advances not only to claim "secular" ground which kingdom-citizens have abandoned, it advances into the "sacred" domain of the church itself. When Christians retreat from the world, they are easily overtaken by the world, which, governed by the kingdom of evil, is always seeking to advance. The only way the church can adequately resist this offensive is to mount a counter-offensive of God's kingdom. This is not the only reason we should make a sustained, prayerful effort to transform society, but it is certainly a sufficient one. The simple truth is, if we do not *confront* the world, we shall be *conformed* to it.

History witnesses that the Christian dynamic is world-transforming. Consider the effect of the early church on its surrounding culture:

The high conception that has been formed of the sanctity of life, the protection of infancy [from Roman infanticide], the elevation and final emancipation of the slave classes, the suppression of barbarous games, the creation of a vast and multifarious organization of charity, and the education of the imagination by the Christian type, constitute together a movement of philanthropy which has never been paralleled or approached in the pagan world.[11]

Christians *transformed* the pagan world.

We could add to Christianity's accomplishments the depaganizing of Europe; its contribution to Western political and religious liberties; its exalting of literacy and education; its establishment of hospitals; its working for social reforms such as abolishing slavery, overturning legalized widow burning (suttee) in India, establishing women's rights and—very recently—attempting to protect the unborn through legislative measures and the creation of homes for unwed mothers and crisis pregnancy centers. This transformational dynamic is both unmistakable and imperative. It is both demanded by Scripture and demonstrated in history.[12]

Parents who remove their child from a public-school classroom which is teaching occult practices *(separation)* must also try to rectify the problem. They should, as much as possible, try to *transform* the situation so that children—Christian or non-Christian—are not indoctrinated into the occult. (For strategies, see chapter seven.)

Conservation

Besides separating from evil and working to transform situations for God's glory, Christians are also called to *conserve* what is God-honoring in their culture. Although sin in the world provokes us to work for its cultural transformation, some pockets of culture are relatively pleasing to God and should be conserved. Properly identifying these areas calls for discernment and wisdom, for we should not conserve what should be rejected or transformed; yet neither should we reject or replace what should be conserved.

The concept of *conservation* is found in Paul's preaching to the Athenians. Though Paul was "greatly distressed" (Acts 17:16) at the Athenians' idolatry, he began his Mars Hill address by commending what was true in their philosophies. He first noted the religiosity evidenced by their worship of many idols, one of which had the inscription, "To an unknown God." Paul then said, "Now what you worship as something unknown I am going to proclaim to you" (v. 23). In proclaiming God as Creator and Lord who is nevertheless "not far from each one of us" (v. 27), Paul favorably quotes from the Cretan poet Epimenides who said, "For in him we live and move and have our being" (v. 28), and from the Cilician poet Aratus who said, "We are his offspring" (v. 28).

Yet after identifying religious themes that should be conserved,

Paul went on to decry the Athenians' idolatry, to call them to repentance and to proclaim the One who is risen from the dead (vv. 29-31).

Paul did not totally reject Greek philosophy. He knew that by God's grace some elements of truth remained—although the whole philosophical system was built on the shifting sands of mere human opinion. In fact, Paul separates himself from worldly thinking, insisting that the gospel is based on God's revelation, not human craftiness (1 Cor 3:19; Col 2:8-9). Yet he does not deny that "all truth is God's truth" wherever it may be found. As Lovelace comments:

> Clearly Paul does not rule out the possibility of encountering value, truth, and beauty in non-Christian culture since he advises Christians to let their minds dwell on "whatever is true, whatever is lovely, whatever is gracious, if there is any excellence [*arete,* the pagan Greek word for moral excellence which was also used in the Jewish and Christian communities for any manifestation of divine glory]" (Phil. 4:8).[13]

In saying that "all truth is God's truth" we do not mean that whatever people take to be true is, in fact, "true for them." That would be relativism; and to that the Bible declares, "Let God be true, and every man a liar" (Rom 3:4). Nor does it mean that human opinion is exalted to the status of biblical revelation. But it should be remembered that aspects of God's truth have been discerned worldwide by all people. This is what theologians call "common grace." Jesus said that God "causes his sun to rise on the evil and the good and sends rain on the righteous and the unrighteous" (Mt 5:45). To reject the truth which God has granted to unbelievers is to reject a gift from the ultimate source of the truth, God himself. But to accept truth from unbelievers is not to accept the ultimately false world view which has adopted it. Truth—wherever it is found—can only be from God.[14]

James Orr brings this together by pointing out that we can best defend Christianity (apologetics) by recognizing the truth wherever found and by integrating it into a distinctively Christian viewpoint. "If apologetic is to be spoken of, this surely is the truest and best form of Christian apology—to show that in Christianity, as nowhere else, the severed portions of truth found in all other systems are organically united, while it completes the body of truth by discoveries peculiar to itself."[15]

Conservation is vital in order that Christians not "throw the baby out with the bath water." First, of course, we need to determine whether there is a baby worth saving at all! Some New Age practices are irredeemable. There is no baby, but a monster! If so, the "baby" should be dumped along with the bath water. But not everything associated with the New Age movement is irredeemable. Some elements of New Age thought should be conserved precisely because they agree with a Christian perspective. For instance, Christian psychologists can agree with the New Age psychologists that humans are more than programmed animals, that they have real spiritual capacities that need to be exercised. Both agree that religious interests are not inherently neurotic. Both will stress "human potential"— although the Christian stresses the human potential of beings made in the image of God as they submit to the wise leadership of their Maker, Savior and Guide, while the New Ager stresses the unlimited potential of self-realized, human "gods."

For instance, although it is sometimes tied in to New Age ideas, Viktor Frankl's "logotherapy" resonates with and reinforces some crucial Christian themes. Frankl stresses the innate and basic human need for meaning and purpose in life, what he calls "the will to meaning." Yet many suffer, thinks Frankl, from an "existential vacuum" or meaninglessness. This may often be furthered by psychologists who fail to recognize the crying human need for an ultimate meaning that transcends lesser goals. The aim of logotherapy is to help people discover a higher purpose for their life. And Frankl is not opposed to Christianity as being someone's higher purpose.[16]

Frankl, although not a Christian, points to our need for God's ultimate direction and purpose, and to the fact that we are lost and alienated apart from a personal relationship with him. Frankl does not put his ideas in this Christian perspective, but many of his insights should be appreciated and *conserved* by Christians.

Someone who sees Frankl commended by a New Ager or who notes Frankl's attendance at a New Age conference might be tempted to dismiss his work entirely. But this would be a great mistake. There is, in this case, a "baby" to be conserved—but also some bath water to be thrown out. Christians often find friends in unlikely places—if they are looking.

Although Christians should help *conserve* a spiritual view of human psychology, they must *separate* themselves from any pantheistic assumptions (humanity is divine) or occultic practices (such as supposed "past-life hypnotic regression") that the Bible forbids. By taking the truths they find in these other psychologies and repositioning them within a system more consistent with Christian truths, they can *transform* psychology for the glory of God.[17]

Critical Engagement

Looking at the themes of separation, transformation and conservation concerning a Christian's relationship to culture, we reach what could be summarized as a position of "critical engagement." Our interaction with culture should be critical; all must be brought under the scrutiny of God's Word. From those things deemed to be evil, we need to *separate* ourselves, both in thought and action. Yet we are also called to be engaged, to *transform* culture for the glory of God and to *conserve* those aspects of culture that please him.

John Stott comments, "We cannot be totally 'world affirming' (as if nothing in it were evil), nor totally 'world-denying' (as if nothing in it were good), but a bit of both, and particularly 'world-challenging,' recognizing its potentiality as God's world and seeking to conform its life increasingly to his lordship."[18]

When separation, transformation and conservation are held in balance, Christians can intelligently and effectively confront the New

Age; yet without this balance they may easily fall into any of six different pitfalls.

Six Pitfalls

The Quarantine Mentality. Those with this tendency are rightly distrustful of the New Age world view and agenda, but they wrongly assume that anything approved by the New Age is therefore intrinsically evil and "off limits" for all Christians. Whatever the New Age touches is quarantined.

The problem with this pitfall is that it tends to tar with too wide a brush and thus paints black what may in fact be white or gray. It fails to recognize our responsibility to *conserve.* Paul warns the early church, "Test everything. Hold on to the good. Avoid every kind of evil" (1 Thess 5:21-22); thus he teaches the value of both *conservation* ("hold on") and *separation* ("avoid evil"). The quarantine mentality overemphasizes separation. For instance, the holistic health movement is significantly polluted by New Age ideas in various areas. Supposed occult energies—or even entities—may be invoked for healing purposes. Yet all that is holistic is not hellish. An emphasis on "the whole person" medically and spiritually is indeed healthy and not, in itself, incompatible with biblical teaching. Yet some have wrongly quarantined everything holistic.[19]

The Taboo Mentality. This second pitfall follows from the first. Since everything related to the New Age is out of bounds, our spiritual/intellectual discernment is exhausted by a simple list of taboo practices, ideas and individuals. Certainly, much that is New Age should be strictly and studiously avoided. No Christian—or non-Christian, for that matter—should ever take part in psychic healing, astrology, past-life therapy or any other occult activity. Christianity has plenty of "don'ts" (witness eight of the Ten Commandments, Ex 20:1-17). But the "taboo mentality" tends to substitute a list of taboos for *learning how to think discerningly.* It invokes simplistic black-and-white rules instead of cultivating the ability to understand critically the issues at hand.

The Paranoid Mentality. Awareness and avoidance of evil is a Christian virtue. But unhealthy fear of evil and vain speculations concerning its extent are not virtues.

This "paranoid mentality" can be both crippling and condemning, as Christians, lacking sufficient evidence, brand other Christians with such labels as "New Age" or "anti-Christ." It is, of course, sadly true that some New Agers hide under the guise of "Christianity" when in fact their teachings deny Christ himself. Such counterfeit Christianity must be unmasked and confronted. But where hurried condemnation replaces careful evaluation, the distinction between brotherly disagreement and heretical teaching may be sadly confused. Those who have sunk into this pitfall have little patience or energy to honor the transformation theme of Scripture. Their paranoid fears immobilize them, and they give up on transforming culture. They simply condemn it. They also misapply the separation theme—separating sheep from sheep instead of sheep from goats. The church is thereby divided against itself and is rendered less effective in all aspects of its mission.

The Chicken Little Mentality. Since the ascension of their Lord into heaven, Christians have expectantly awaited his descending from heaven at the end of the age (Acts 1:11). It is the "blessed hope" of all believers (Tit 2:13). Yet some believers have invested too much in calculating how New Age activities relate to particular end-time events. Some condemn the New Age primarily because they believe it fulfills biblical prophecy concerning the rise of evil in the world before the Second Coming. They have little more than this in their apologetic arsenal. Like those with the "paranoid mentality," they ignore the transformation theme. We shouldn't assume that God has given up on our or any other culture, although the threat of judgment should drive us to our knees and into the streets.

Jesus said to occupy until he comes again, not to be preoccupied with his coming.[20] The kingdom will come in its fullness only when

Jesus Christ returns; yet there is kingdom work to be done here and now. Apocalyptic speculations may narrow the vision of the church only to saving a few souls, rather than advancing as an army on earth for Christ, the King of creation. An apocalyptic apologetic may also seem hollow if the scenarios fail to materialize. Jesus calls us to transform the world for his glory, not to sit on our hands with eyes upraised to heaven, oblivous to our kingdom duties here on earth.

The Ostrich Mentality. The fifth pitfall differs in spirit from the first four. The "ostrich mentality" comes from a lack of awareness of the need for _separation_ and _transformation._ Some Christians dismiss the advance of the New Age into our culture as merely the figment of overactive imaginations. They stick their heads comfortably in the sands of ignorance. Their ignorance then ossifies into a spiritual impotence which leaves them helpless to unmask and confront New Age activity. Having not identified the phenomena, they cannot hope to transform a bad situation into a better one for Christ. "It couldn't happen here," they say—until a friend or relative joins a cult, or begins to consult a channeler, or learns to meditate in school, or signs up for TM training.

The Chameleon Mentality. The sixth pitfall is a cousin to the ostrich mentality because it misunderstands the Christian's separation and transformation responsibilities. Those affected are "trendier than thou" and equate human (or demonic) innovation with spiritual insight. They passively absorb their environment, changing colors in accordance with popular New Age practices or ideas. So we hear calls for "Christian yoga," "Christian zen" or less blatant compromises with non-Christian presuppositions involving such things as certain self-esteem teachings (to be taken up in chapter nine). Although it is true that "all truth is God's truth," all that glitters is not God's gold; fool's gold abounds.

The challenge of the New Age demands a world-challenging faith. This involves spiritual discernment and empowering regarding spiritual warfare, and intellectual renewal and a critical engagement of our culture for the greater glory of God. In the next chapter we will consider what specific points must be faced in convincing the New Agers to reconsider their world view and embrace Jesus Christ as their Lord.

Notes

[1]Richard Lovelace, *Dynamics of Spiritual Life* (Downers Grove, Ill.: InterVarsity Press, 1979), p. 183.
[2]Henry Van Til, *The Calvinistic Concept of Culture* (Grand Rapids, Mich.: Baker, 1959).
[3]Francis A. Schaeffer, *How Should We Then Live?* (Old Tappan, N.J.: Revell, 1976), p. 19.
[4]See Phylis Schlafly, *Child Abuse in the Classroom* (Westchester, Ill.: Crossway Books, 1984), pp. 209-10.
[5]James Orr, *The Christian View of God and the World* (Grand Rapids, Mich.: Eerdmans, 1947), p. 4.
[6]Calvin Seerveld, *Rainbows for a Fallen World* (Downsville, Ontario: Toronto Tuppence Press, 1980), p. 24.
[7]Hans Rookmaaker, *Modern Art and the Death of a Culture* (Downers Grove, Ill.: InterVarsity Press, 1970) p. 37.
[8]John Stott, *Involvement,* Vol. 1 (Old Tappan, N.J.: Revell, 1985), p. 46.
[9]See Wimber with Springer, *Power Evangelism,* pp. 1-14.
[10]Francis A. Schaeffer, *A Christian Manifesto* (Westchester, Ill.: Crossway, 1981), p. 19.
[11]W. E. H. Lecky, *History of European Morals from Augustus to Charlemagne,* Vol. 2 (New York: D. Appleton, 1906), p. 100.
[12]On Christianity as "the project of God" see William Dyrness, *Christian Apologetics in a World Community* (Downers Grove, Ill.: InterVarsity Press, 1983), pp. 74-84.
[13]Lovelace, *Dynamics,* p. 173.
[14]See Arthur Holmes, *All Truth Is God's Truth* (Downers Grove, Ill.: InterVarsity Press, 1983).
[15]Orr, *Christian View,* p. 12.
[16]See Donald Tweedie, *Logotherapy and the Christian Faith* (Grand Rapids, Mich.: Baker, 1965).
[17]Groothuis, *Unmasking,* pp. 71-91.
[18]Stott, *Involvement,* Vol. 1, p. 49.
[19]Groothuis, *Unmasking,* pp. 57-70.
[20]I owe this phrase to Jimmy Williams.

Witnessing
to the
New Age

II

Developing
a Strategy

4

Each age offers its own particular challenge to christianity. Because unbelief can take many forms, those longing "to give the reason
for the hope that [they] have" (1 Pet 3:15) need to be sensitive to the
audience they are addressing—yet not so "sensitive" that the gospel
is altered to suit modern tastes. As J. B. Phillips said, "I am *not* concerned to distort or dilute the Christian faith so that modern under-
graduates, for example, can accept it without a murmur. I am concerned with the truth revealed in and through Jesus Christ. Let the
modern world conform to him, and never let us dare to try to make
him fit into our clever-clever modern world."[1] Christian defenders of
the faith should discern the issues at hand and respond to them with
the uncompromised, undiluted Word of God.

Although their gospel is timeless, many Christians are behind the
times. Some friends of mine passed out evangelistic tracts at one of

Shirley MacLaine's New Age seminars that was oriented toward finding your "Higher Self" (the God within). One well-meaning man, recently trained in lay evangelism, gained the attention of a participant. Following the method he had just learned at his church he asked her, "If you should die and stand before God and he asks you why he should let you into his heaven, what would you say?" Much to my friend's surprise, the woman replied that she didn't believe in such a God and that everyone had her own god-concept. She didn't see herself as accountable to any Higher Power. She was "a god of her own universe." She could barely understand his question!

This embarrassing situation underscores the need for appropriate evangelism and apologetics. The evangelistic strategy used by our perplexed friend is appropriate for the nominal Christian who believes in a personal, moral God, but who has not confessed Christ as Lord and Savior. Yet the strategy falls on deaf ears when used on many New Agers.

Before developing an appropriate strategy for communicating Christ to the New Ager, we should quickly define and differentiate the terms *apologetics* and *evangelism.*

Apologetics has to do with defending the truth of the Christian faith. The classic New Testament text for apologetics is 1 Peter 3:15: "But in your hearts set apart Christ as Lord. Always be prepared to give an answer to everyone who asks you to give the reason for the hope that you have. But do this with gentleness and respect." This includes rational persuasion that Christianity is true. Apologetics concerns a variety of issues, but can be divided into two categories, *positive apologetics* and *negative apologetics.*

Positive apologetics presents *reasons for* Christianity, such as evidence for the resurrection of Christ, the reliability of Scripture, the existence of God and so on. It does not deny the crucial role of faith but seeks to present a faith that is reasonable. Luke, the careful historian (Lk 1:1-4), exemplifies this approach when he says that after Jesus' suffering, Jesus "showed himself to these men [the apostles] and gave many convincing proofs that he was alive" (Acts 1:3). We also find Stephen defending his faith before Jewish detractors who "could not stand up against his wisdom or the Spirit by whom he spoke" (Acts 6:10). This fullfilled the promise of Jesus, who said to his disciples, "I will give you words and wisdom that none of your adversaries will be able to resist or contradict" (Lk 21:15). We should seek the same.

Negative apologetics presents *reasons against* non-Christian perspectives. It assumes that "unless the LORD builds the house, its builders labor in vain" (Ps 127:1); that is, if non-Christain world views arc largely based on false ideas, the weakness of those world views can be highlighted through argumentation (as we will see concerning certain New Age ideas). Any world view not based on the truth of God's revelation in the Bible will prove itself faulty at key points. As F. F. Bruce comments in reference to the book of Jude's denunciation of false religion: "There are times when it is not enough to hold and expound the truth; the war must be carried into the enemy's lines so that the error may be attacked, exposed and refuted."[2] Negative apologetics says, "Your perspective doesn't make sense; and it doesn't fit the facts. Therefore, you shouldn't believe it." Negative apologetics is not an end in itself—lest we become mere critics—but it can often serve as an introduction to positive apologetics and evangelism.

Apologetics is only necessary when someone is hindered, through some intellectual snag, from embracing Christ. Many times apologetic arguments are unnecessary; a clear presentation of the gospel of Christ may be all that is needed. If so, fine! *Evangelism,* then, simply means the proclamation—as opposed to the argumentation—of the saving truth of Jesus Christ. For instance, when Philip was led to the Ethiopian eunuch who was reading Isaiah 53 while riding in his chariot, all Philip needed to do was explain that the passage referred to Christ. The man then gladly accepted Christ (Acts 8:26-39). No extended apologetic arguments were necessary, just a simple lesson in fulfilled prophecy.

A sensitive Christian witness will first try to discern how much convincing a person needs before he or she is ready to confess Christ. This will help prevent the mistake of either pressing for a decision before the person is ready, or the opposite error of wasting time arguing for what the person is already beginning to believe!

Both apologetics and evangelism may be called "Christian witness": we are witnessing to the saving truth of Jesus Christ and the veracity of the Christian world view. But what form should our witness to the New Ager take?

In this and the following two chapters we will address basic evangelistic considerations along with negative and positive apologetics, which in some cases overlap. We will argue against (negative apologetics) the New Age views of the Bible and spiritual exploration and the New Age views of Christ and relativistic morality. But in so doing we will also be arguing for (positive apologetics) the Christian viewpoints.

Evangelistic Concerns

First, as mentioned in chapter two, we need to remember that the Christian witness to the New Ager is a spiritual offensive into enemy territory. Any arguments or appeals are only as existentially effective as the Holy Spirit causes them to be (Acts 1:8). In fact, we should be open to the fact that the Holy Spirit may work in unexpected, supernatural ways to demonstrate the truth.[3]

Second, in spiritual battle the effective soldier should be inspired by a principled indignation when facing New Age teachings. We find that the apostle Paul was "greatly distressed" by the idolatry of Athens (Acts 17:16). However, Paul did not issue a tirade against paganism but rather reasoned with the idolaters and proclaimed the gospel to them. His anger over error inspired outreach, not cheap condemnation. We can be spiritually angry in two senses; first, because people are being led down the broad path that leads to hell;

and second, because God himself is being mocked by "hollow and deceptive philosophy" (Col 2:8). The great theologian and apologist of the previous generation, J. Gresham Machen, drives this point home:

Every true man is resentful of slanders against a human friend. Should we not be grieved ten times more by slanders against our God? How can we possibly listen with polite complacency, then, when men break down the distinction between God and man, and drag God down to man's level? . . . We should never say with regard to a human friend that it makes no difference whether our view of him is right or wrong. How, then, can we say that absurd thing with regard to God?[4]

As has been often said, we hate the sin that destroys lives and defames God, while loving the sinner who needs the Savior.

Third, principled anger must be combined with a love for the lost. We witness to the New Ager not to win arguments, but to see people made whole in Christ; not to score apologetic points, but to give the angels another converted soul to rejoice over. Ultimately, we witness for and about Christ because of our love of God, whom we desire to glorify through outreach (1 Cor 10:31).[5]

If I proclaim sound doctrine with evangelistic fervor but have no love, my explanations, exhortations and arguments will profit little (1 Cor 13:1). The *way* the gospel is presented is as important as *what* is presented. Our attitude should be that of Jesus, the great seeker of the lost, who, "when he saw the crowds . . . had compassion on them because they were . . . like sheep without a shepherd" (Mt 9:36; see also 14:14; 15:32). Many New Agers jump from one costly therapy, seminar or technique to another in the pathetic pursuit of their ever-elusive "Higher Self"—a mad dash for divinity that easily becomes a demolition derby of dissatisfaction.[6] They are—as all Christians once were—"sheep without a shepherd" in need of hearing the truth spoken in love, the truth of Jesus Christ.

Fourth, Christians should be careful not to stereotype those they encounter. You may know (or think you know) more about the New Age movement than some New Agers. However, you are not addressing an abstract system of thought, but a person who holds New Age ideas near and dear. You are dealing with a way of life. A good understanding of New Age thought is helpful, of course, but the person should be honored and not just classified under the impersonal category of "New Ager." People, not world views, are in danger of going to hell. Although we outlined in the first chapter a distillation of New Age beliefs, the movement is eclectic and diverse. Treat each person individually, as you would want to be treated yourself. For instance, if you discover that a coworker has been through a New Age human-potential seminar, such as est, don't lecture her on its error, but engage her in conversation about her experiences and beliefs. A real and loving interest in a person's viewpoint will win more respect than a ready-made anti-New Age lecture.

Nevertheless, fifth, as a point of contact Christians can find some common ground with New Agers (but not for compromise). Just as Paul appealed to selected statements by the Stoic and Epicurean philosophers when he preached to the Athenians (Acts 17:28), so we can highlight some areas of agreement with New Agers, such as the reality of the spiritual realm, life after death, and the need for spiritual growth and social change. But, as Paul did at Athens, we must also be careful to highlight the crucial points of conflict between biblical Christianity and New Age thought, as discussed below.[7]

Sixth, in dialoging with and proclaiming the gospel to a New Ager, be extremely careful to define your terms clearly and carefully. New Age vocabulary is brimful of "spiritual" words and phrases. Terms such as _God, Christ, spirituality_ and even _born again_ (referring to reincarnation) may be used with great frequency, yet with a distinctly non-Christian meaning. We should be alerted to semantic camouflage. I was in a radio discussion with a Religious Science minister who told the audience that he believed in heaven and hell, but added that we create heaven and hell through our thinking. He did not view heaven and hell as real places where people will spend eternity, in accordance with their response to God. Yet in a casual conversation someone might assume that he does think of heaven and hell in the biblical sense.

Unlike atheists, New Agers speak enthusiastically about "God." This can give the wrong impression. Having been buffeted by atheists, skeptics and agnostics, the Christian may warmly embrace an apparent fellow believer in God. But what kind of God? New Agers demote the Deity to a cosmic It, an impersonal force, energy, principle or process. Further, they identify themselves with this demoted deity, thus attempting to promote their own metaphysical status. So the New Age affirmation "I believe in God" may well mean "I believe in Me"!

Similar suspicion should be cast on the New Age use of the word *Christ.* In the radio program just mentioned, the Religious Science minister confessed that he believed that "Jesus was the Christ." It sounded orthodox; yet it rang hollow. I alerted the audience that in Religious Science doctrine Jesus was just a man who attained an awareness of "Christ consciousness"—the impersonal divine essence. So to this minister, "Jesus is the Christ" only because he realized his divine potential; but we too can realize our divine potential just as Jesus did. To the New Age, Jesus is not "the *one and only* Son" (Jn 3:16; emphasis mine); we are all "sons of God." In fact, we are all gods.

Even a word at the very core of Christianity—*atonement*—can be used in a radically unbiblical manner. Instead of believing that Christ atoned for our sins by suffering on the cross so we would not have to pay the penalty ourselves, the New Ager believes in "at-one-ment," which is an awareness that "all is one." No blood atonement is necessary because there is no real separation to be healed; there is no sin, only ignorance of the great cosmic Oneness.

The popular New Age text *A Course in Miracles* claims that Christ's atoning work had nothing to do with his taking upon himself the punishment for our sins. Yet it uses the word *atonement.*[8]

The Rational and Intuitive

If we can get beyond semantic issues, we also need to face the fact that New Agers often sink in the sands of subjectivism, resulting in illogic and amorality. New Agers should be pressed when making illogical statements. Later we will give examples of the logical weakness of New Age views on reincarnation, the Bible and relativism. It's interesting to note that non-Christian skeptical literature can often be of great help. Journals such as *Free Inquiry* and *Skeptical Inquirer* often set their gun sights on extravagant New Age claims and hit the target in exposing their inadequacies. (Of course, for the secular humanist,[9] all spirituality is bogus, and so we also find articles rejecting Christianity as well.) A sterling example of helpful skepticism is the debunking of the "hundredth monkey phenomenon" by University of Hawaii professor of philosophy, Ron Amundson.

Amundson set out to investigate some fantastic claims made about a troop of monkeys (Macaques) on Japanese islands in the 1950s. The New Age folklore has it that when one hundred monkeys on Koshima Island learned a new behavior—washing sweet potatoes in water—this produced a "critical mass" of consciousness that transferred paranormally to other islands, psychically initiating other monkeys into the mysteries of improved sanitation and culinary enjoyment. The cosmic upshot is that a "critical mass" of consciousness can likewise be developed by humans to bring about world peace and eliminate the possiblity of nuclear war. Ken Keyes's popular book, *The Hundredth Monkey,* puts it this way: "You may be the 'Hundredth Monkey.' . . . You may furnish the added consciousness energy to create the shared awareness of the urgent necessity to rapidly acheive a nuclear-free world."[10] Thus the "hundredth monkey phenomenon" has spread like wildfire in New Age circles and is affirmed as if it were an established scientific law.

This monkey business was the operative philosophy behind the World Peace Events held worldwide on December 31, 1986 (see first chapter). If enough people would "think peace," peace would break out globally. The idea has tremendous motivating power—but little truth.

Dr. Ron Amundson was so bold as to read the original scientific journal articles cited by Lyall Watson in his book *Lifetide.* He then found that Watson, the principle perpetrator of the idea, had not accurately represented the material.[11]

First, the original articles reveal that the Japanese primatologists conducting the study found nothing extraordinary to report about the monkeys. All the factors relevant to the monkeys' behavior are documented, and none of them intimate anything paranormal. It is not the case, as Watson says, that the researchers feared ridicule in reporting the paranormal and "are still not quite sure what happened." They claimed to know exactly what happened.

Second, potato washing was found in other monkey troops on other islands but there was no indication that this behavior was paranormally transferred to them from the Koshima spud-dunkers. A better explanation is that these resourceful creatures independently thought up the practice. According to Amundson, the articles Watson cites also mention that "in 1960 a potato washer named 'Jugo' swam from Koshima to the island on which the Takasakiyama troop lives. Jugo returned four years later. Watson does not mention this. The Japanese monkeys are known to be both clever and mobile, and either characteristic might explain the interisland spread of potato washing. Watson ignores both explanations, preferring to invent a new paranormal power."[12] The activity of monkey missionaries would explain the situation better than recourse to the paranormal.

The reader will want to consult Amundson's article for more specifics, but it seems he has nailed Watson to the wall. Watson's own published response to Amundson admits as much by saying that the whole idea is "a metaphor of my own making, based—as he rightly suggests—on very slim evidence and a great deal of hearsay."[13] In another article, Amundson points out that while Watson claims he was improvising as he went along, his original comments in *Lifetide* make it appear that the "hundredth monkey phenomenon" was backed up by scientific evidence. But it was not.[14]

Yet the monkey business has taken the form of a New Age fable, inspiring the faithful to pump up that "critical mass" of consciousness to transform the planet. In fact, the story gets better with the telling.[15] Sources that depend on Watson inflate the idea even further. Falsehoods seem "true" when indiscrimately broadcast in the media.[16] We should remember the proverb: "The first to present his case seems right, till another comes forward and questions him" (Prov 18:17).

Here thoughtful Christians can politely puncture this paranormal propaganda by simply citing carefully researched material. Even journals that tend to be New Age in orientation, such as *The Journal of Humanistic Psychology* and *The Whole Earth Review* (which carried Amundson's article), will sometimes police their own ranks and print articles critical of various aspects of New Age thought. Christians can get good apologetic mileage from these sources. (At the same time we should remember Peter's injunction to conduct ourselves "with gentleness and respect," 1 Pet 3:15).

While rational refutation of New Age aberrations and rational arguments for the truth of Christianity are both crucial, it is legitimate for the Christian to appeal to the mysterious and subjective aspect of Christian faith in communicating to New Agers.[17]

First, although rationality should be affirmed, rationalism should be avoided. Arguments may need to be made, but more than arguments are required. Christianity is a world view capable of rational defense, but it is also a way of salvation.[18] New Agers endlessly quest after spiritual experience. Christ offers abundant life (Jn 10:10) to those who put their trust in him as Savior, and throughout the centuries millions have testified to this wonderful fact. Of course, the Christian must affirm that the experience of Christ's love is real only because Christ himself is objectively real. The subjective experience of knowing God is grounded in the objective truth of God's justice and love.

The Christian does not entirely rule out powerful spiritual experiences[19] so long as they meet all the following criteria. Any special divine communication or inspiration, following the biblical model (Is 6; Rev 1:12-19), must be:

1. *Personal.* God communicates personally to persons made in his image. Personality—either divine or human—is not dissolved into a mystical oneness. The experience is one of dialog, not monolog.

2. *Moral.* God's moral holiness is repeatedly emphasized in Scripture. This is seen in Isaiah's confession of sin when God was revealed to him. The interaction is between a morally perfect Being and a sinful creature. Moral categories do not dissolve, New Age amoralism to the contrary. The true spiritual experience of a holy God involves a sense of his majesty, wonder and power in relation to human frailty and sin.[20]

3. *Cognitive.* Truths are communicated in propositions. It is not an ineffable experience, but one that can be reported (even if not completely recaptured) and discussed logically. It is not an irrational experience, no matter how symbolic some visions may be.

4. *Doctrinally correct.* The apostle Paul says that even if an angel from heaven should preach another gospel than the true gospel, that angel and the false gospel should be rejected (Gal 1:8). John tells us to "test the spirits" by biblical doctrine (1 Jn 4:1-4). A spiritual experience in itself does not guarantee its truth, nor are intense spiritual experiences a requirement for a godly life.[21]

Second, in presenting the logic of the Christian position, Christians should be careful not to oversimplify the message. Christianity does encompass the mysterious. It is not an arid rationalism.[22] God has revealed in Scripture truths unreachable through human logic alone (though not in opposition to human logic). Since God is infinite and we are finite, many crucial Christian doctrines—such as the Trinity and Incarnation—are mysterious in some ways. Yet mystery need not be absurdity. C. Stephen Evans explains: "If God were going to give humans a special revelation, would it not contain some truth that humans would be unable to discover on their own? Otherwise, why would he bother? In other words, we would expect a *genuine* revelation from God to contain mysteries."[23]

Evans goes on to say that Christians insist that "the basic mysteries of the faith are *above* reason, but not *against* reason. That is, although we cannot fully understand them or prove their truth, they do not contradict what *is* known to be truth."[24]

Pascal put it this way: "The last proceeding of reason is to recognize that there is an infinity of things which are beyond it. It is but feeble if it does not see so far as to know this."[25]

Christians should remember that sensitivity to the leading of the Holy Spirit is crucial for any apologetic or evangelistic encounter so that, in Paul's words, "your faith might not rest on men's wisdom, but on God's power" (1 Cor 2:5).

Spiritual Dangers

Those who trust in Christ are given access to spiritual discernment and power in spiritual combat. Yet those outside of Christ are fair prey of the enemy. In communicating to New Agers it is sometimes wise to warn them that psychic sojourns may lead them into raging spiritual storms.

As New Age seekers dive into their spiritual experiences, they leave themselves vulnerable to both fraud and spiritual deception. Some seekers are primed for deception because they are desperate, hurting people looking for an answer—any answer. If Christians encounter such souls, a word of warning is a good tonic. Even if we can't lead them to Christ just then, we can warn them of occult dangers and offer the safety of knowing Christ as victor over sin and Satan.

It should be made clear that the Bible prohibits all occult activities for at least two reasons. First, God alone is worthy of worship, and he is rightfully jealous of our affections and obedience. Since he is supremely good, this jealousy translates into a desire both to glorify himself and to have his creatures live as they ought to live. Second, God also knows the reality of fallen spiritual beings who entice humanity to follow their destructive ways. For these reasons he vetoes any suggestion of occult involvement. Although many biblical passages condemn the occult, this passage from Deuteronomy, originally given to God's people who were to possess the Promised Land, is the most exhaustive:

> When you enter the land the LORD your God is giving you, do not learn to imitate the detestable ways of the nations there. Let no one be found among you who sacrifices his son or daughter in the fire, who practices divination or sorcery, interprets omens, engages in witchcraft, or casts spells, or who is a medium or spiritist or who consults the dead. Anyone who does these things is detestable to the LORD, and because of these detestable practices the LORD your God will drive out those nations before you. You must be blameless before the LORD your God. (Deut 18:9-13; see also Lev 19:31; 20:6)

Isaiah echoes this and points us in the right direction: "When men tell you to consult mediums and spiritists, who whisper and mutter, should not a people inquire of their God? Why consult the dead on behalf of the living? To the law and the testimony! If they do not speak according to this word, they have no light of dawn" (Is 8:19-20; see also 47:8-15).

Although there are scores of other biblical warnings, consider the stark finality of Jesus Christ's words concerning those who will not enter the eternal city: "Outside are the dogs, those who practice magic arts, the sexually immoral, the murderers, the idolaters and everyone who loves and practices falsehood" (Rev 22:15).

If the biblical warnings are not heeded, cautions can be given from New Age literature itself. For instance, if a friend wants to take a yoga class at the local YMCA to help calm her nerves, we might quote the following, written by an *advocate* of yoga: "Yoga is not a trifling jest if we consider that any misunderstanding in the practice of yoga can mean death or insanity."[26] Practitioners of yoga often warn of the power of the kundalini energy, represented as a serpent coiled at the base of the spine. The purpose of many forms of yoga is to "awaken the kundalini" and release its energy upward through the seven chakras (energy centers) of the body. But the yogis themselves caution that this is no child's play. One might get burned (literally!) by the serpent's hot breath—or go insane.[27]

In an issue of *ReVision,* a scholarly New Age journal, consciousness researchers Christina and Stanislav Grof speak of "transpersonal crises" that are often linked to "various meditative practices which are specifically designed to activate spiritual energies." These include "the practice of yoga, Zen, various movement meditations, pranayama, Kundalini maneuvers, Tibetan Buddhist psychoenergetic exercises, Christian prayer and other forms of deep and systematic spiritual involvement and self-exploration."[28] (Given the substance of their article, it is clear their concept of "Christian prayer" is not a biblical spirituality, but pantheistic introspection falsely labeled *Christian.*)

The Grofs believe these "emergencies" are merely difficult stages often required for greater growth, which they interpret as New Age enlightenment. Yet their descriptions of the "crises" are bone chilling, especially when describing the "awakening of the Serpent Power (Kundalini)" which they say "can be accompied by dramatic physical and psychological manifestations called *kriyas,"* which include "powerful sensations of heat and energy streaming up the spine, associated with tremors, spasms, violent shaking, and complex twisting movements." They also mention "involuntary laughing or crying, chanting of mantras or songs, talking in tongues, emitting of vocal noises and animal sounds, and assuming spontaneous yoga gestures (mudras) and postures (asanas)." Other physical manifestations include "nausea, diarrhea or constipation, anal or uterine contractions, clenching of the jaws, rise and drop of temperature, and bulimia or loss of appetite. The entire body can be rigid or limp, and feel unusually large or small."[29]

Although the Grofs also list supposedly positive benefits of kundalini such as "ecstasy, orgastic raptures, and states of indescribable peace and tranquility,"[30] one must risk a total breakdown (or worse) for that prize. Yet all the subjective enjoyment in the world cannot yield the forgiveness of sins or the peace of mind offered by Jesus Christ, who requires no such psychological and physical violence from his followers.

The Grofs found these "transpersonal emergencies" prevalent enough among New Agers that in 1980 they founded "the Spiritual Emergency Network" to help enlighten the "psychotherapeutic community" to the reality of the issue and to offer assistance through education and referrals to those undergoing various crises. The headquarters for the Spiritual Emergency Network is on the campus of the California Institute of Transpersonal Psychology in the San Francisco area and has 42 regional centers worldwide.[31]

Yoga may also open up a person to spiritual contacts and all manner of occult activity. Transcendental Meditation—while claiming to be a neutral, psychological technique—uses yogic methods to alter consciousness. Maharishi, its founder, has said that the purpose of chanting the mantra in Transcendental Meditation is "to produce an effect in some other world, to draw the attention of those higher beings or gods living there. The entire knowledge of the mantra . . . is devoted to man's connection, to man's communication with the higher beings in a different strata *(sic)* of creation."[32]

If a person says he is interested in yoga simply as a physical discipline, he should be told that it was not invented by the mystic masters of old simply to cultivate better physiques. Yoga teachers such as R. L. Hittleman admit that any health benefits are secondary. He also admits to having used the health angle to hook Westerners on the Hindu world view.[33]

An article in *Yoga Journal* on parapsychology even warns psychic sojourners that the use of divination (through Ouija boards, automatic writing and other methods) "in a frivolous or disrespectful manner" makes one "liable to attract 'lower' discarnate communicators, including ghosts or poltergeists, and one runs the risks of becoming obsessed or possessed."[34] Christians need not use quotation marks for the word *lower*, because they believe in an active "Lowerarchy"[35] of demonic mischief-makers capable of possessing, obsessing and oppressing those outside the protection of the risen Christ. Although the article in *Yoga Journal* issues a small warning, it falls tragically short of Christian discernment. It tantalizes readers by saying that "two of the most famous 'channeled' teachings of recent years—the Seth books and the 'messages from Michael'—got their start on the Ouija board."[36]

Christians may challenge New Age aspirants by concretely relating dangers of various New Age practices. Many of these—channeling, psychic healing, mind-altering meditations and so on—are nothing but modernized occultism, and occultism exacts too high a price in the end. The late Kurt Koch, Christian theologian and occult counselor for over forty-five years, has given hundreds of examples of occult bondage in his many writings. His seasoned analysis was that "no one makes use of occult powers without harm."[37] We are not suggesting that all people involved in some occult/New Age practice will suffer similar symptoms, but that these practices are outside the will of God and thus generally dangerous. In the chapter "Effects of Occult Movements and Devices" from *Occult ABC*, Koch lists different spiritual maladies caused by occult involvement (some of the following illustrations are drawn from other sources):

1. *Mediumistic Affinity.* Those who open up themselves to the occult in any form may develop mediumistic powers that subject them to malignant spiritual influences. For instance, two "channelers"— Kevin Ryerson and Jach Pursel—claim to have been "contacted" by spirit guides while meditating. Demons "stand at the door and knock" as well, eagerly waiting quickly to take up residence once they get their feet in the door.

2. *Resistance to the Things of God.* Those ensnared by the occult often find it difficult to turn from their practices and to God. Through

seeking spiritual freedom, they submit to bondage. The lowerarchy often doesn't relinquish its prisoners easily. Johanna Michaelson relates her struggle to commit herself fully to Christ after hands-on involvement with psychic healing in Mexico. Having come to the Christian L'Abri fellowship in Switzerland, she was challenged to read the Gospel of John. Her first attempt only got as far as the fourth verse before she was inexplicably exhausted. Later she was harassed by spirits telling her Jesus couldn't help her. They gripped her throat such that she could not cry out. Yet after the struggle, Jesus did prevail, and Johanna committed herself fully to Christ.[38] Koch's writings report dozens of such cases.

3. *Character and Emotional Disorders.* Koch says that occult healings, for instance, often result in "compulsive lying, compulsive stealing (kleptomania), and compulsive arson (pyromania)."[39] He believes that any physical healing is offset by a transference of the physical malady to a spiritual malady.[40]

4. *Breeding Ground of Mental Illness.* From his extensive counseling experience, Koch believes that occult activity makes one vulnerable to mental illness. In a newspaper article on "Witches in Wisconsin," Jonathan, the high priest of a coven in Madison, relates that the initiation ritual into witchcraft puts the neophyte into a trial to see if he or she has the stamina. He notes that spiritual power is transferred from the coveners to the initiate. He says, "You are getting a lot of energy, a lot of power, and you have to know how to handle it. If you don't know how to handle it you overload." Jonathan says he has encountered four people who turned psychotic because they were not prepared for the occult overload.[41]

5. *Oppression of Descendents.* Koch's writings often stress the reality of generational curses whereby descendents sometimes inherit a predilection for occult phenomena (see Ex 20:4). Johanna Michaelson, in fact, seems to have inherited her psychic predilections from her spiritualist great-great aunt who predicted that a third generation child would inherit her occult "gifts."[42]

6. *Suicide.* Since Satan's supreme strategy is to kill and destroy (Jn 10:10), it isn't surprising that his charms would lead to self-slaughter. In addition to examples given by Koch, psychic Dr. H. H. Bro states that persons who try to develop psychic powers for the wrong reasons "embark on a course of increasingly distraught behavior, compulsive actions, alienation from friends and relatives, and finally multiple personality symptoms [possession] or suicide."[43]

7. *Ghosts and Poltergeists.* If the occult world is freely consulted it may, in turn, freely consult New Age seekers in consuming ways. "Poltergeists" refer to particularly disruptive spirits that tend "to go bump in the night"—or daytime, for that matter. "Ghosts" or "spooks" refer to less openly obnoxious, but nevertheless demonic, entities. Koch says that "in all cases of spooks which I have been able to investigate, occult practices lay at the root of spook phenomena."[44]

Weldon and Wilson's book, *Occult Shock and Psychic Forces,* lists many warnings given by parapsychologists and occultists concerning poltergeists, insanity and other rotten fruits of the forbidden.[45]

8. *Frequent Diseases.* Koch warns that not all illness is directly demonic, yet "people who come under the curse of sins of sorcery are frequently plagued with illness of every sort."[46] We can see this dynamically expressed in the curses of Deuteronomy 28:15-68, especially verses 21-22. When people rebel against God—and especially when they court the occult world for spiritual power apart from God—they place themselves in a perilous situation, for time and eternity.

Satan, "the prince of darkness grim" (Luther), "masquerades as an angel of light" (2 Cor 11:14); yet being truly evil, his counterfeit light eventually fades, revealing a consuming blackness. His true darkness is exposed as Christians shine forth the light of the gospel. As Paul says,

> Have nothing to do with the fruitless deeds of darkness, but rather expose them. For it is shameful even to mention what the disobedient do in secret. But everything exposed by the light becomes

visible, for it is light that makes everything visible. This is why it is said: "Wake up, O sleeper, rise from the dead, and Christ will shine on you." (Eph 5:11-14)

Notes

[1]J. B. Phillips, *The Ring of Truth* (New York: Macmillan, 1967), pp. 9-10.

[2]F. F. Bruce, *The Defense of the Faith in the New Testament,* Rev. ed. (Grand Rapids, Mich.: Eerdmans, 1977), p. 80.

[3]See Wimber with Springer, *Power Evangelism.*

[4]J. Gresham Machen, *The Christian Faith in the Modern World* (Grand Rapids, Mich.: Eerdmans, 1968), p. 120.

[5]On the importance of the witness of love for Christians see Francis Schaeffer, *The Mark of the Christian* (Downers Grove, Ill.. InterVarsity Press, 1970).

[6]Compare this with the frenzied futility of the self-mutilating Baal worshipers that Elijah challenged to a religious showdown (1 Kings 18:25-29).

[7]For an excellent study of Paul's method in relation to non-Christian religions, see Ajith Fernando, *The Christian's Attitude toward Non-Christian Religions* (Wheaton, Ill.: Tyndale, 1987).

[8]*A Course in Miracles: Text* (Tiburon, Calif.: Foundation for Inner Peace, 1981), pp. 32-34.

[9]It should be noted that not all contributors to skeptical literature are atheistic secularists. A constant critic of the paranormal such as Martin Gardener is a non-Christian theist.

[10]Ken Keyes, Jr., *The Hundredth Monkey* (Coos Bay, Oreg.: Vision Books, 1984), p. 18.

[11]Ron Amundson, "The Hundredth Monkey Debunked," *Whole Earth Review* (Fall 1986), pp. 19-24.

[12]Ibid., p. 23.

[13]Lyall Watson, "Lyall Watson Responds," *Whole Earth Review* (Fall 1986), p. 25.

[14]Ron Amundson, "Watson and the 'Hundredth Monkey Phenomenon,' " *The Skeptical Inquirer* 11 (Spring 1987), pp. 303-4.

[15]See Amundson, "Hundredth Monkey Debunked," p. 23.

[16]See Jacques Ellul, *The Presence of the Kingdom* (New York: Seabury, 1967), p. 100.

[17]David Hesselgrave, *Communicating Christ Crossculturally* (Grand Rapids, Mich.: Zondervan, 1981), pp. 218-19.

[18]Ibid.

[19]See Francis Schaeffer, *True Spirituality* (Wheaton, Ill.: Tyndale, 1976), pp. 54-55; and Richard Lovelace, *Renewal as a Way of Life* (Downers Grove, Ill.: InterVarsity Press, 1985), pp. 15-33.

[20]See Calvin *Institutes* 1.1.3.

[21]See also Howard Ervin, *This Which Ye See and Hear* (Plainfield, N.J.: Logos, 1972), pp. 95-103 on "spiritual versus psychic experiences."

[22]Hesselgrave, *Communicating Christ Crossculturally,* pp. 214-22.

[23]C. Stephen Evans, *Quest for Faith* (Downers Grove, Ill.: InterVarsity Press, 1986), p. 115.

[24]Ibid.

[25]Blaise Pascal, *Pensées* 4.267 (Great Books Edition).

[26]H. Reiker, *The Yoga of Light* (Los Angeles: Dawn House, 1974), p. 9; quoted in John Weldon and Clifford Wilson, *Occult Shock and Psychic Forces* (San Diego: Master, 1980), p. 72.

[27]See Weldon and Wilson, *Occult Shock,* pp. 71-74.

[28]Christina and Stanislav Grof, "Spiritual Emergency: The Understanding and Treatment of Transpersonal Crisis," *ReVision* 8, no. 2 (Winter/ Spring 1986), p. 7.

[29]Ibid., p. 9.

[30]Ibid.

[31]Megan Nolan, "Spiritual Emergency Network," *ReVision* 8, no. 2 (Winter/Spring 1986), p. 89.

[32]Maharishi Mahesh Yogi, *The Meditations of Maharishi Mahesh Yogi;* quoted in John Allan, *Yoga: A Christian Analysis* (Leicester, Eng.: Inter-Varsity Press, 1983), p. 29.

[33]Richard Hittleman, *Guide to Yoga Meditation* (New York: Bantam, 1969), pp. 9-14; quoted in Hexam and Poewe, *Understanding Cults,* p. 80.

[34]John Llimo, "A Primer of Parapyschology," *Yoga Journal* (July/August 1986), p. 40.

[35]See C. S. Lewis, *The Screwtape Letters* (Old Tappan, N.J.: Revell, 1976), p. 97.

[36]Llimo, "A Primer of Parapyschology," p. 40.

[37]Koch, *Occult ABC,* p. 40.

[38]Johanna Michaelson, *The Beautiful Side of Evil* (Eugene, Oreg.: Harvest House, 1982), pp. 131-49.

[39]Koch, *Occult ABC,* p. 271.

[40]Kurt Koch, *Demonology Past and Present* (Grand Rapids, Mich.: Kregel, 1973), pp. 121-29; quoted in John Weldon and Zola Levitt, *Psychic Healing* (Chicago: Moody, 1982), pp. 193-94.

[41]Mette Hammer, "Witches in Wisconsin: Magic Is the Medium for Area Practitioners of Wicca," *Isthmus* (July 25-31, 1986), p. 10.

[42]Michaelson, *Beautiful Side of Evil,* pp. 15-16.

[43]H. H. Bro, *Fate* (February 1971), pp. 102-3; quoted in Weldon and Wilson, *Occult Shock,* p. 443.

[44]Koch, *Christian Counseling,* p. 181.

[45]Weldon and Wilson, *Occult Shock,* pp. 444-53.

[46]Koch, *Occult ABC,* p. 280.

The Bible and Reincarnation

5

In WITNESSING TO NEW AGERS, CHRISTIANS OFTEN FACE THE "BUT THAT'S JUST your interpretation" problem. Suppose you have persuaded someone that the New Age meaning of *Christ* is infinitely removed from your meaning. What do you say when the retort is, "I interpret the Bible to mean that 'Christ' is the impersonal divinity within all people that we can tap into"?

This is a crucial area of New Age apologetics, because New Agers often want to include the Bible in their smorgasbord of religious traditions which support their point of view. Christians must make it clear that the Bible cannot be digested along with New Age fare.

I have been afflicted with the but–that's–just–your–interpretation response more times than I wish to remember, and I must admit I have not always been successful in making the following point. Nevertheless, we must valiantly press it home: Yes, everyone is entitled to his or her own interpretation of the Bible. But no, not all interpretations are equally correct. You may, in fact, "interpret" the bright, large orb that irradiates the solar system as being a remarkably durable and powerful satellite constructed by Peruvian peasants in A.D. 300. You have a "right," so to speak, to interpret things that way; but that in no way makes your view correct. Your interpretation is either true or false; you are either right or wrong.

The same is true when we come to the Bible. You either interpret it correctly or incorrectly. There is a difference between proper interpretation and misinterpretation. Having "your own interpretation" about the Bible does not, in itself, legitimate that interpretation as true any more than "your interpretation" of your IRS return legitimates itself before the penetrating eyes of an income-tax auditor. He goes by "*the* book," not your book. The its-my-interpretation cop-out may land you a big fine or even time behind bars (which no amount of creative interpretation will dissolve).

The idea that there are right and wrong interpretations is astonishingly simple. Rational adults live by it in order to forge their way through everyday life. Yet when the Bible becomes the subject matter, New Agers often throw all common sense to the winds of relativism. But we can and must return people to reality by giving examples of how they read other written documents.

If I am following a recipe for cheesecake, it is essential that I follow the recipe as it was intended to be followed; that is, I must honor the intention of the cook who wrote the recipe. If I use the interpretive license of the New Age, I could end up with almost anything—but not a palatable cheesecake.

Similarly, a college student studying for a final examination on the French Revolution must understand his history text in terms of what it actually says. He wants to *discover* what has been said. The teacher will grade his work accordingly, and no excuse such as "but that's what it means *to me*" will hold up. Interpretive relativism deserves a failing grade.

The subject of exegesis (the interpretation of a text) is too extensive to cover completely here.[1] Yet we must emphasize the crucial need for intellectual honesty in looking at the Bible. The first principle in interpretive integrity is the desire to see what is objectively there, pure and simple; that is, to discern what the author intended to communicate. The Bible is not meant to be a Rorschach test. Gordon Lewis simply but profoundly makes this point: "When we claim Biblical authority for an idea, we must be prepared to show from the grammar, the history, the culture and the context that the writer in fact taught that idea. Otherwise the Bible is not used but abused."[2] Consider Shakespeare's words:

In religion
What damned error, but some sober brow
Will bless it and approve it with a text
Hiding the grossness with fair ornament.

Although any biblical passage may have many *applications*, it can have only one true *meaning* (correct interpretation).

Esoteric Interpretation

At this point the New Ager may search for several escape routes. He may say that he is seeing the deeper or "esoteric" meaning of Scripture. In *The Planetary Commission*, John Randolph Price gives us his "interpretation" of John 14:6, a crucial passage on the uniqueness of Jesus Christ. Price says that while meditating he realized that "when Jesus said 'I am the Way'—it was not his personality speaking. It was the High Soul, the Christ Consciousness, that which I am. And when he said 'No one cometh unto the Father but by me'—that too was the voice of the Spiritual Ego."[3]

Price's interpretation is arguing that the man Jesus tapped into the universal and impersonal "Christ consciousness." Price goes on to say that he too is part of that Christ consciousness; it is "that which I am" (pantheism). He thus stands the text on its head. His conclusion is that we must look within to find our "absolute self,"[4] rather than look to Christ who is outside our self.

Yet if we look at the verse in context, we see that the disciple Thomas asked Jesus, "Lord, we don't know where you are going, so how can we know the way?" (Jn 14:5). Jesus replied, "I am the way and the truth and the life. No one comes to the Father except through me" (v. 6). Despite Price's meditatively derived insight, Jesus is clearly speaking of himself, his personality, as the one and only Christ and the one and only way to the Father. Since there is no evidence to the contrary, we should understand the words *I* and *me* in their plain and simple meaning. Elsewhere Jesus says that he is the "gate" and that "whoever enters through me will be saved" (Jn 10:9). To assert that Jesus is speaking of "the Christ consciousness" is to insert a meaning alien to the text. Gordon Lewis comments: "To introduce into any piece of literature 'key' ideas unknown to the author is to destroy the intended meaning."[5]

Yet Price tries to gain credibility by warping the Bible to support his New Age ideas. It is also interesting to note that Price rarely cites which verse he is misinterpreting. This is done by other New Age writers as well, and it gives the reader who is only vaguely familiar with the Bible the impression that Price's views are biblical. The reader is not able—unless she consults a concordance (something she's probably never heard of)—to look up what is quoted. With a little common sense, the act of looking up the text in its original context could well result in Price's theological downfall.

The "esoteric" interpretation suffers from the fact that it cannot be rationally *argued;* rather, it is simply *asserted:* "This is what Jesus *really* meant" or "This is the deeper meaning." If we ask why we should believe it, given the text before us, the answer will probably be, "You will know when you are more spiritual." That is an irrational evasion, not an enlightened evaluation. The rational interpreter says, "This is how I interpret it. I look at the grammar, the literary context, the cultural background, the plain meaning of the words used and the whole context of Scripture. I'm open to correction, but if and only if you can prove me wrong from the text itself." For the rational interpreter, debate and discussion are possible without an appeal to some mystical illumination devoid of cognitive content. James Sire comments that "the key to the fallacy of esoteric interpretation" is that "it is totally private. There is no way to check it out. There is no way to tell if the system that derives from esotericism is really so or merely a figment of the esotericist's imagination—or worse—a direct plant by the Father of Lies."[6]

Peter Kreeft further expands on the fallacy of "esoteric interpretation":

It is true that Eastern religions are esoteric, but Western religions are not; they are religions of a Book, a public revelation. An esoteric Christianity is a pure invention of the modern orientalizer. There is no evidence in Scripture or tradition for it. It is a hypothesis invented to save a dogma; a rationalization. But even if it were true, it would not be true; it is self contradictory. For it would not make Christ a guru but a fool, because His esoteric teaching led His followers in exactly the opposite direction from the [supposed] truth (pantheism)."[7]

In other words, if the esoteric interpreters are correct, Jesus wasn't much of a teacher since his explicit teachings led his disciples in the opposite direction of what esoteric interpreters find in his words. If we are to revere Jesus as a spiritual master, as New Agers claim to do, we must take him at his word (more on this below).

Furthermore, the esoteric interpreter of the Bible would strongly object if the orthodox Christian interpreted the Eastern mystical texts esoterically. If I read through the Hindu holy books and concluded that all references to Brahman (the impersonal, pantheistic god) were really references to the God of Abraham, Isaac and Jacob (the personal, transcendent God of the Bible), I should rightly be rebuked by the New Ager. I would be twisting the *objective* meaning of the texts in accordance with my *subjective* desire to read in what isn't even there. If New Agers cry "Foul!" at this silliness, they should likewise disqualify themselves from similar stunts with the Bible. The golden rule applies here as well: Interpret others' texts as you would have them interpret your own.

The Bible itself warns its readers to interpret it correctly. It is like a manufacturer's handbook that says, "Warning: Read the directions carefully." The prophet Jeremiah was called by God to prophesy against the religious apostasy of his day. He rhetorically asked those who were to guard the law of God, "How can you say 'We are wise, for we have the law of the LORD,' when actually the lying pen of the scribes has handled it falsely? The wise will be put to shame; they will be dismayed and trapped. Since they have rejected the word of the LORD, what kind of wisdom do they have?" (Jer 8:8-9).

Jesus rebuked some of the religious leaders of his day (the Sadducees) for trying to trick him concerning a question about the resurrection of the dead. He began his response by saying, "You are in error because you do not know the Scriptures or the power of God" (Mt 22:29), and then went on to disprove their charge. Jesus also strongly corrected the Pharisees and teachers of the law for substituting human tradition for the commandment of God found in the Scriptures (Mt 15:1-9).

The apostle Peter, speaking of the apostle Paul, warned that some "ignorant and unstable people" distort his writings "as they do the other Scriptures, to their own destruction" (2 Pet 3:16). Mishandling God's Word is spiritually dangerous. Paul himself defended his ministry by arguing that "we do not use deception, nor do we distort the word of God" as did the false teachers at Corinth (2 Cor 4:2).

Proverbs says that even wisdom can be distorted: "Like a lame man's legs that hang limp is a proverb in the mouth of a fool. . . . Like a thornbush in a drunkard's hand is a proverb in the mouth of a fool" (Prov 26:7, 9).

The craftiest misinterpreter of God's Word is God's enemy, the devil himself. After Jesus was led by the Spirit into the wilderness to fast and pray, the devil tempted him to disobey his heavenly Father. The tempter's method was misinterpretation: he hurled two out-of-context passages at the Savior in hopes of using God's Word against God's Son. But Jesus knew better (Mt 4:1-11) and relied on the real written Word. So should we.

Trustworthiness of the Bible

Another escape route which may be used by the New Ager is the objection, "Well you can't really trust the Bible. It was written so long ago, and it's been translated so many times." New Agers often rely more on experience than historical considerations, but if they are going to reject the Bible for historical reasons, historical arguments should be marshalled. Many people who raise this objection are only parroting clichés. It sounds like an easy out—unless, of course, you think it through and consult the evidence.

First, New Agers themselves often rely on or appeal to ancient texts for many of their ideas. Proponents of reincarnation claim it is taught in Hindu writings and other ancient texts. So it seems that being written long ago isn't a sufficient reason to reject the Bible, unless the New Ager wants likewise to throw out all ancient documents used to support New Age beliefs. Much talk of *"ancient* wisdom" would then be banished.

Second, neither is it logical to reject the Bible simply because we read it as a translation from the original languages. If we rejected as unreliable all translated works we would lose hundreds of authors and religious texts, including many cherished in New Age circles. A perfectly accurate translation may be difficult to acheive, but it is not impossible. The New International Version (NIV) of the Bible, for example, was completed by a team of topnotch scholars working for a number of years. And because these scholars were Christians who believe the Bible to be God's Word to us, they exercised the greatest care to translate the text accurately. They did not want to misrepresent their God, the God to whom they are accountable.[8]

Third, many different biblical translations can be consulted today.

Except for those few translations perpetrated by nonscholars to advance unbiblical ideas (such as the Watchtower's *New World Translation*),[9] there is great agreement in meaning. The overwhelming majority of differences between translations are only a matter of style, not substance.[10]

Fourth, there is greater evidence for the historical accuracy of the New Testament than for any other piece of ancient literature. Although I can only quickly paint the picture with a few wide but bright strokes, it can be shown that the New Testament passes three crucial tests for historicity: the biographical, internal and external tests.

The *biographical test* considers (a) how many manuscript copies we possess of a document and (b) the time gap between the documents and the originals. Although it is a well-kept secret, the New Testament is highly attested in the number of extant manuscripts (over 5,000), much more so than other pieces of classical literature.[11] Because of recent discoveries of ancient documents, biblical scholars today have more manuscripts to work with than scholars did two hundred years ago. So, paradoxically, the further we are in time from the life of Christ, the more early manuscripts we have that confirm the biblical records![12]

The time gap between the original writing and the earliest copies is also quite short, with manuscripts dating as early as A.D. 120, 200 and 350. Here again the New Testament leaves other ancient documents—with time gaps averaging a thousand years—in the historical dust.[13]

Concerning *internal evidence*, the New Testament claims to be written by eyewitnesses or by those who based their writing on the testimony of eyewitnesses (Lk 1:1-4; Gal 1; 2 Pet 1:16; 1 Jn 1:1; and so on). The style and content of the documents do not indicate fraud or deception. The writers had nothing to gain and much to lose by inventing a new religion that was so quickly and violently opposed by Judaism. Paul, who wrote more New Testament books than anyone else, suffered greatly for his faith (2 Cor 11:23-29) and declared that if Christ had not been raised from the dead, Christian faith was futile (1 Cor 15:17). The early church appealed to the historical knowledge of unbelievers (Acts 2:22) and Paul confidently affirmed that over five hundred people witnessed the resurrected Christ and that many of them were still living at the time in which he wrote (1 Cor 15:6). The accounts read as legitimate historical documents, not myths.[14] Furthermore, the New Testament books all may be safely dated before A.D. 95 and possibly even before A.D. 70, putting them quite close to the time of the events they record.[15]

The New Testament is also substantially corroborated by the *external evidence* of archaeology and extrabiblical historians. The Jewish historian Josephus, the Roman historians Tacitus and Suetonius, the Greek satirist Lucian, and others comment on the historicity of Christ and other events recorded in the New Testament.[16] Renowned archeologists such as William F. Allbright, Sir William Ramsay and others have also testified to the historicity of the New Testament documents and the Old Testament as well.[17]

Finally, on the presuppositional level, if a personal God exists who is interested in truthfully communicating with us, creatures made in his image, it is not unreasonable to believe that he would sovereignly preserve his Word for his purposes and our good.[18]

In light of all this, we should scarcely take seriously the purported revelations of "the lost years of Jesus," in which, supposedly, Jesus traveled to the East for enlightenment. These revelations are generally culled from one exotic (and erroneous) source after another which claim that the biblical accounts of Jesus got it all wrong and omitted his journeys East. Should any supposed record of Jesus' life come to the fore, let it marshal its historical merits in competition with holy writ. The competitors have an uphill battle against the incumbent.

Although it was discredited long ago, the "Unknown Life of Christ" still turns up to cause trouble. Originally published in 1894 in France by the Russian Nicolas Notovitch, it speaks of an ancient manuscript in India called "The Life of Issa" which describes Jesus' ministry in Palestine and his supposed trek to India. A story in *Heart* called "The Lost Years of Jesus" claims that this discovery will "shake the foundations of modern Christendom."[19]

Unfortunately for the New Age revisionists, this Eastern "Gospel" has nothing but imagination going for it. Noted Bible scholar Edgar Goodspeed commented that "on the whole, as an ancient document the 'Life of Issa' is altogether unconvincing. It reads more like a journalistic effort to describe what might have happened if Jesus had visited India and Persia in his youth, and what a modern cosmopolite thinks Jesus did and taught in his ministry in Palestine."[20] The internal evidence is unconvincing.

In addition, there is no bibliographical evidence for the veracity of "The Life of Issa." Notovitch supposedly copied what was read by a lama as heard through an interpreter. Even according to Notovitch, the manuscript was not deciphered and translated by a bona fide scholar.[21] In fact, no manuscript can be found at all, as Notovitch admitted.[22] If Notovitch was not tricked, he was a fraud, and Goodspeed gives good reason to suggest this.[23]

But whether he was a fraud or a fool, Notovitch's "Unknown Life of Christ" cannot compete with the New Testament as a reliable record of Jesus' life; nor can other purported gospels outside Matthew, Mark, Luke and John.[24] These have stood the test of time for good reason.

Reincarnation in the Bible?

In some cases, the New Ager may attempt to extract a New Age doctrine from the Bible without resorting to esotericism. For example, New Agers often say that the Bible teaches reincarnation, despite the flaming fact that there is a qualitative difference between the doctrine of reincarnation and the biblical teaching of resurrection. As James Sire puts it, "Reincarnation is the successive embodiment of the soul in a series of different mortal bodies; resurrection is the transformation of a person's one mortal body to an immortal one."[25] We should also add that reincarnation is thought to be an ongoing process whereas resurrection is a one-time and final event. Moreover, the sovereign Lord is in control of the time and type of resurrection; whereas an impersonal law of karma or the discarnate soul itself is the active agent in the case of reincarnation.

The Bible's insistence that we have but one life in which to make our peace with God through Christ (Heb 9:27) is radically at odds with the teaching that we have an unlimited number of opportunities (incarnations) for our spiritual evolution. While Scripture declares, "Today, if you hear his voice, do not harden your hearts" (Heb 3:7-8), reincarnation declares, "You have plenty of time to hear your inner voice and save yourself."

New Agers cite several passages in their attempt to argue reincarnation from the Bible, but we will consult the most important ones—because if these texts don't prove their point, none will.[26]

In several biblical passages Jesus says that John the Baptist is Elijah. In Matthew 11 he teaches his disciples concerning the ascetic prophet and forerunner for Christ: "And if you are willing to accept it, he is Elijah who was to come" (v. 14; see also Mk 9:11-14). In her book *It's All in the Playing* Shirley MacLaine refers to a similar statement in Matthew 17 (to be discussed below) and says, "As I read these verses in Matthew, it was clear to me that Jesus and his disciples were talking about reincarnation. They were saying that John the Baptist had lived in a previous incarnation as Elias [King James for Elijah]."[27]

On the surface, these verses do seem to teach reincarnation: Elijah had come back as John the Baptist this time around. Didn't Jesus say so? But several factors clash with this conclusion.

First, if we consult the account of the prophet Elijah's exit from earth recorded in 2 Kings 2:9-18, we find that he never died, but was taken bodily (or translated) into heaven. This was common knowledge in the Israel of Jesus' day, which explains why many awaited

Elijah's coming. But in the standard reincarnation theory, someone must first die in order for her soul to be released from her body and then incarnated into another body. Since Elijah never died, he could not be reincarnated. Matthew 17 makes this crystal clear. Jesus took Peter, James and John up to a high mountain where he "was transfigured before them. His face shone like the sun, and his clothes became as white as the light. Just then there appeared before them Moses and Elijah, talking with Jesus" (vv. 1–3).

We must remember that by this time John the Baptist had already lived and died. If he had been the reincarnation of Elijah, then Elijah could not have appeared with Moses on the Mount of Transfiguration. Therefore, John the Baptist could not have been the reincarnation of Elijah.

Some may want to say at this point that the transfiguration account did not involve the actual personages of Moses and Elijah, but was rather a hallucination of some kind. But the text reports that Jesus was actually transfigured before them, that Moses and Elijah appeared and talked with Jesus (Lk 9:31 adds that they spoke of his upcoming death) and that the Father pronounced Jesus as his Son (Mt 17:5). This event cannot easily be splintered into hallucinogenic and historic elements. The context demands that Moses (representing the Old Testament law) and Elijah (representing the prophets) actually conversed with Jesus Christ on the mount. Jesus wasn't mumbling to himself. Moses, Elijah and Jesus all were objectively there, as publicly observed by Peter, James and John. Peter was so convinced of their personal presence that he voiced a desire to build shelters for them (v. 4).[28]

Some may respond that the King James Version of the Bible calls the event a "vision" (v. 9), and so it is not to be seen as objective. Yet the New International Version substitutes "what you have seen" for "vision" and for good reason; the Greek word in question, *horama,* is best defined as something seen with the eyes, not a hallucination.[29]

We should add to this John the Baptist's own confession that he was not literally Elijah (Jn 1:21). He was neither the reincarnation of Elijah, nor the original Elijah incognito.

This idea helps us explain Jesus' affirmation that John was Elijah. Jesus was speaking of John the Baptist's function or office as a prophet, not of his actual identity as a person. Second Kings 2 illustrates this distinction. Before Elijah was taken "up to heaven in a whirlwind" (v. 1), Elisha, his protégé, requested of Elijah that he "inherit a double portion of your spirit" (v. 9). This request was granted as indicated by the "company of the prophets" who said "the spirit of Elijah is resting on Elisha" (v. 15). Elisha asked for—and received—the prophetic spirit of Elijah from the Lord. He too would be a prophet. He certainly was not the reincarnation of Elijah. Neither was John the Baptist.

A passage in Luke 1 explains this. The angel of the Lord appeared to Zechariah in the Temple and prophesied concerning the mission of John the Baptist. He said, "He will go on before the Lord, in the *spirit and power* of Elijah, to turn the hearts of the fathers to their children and the disobedient to the wisdom of the righteous—to make ready a people prepared for the Lord" (v. 17). John would thus fulfill the prophecy of Malachi 4:5-6. "The spirit and power of Elijah" meant that he would have the same office and function as Elijah, and so *in that sense* he was Elijah.

Given the biblical context and Jesus' adherence to the Scriptures (Mt 5:17-20; Jn 10:35), he could not have meant that John the Baptist was the reincarnation of Elijah, anymore than when he said that "whoever does the will of my Father in heaven is my brother and sister and mother" (Mt 12:50) he meant that all Christians were literally his blood brothers, sisters or mother. A "this is" (identification) statement can be metaphorical, and in this case the metaphorical interpretation makes the most sense in light of the whole of Scripture. John Snyder offers an explanatory paraphrase of the passage in Matthew 11:14: "That which you were anticipating to be accomplished in the person of Elijah was virtually fulfilled in the person of John the

Baptist."[30]

This does not contradict the idea that John the Baptist had an Elijah-like ministry such that in some sense he could be called Elijah. The way we use nicknames today illustrates this. If a power-hitting, rookie baseball player named John Jones, for example, reminds us of Babe Ruth, we might call him "Babe" Jones or even "the Babe." He bats in "the spirit and (homerun) power" of the Babe himself, but he is not the Babe himself.

In addition to this, many passages of Scripture clearly teach resurrection, not reincarnation.[31] In speaking of God's separation of the sheep from the goats, Jesus says that the goats "will go away to eternal punishment, but the righteous to eternal life" (Mt 25:46). The book of Daniel says that "multitudes who sleep in the dust of the earth will awake: some to everlasting life, others to shame and everlasting contempt" (Dan 12:2). Those who embrace Christ as Savior will live forever with him; those who continue to rebel against God will suffer eternal punishment.

The New Ager needs to be honest and admit that the Bible's teaching on resurrection is incompatible with the New Age teaching and not be so deceived as to think that reincarnation is in harmony with the Bible. Then at least the real disagreement will be highlighted, rather than being obscured by the esoteric indiscretions of playing fast and loose with the revealed truth.

Reincarnation and the Conspiracy Theory of the Bible
New Agers sometimes object that reincarnation was once in the Bible but was deleted at a later time. This censoring was supposedly performed by manipulative clerics who feared the doctrine of multiple lives might loosen their power over the masses who believed they must obey the church in their one life to gain heaven and avoid hell.

This assertion has become an old saw in New Age circles. It often functions at what sociologists call the "taken for granted" level. I have already cited Ruth Montgomery's version of it in chapter one. As another example, consider Kenneth Ring's passing remark in his book *Heading toward Omega:* "Although variants of this doctrine were acceptable to and promulgated by the early Church Fathers, reincarnation was declared heretical and expunged from Christian dogma in the sixth century."[32] Ring's undocumented comment illustrates the cavalier manner by which many writers rewrite history without a second—or even a first—thought.

This "conspiracy" view of the formulation of the Bible has several imaginative versions. One is that reincarnation was erased from the Bible at the Council of Nicea (A.D. 325); another is that it was edited out at the Second Council of Constantinople (A.D. 553). Some say all the reincarnation teachings were destroyed completely by the church; others say the writings were simply rejected. But the real conspiracy seems to be one of ignorance—or worse—of the New Age consensus.

Before consulting the historical material, we should first question the very rationale of the conspiracy theory. In MacLaine's *Out on a Limb,* her friend David enlightens her to the notion that "it was to the advantage of the Church to 'protect the people' from the real truth . . . [of] each soul's responsibility for its own behavior in the realization of its own divinity."[33] David's assertion jumps to the purported motives of the manipulating clergy, rather than to any factual considerations. It is a crass case of psychologizing at the expense of historical interest.

If the early church—which, for some reason, is assumed to be uniformly deceptive—wanted to control the ignorant masses, they could just as easily have used the doctrine of reincarnation to that end. In fact, this was done for centuries in India. The entire caste system was based on reincarnation: people's castes were thought to be assigned according to their good or bad karma. If one had been born a Brahmin (the highest class), he deserved it and should not be demoted in this life; if one had been born an Untouchable, she deserved it and should not be promoted in this life. Social mobility in the present lifetime was impossible. The Brahmins ruled; others obeyed. Even if it were granted that both Brahmins and Untouchables were, in essence, God, they were viewed as being at different levels of god-realization. Reincarnation need not be egalitarian; historically it seldom has been.

Reincarnation can easily be used to oppress the masses. The theory that the church expunged reincarnation from the Bible in order to control the masses, therefore, loses much of its force. The clergy could have exerted just as much control if they had taught reincarnation—assuming they had only malignant motives. So the supposed necessity to rub out reincarnation doesn't bear up under closer scrutiny.

Furthermore, the biblical texts that were canonized proclaim the liberty bestowed by the gospel: that anyone can be born again and assured of heaven simply through faith in Jesus Christ, independent of any church authority. Sad to say, this teaching was later largely lost, and the Bible itself became inaccessible to many. But if the canonization of the Bible had been strictly according to what texts would have best enslaved the masses to the church, an epistle like Galatians would never have survived! Here Paul stresses that salvation comes through faith in Jesus Christ, not through obeying the law. Salvation is dependent on no human institution, but rather on God who offers it freely to all. New Age conspiracy ideas to the contrary, there is no reason to assume that the early church leadership was only concerned with suppressing that which would jeopardize its power.

If the church had been adamantly concerned to fumigate the Bible of anything even hinting at reincarnation, why would it have missed Jesus' statement that John the Baptist was Elijah? We have shown that this passage does not truly teach reincarnation; yet it appears to do so at first glance (or at a jaundiced second glance). If the church fathers aimed to extract anything remotely reincarnational, they should have destroyed that one! But they did not.

Although the rationale for "the conspiracy view" is weak, the historical case for it is even more problematic. Whatever later church councils decided about the Bible is in one sense irrelevant because, as John Snyder points out, we can "go directly to the most ancient texts that preserve the gospel for us. Those texts that are the earliest surviving manuscripts in Greek show that the verities of faith antedate any medieval attempts at revision. Many of these manuscripts are *older* than the major councils of the church. The ancient world was so flooded with copies of the New Testament that it was well beyond the power of any officials to expunge certain uncomfortable doctrines from them."[34]

The New Testament documents were selected for good reasons: they had to be written by an apostle or endorsed by one; they had to have been recognized early on as authoritative in the early Christian congregations; and they had to contain teaching consistent with apostolic doctrine.[35] It is simply historically false that corrupt councils of conniving clerics whipped up the biblical canon in accordance with their own whims; rather, they formally recognized what the churches already practiced. Noted biblical scholar F. F. Bruce explains:

> One thing must be emphatically stated. The New Testament books did not become authoritative for the Church because they were formally included in the canonical list; on the contrary, the Church included them in her canon because she already regarded them as divinely inspired, recognizing their innate worth and general apostolic authority, direct or indirect.[36]

Bruce adds that the first two church councils called to codify the canon in North Africa in the late fourth century did not assert anything novel. They simply identified the practice of the churches.[37]

None of the New Testament documents teach reincarnation. We should see that Jesus' commitment to the Old Testament Scriptures prohibited him from teaching reincarnation, since, like Jesus himself, the Old Testament clearly teaches resurrection (Job 19:26;[38] Dan 12:1-2); in fact, Jesus upbraided the Sadducees for denying the resurrection by quoting to them Exodus 3:6 (Mt 22:23–32).

The early church fathers also taught resurrection, and only explicitly opposed reincarnation when it was necessary to defend truth from error. The teaching of reincarnation had no roots in historical Judaism or Christianity; only after the fact did certain heretical thinkers—influenced by Platonic, Pythagorean or other Hellenistic or Eastern thought—attempt to graft it into Christian theology. Irenaeus opposed reincarnation as did Justin Martyr, Jerome, Tertullian, Gregory of Nyssa and Augustine.[39] Augustine rejected Porphyry's reincarnation ideas by saying of Porphyry, "It caused him no embarrassment to hold a belief which would admit the risk of a mother returning as a girl and marrying her own son." He then eloquently presents the biblical view:

> How much more honourable is the belief taught by the holy and truthful angels, spoken of by the prophets under the guidance of the Spirit of God, and by him whose coming as Saviour was foretold by heralds in advance, and by the apostles who were sent out and who filled the whole world with the teaching of the gospel. The belief that souls return once for all to their own bodies is far more honourable than that they return time after time to different bodies.[40]

When New Agers say that the church condemned reincarnation at the Second Council of Constantinople (A.D. 553), they are referring to a pronouncement against a certain teaching by the early church father Origin (185–254). What actually happened was that either in 543 or in 553, fifteen anathemas (condemnations) were adopted against Origin, none of which refers to reincarnation. Yet one of them reads, "If anyone asserts the fabulous pre-existence of souls . . . let him be anathema."[41] New Age writers take this to mean a rejection of a strong current of reincarnation in the early church. This is just not so. The anathema only concerned Origin's teaching that human spirits predated their existence in human bodies. Origin did not hold to reincarnation, but simply spiritual pre-existence. This is what the

Council rightly condemned as unbiblical.[42] In fact, Origin explicitly rejected reincarnation in several of his writings. For instance, in commenting on the Matthew 17 verse disscussed above he said,

In this place it does not appear to me that by Elijah the soul is spoken of, lest I should fall into the dogma of transmigration [reincarnation], which is foreign to the Church of God and not handed down by the Apostles, nor anywhere set forth in Scriptures.[43]

Although all reincarnationists hold to the pre-existence of the soul (before bodily reincarnation), not all who hold to the pre-existence of the soul, like Origin, hold to reincarnation.[44] New Agers typically miss this logical distinction.

Flying in the face of facts is Shirley MacLaine's popularization and distortion: "I read that Christ's teachings about reincarnation were struck from the Bible during the Fifth Ecumenical Council meeting in Constantinople in the year A.D. 553."[45]

First, the Council pertained to Origin's teachings, not Christ's. (Origin never purported to write a gospel account either.) Second, since Origin's writings were never a part of the Bible (nor even considered as candidates for the canon), they could not be "struck from the Bible." Third, Origin didn't teach reincarnation. Ms. MacLaine packs errors tighter than sardines in a squashed can. Yet because of her great media exposure, she is believed by millions.

Let us pray that millions of alert Christian witnesses will lovingly but insistently marshal the truths of Scripture, logic and history in order to "demolish arguments and every pretension that sets itself up against the knowledge of God" (2 Cor 10:5), that New Age error may be stopped dead in its tracks.

Notes

[1]See Walter Kaiser, *Toward an Exegetical Theology* (Grand Rapids, Mich.: Baker, 1981).
[2]Gordon L. Lewis, *Confronting the Cults* (Phillipsburg, N.J.: Presbyterian and Reformed, 1985), p. 137.
[3]Price, *Planetary Commission*, p. 75.

[4]Ibid.

[5]Lewis, *Confronting the Cults,* p. 169.

[6]James W. Sire, *Scripture Twisting* (Downers Grove, Ill.: InterVarsity Press, 1980), p. 113.

[7]Peter Kreeft, "The Most Important Argument," in *The Intellectuals Speak Out about God,* ed. Roy Abraham Varghese (Chicago: Regnery Gateway, 1984), p. 251.

[8]See the preface to *The NIV Study Bible,* ed. Kenneth Barker (Grand Rapids, Mich.: Zondervan, 1985), pp. xi–xiii.

[9]See Robert H. Countess, *The Jehovah's Witnesses' New Testament* (Phillipsburg, N.J.: Presbyterian and Reformed, 1982).

[10]On the issue of textual criticism and biblical authority see Gleason Archer, *Encyclopedia of Biblical Difficulties* (Grand Rapids, Mich.: Zondervan, 1982), pp. 32–44.

[11]See J. P. Moreland, *Scaling the Secular City* (Grand Rapids, Mich.: Baker, 1987), pp. 135–36.

[12]Walter Martin, *Essential Christianity* (Ventura, Calif.: Regal Books, 1980), pp. 15–24.

[13]Moreland, *Scaling the Secular City,* pp. 135–36.

[14]Ibid., pp. 137–47; and William Lane Craig, *Apologetics: An Introduction* (Chicago: Moody, 1985), pp. 167–206, specifically on the testimony for the resurrection.

[15]Moreland, *Scaling the Secular City,* pp. 146–57.

[16]Norman Geisler, *Christian Apologetics,* pp. 323–25.

[17]Ibid., pp. 325–27; and Josh McDowell, *Evidence That Demands a Verdict,* Rev. ed. (San Bernardino, Calif.: Campus Crusade for Christ, 1979), pp. 65–78.

[18]On propositional revelation see Francis Schaeffer, *He Is There and He Is Not Silent* (Wheaton, Ill.: Tyndale, 1975), pp. 91–100; and, in greater detail, Henry, *God, Revelation, and Authority,* Vols. 2–4.

[19]"The Lost Years of Jesus," *Heart* (Spring 1983), pp. 6ff.

[20]Edgar Goodspeed, *Modern Apocrypha* (Boston: Beacon Press, 1956), p. 9.

[21]Ibid.

[22]Ibid., p. 11.

[23]Ibid., pp. 10–14.

[24]See Groothuis, *Unmasking,* pp. 148–50.

[25]Sire, *Scripture Twisting,* p. 92.

[26]For a thorough treatment of all relevant passages see Norman L. Geisler and J. Yutaka Amano, *The Reincarnation Sensation* (Wheaton, Ill.: Tyndale, 1987), pp. 133–54. I'm indebted to their work for some of my arguments.

[27]Shirley MacLaine, *It's All in the Playing* (New York: Bantam, 1987), p. 222.

[28]For an elaboration on the transfiguration see Francis Schaeffer, *True Spirituality,* pp. 45–59.

[29]See Robert A. Morey, *Death and Afterlife* (Minneapolis: Bethany, 1984), p. 207.

[30]John Snyder, *Reincarnation vs. Resurrection* (Chicago: Moody, 1984), p. 51.

[31]For a comprehensive treatment of the biblical view of death and afterlife see Morey, *Death and Afterlife.*

[32]Kenneth Ring, *Heading toward Omega* (New York: William Morrow, 1985), p. 158.

[33]Shirley MacLaine, *Out on a Limb* (New York: Bantam, 1983), p. 205; see also p. 237.

[34]Snyder, *Reincarnation vs. Resurrection,* p. 83.

[35]Albrecht, *Reincarnation,* p. 42; see also R. Laird Harris, *Inspiration and Canonicity of*

the Bible (Grand Rapids, Mich.: Zondervan, 1975), pp. 219–71.

[36]F. F. Bruce, *The New Testament Documents: Are They Reliable?* (Downers Grove, Ill.: Inter Varsity Press, 1967), p. 27; see also Henry, *God, Revelation, and Authority,* 4:405–449, on canonicity in general.

[37]Bruce, *New Testament Documents,* p. 27.

[38]For a defense of the idea that this teaches resurrection see Gleason Archer, *Encyclopedia,* pp. 240–41; and Walter Kaiser, *Toward an Old Testament Theology* (Grand Rapids, Mich.: Zondervan, 1978). pp. 180–81.

[39]See Albrecht, *Reincarnation,* pp. 44–49; and Joseph P. Gudel, Robert M. Bowman, Jr., and Dan Schlessinger, "Reincarnation: Did the Church Suppress It?" *Christian Research Journal* 10, no. 1 (Summer 1987), pp. 8–12.

[40]Augustine, *City of God* 10.30.

[41]Quoted in John Hick, *Death and Eternal Life* (San Francisco: Harper and Row, 1980), p. 394.

[42]See ibid., pp. 392–94; and Albrecht, *Reincarnation,* pp. 46–47.

[43]Allan Menzies, ed., *The Ante-Nicene Fathers of the Christian Church,* vol. 4 (Grand Rapids: Eerdmans, 1978), pp. 474–75; quoted in Albrecht, *Reincarnation,* pp. 46–47.

[44]See Joseph Wilson Trig, *Origin: The Bible and Philosophy in the Third-century Church* (Atlanta: John Knox, 1983), pp. 107, 209, 213.

[45]MacLaine, *Out on a Limb,* p. 249.

Comparing
Gods

6

ONCE WHILE I WAS TEACHING A CLASS ON THE NEW AGE MOVEMENT, A STU-
dent mentioned that he thought Jesus was a manifestation of God.
That's a start, I thought. But when I pressed him further he said that
Jesus was a personal manifestation of the impersonal essence of the
universe. For him, John 1:1 could be rewritten, "In the Beginning was
the It, and the It became a he." That is not the Christ of the Bible.

God, sin, Jesus, atonement, love, justice—often Christians and New
Agers mean different things by these terms. Discussing these differences not only aids communication but also pinpoints the strengths
and weaknesses of the positions. Frequently I have found that New
Agers have not thought through completely what they believe and
that they unconsciously still carry many theistic assumptions. This
can provide for fruitful apologetic and evangelistic discussions.

Is God Personal?

The God of the New Age is merely the Ultimate It, not a personal being. No matter how many nouns we capitalize—such as *Force, Energy, Essence, Consciousness, Vibration, Principle, Being*—a pantheistic God remains impersonal—infinite, but impersonal. Existentially, psychologically and logically, an impersonal God is ultimately unsatisfying.

As Marilyn Ferguson says, "In the emergent [New Age] spiritual tradition God is not the personage of our Sunday-school mentality."[1] Although this view may at first titillate the psychic explorer who seeks joyfully to escape from the moralism of a doting deity, the insignificance of a world bereft of a personal God may prove unsettling. The New Age deity is ill-equipped for personal communion. This displays what might be called "the religious inadequacy" of the position.

In his critical look at "the marketing of the mystic East," Gita Mehta notes this phenomenon: "The Buddha had said, 'God is Nothing!' and been elevated to divinity. The more the Buddha explained the Void, the faster his disciples rushed to fill the Void with the Buddha. Groupies hate a vacuum."[2] The popular piety of much of Hinduism also shows its hatred of a vacuum by its pantheon of personal gods (polytheism) as opposed to the impersonalist "pure pantheism" of some of the Hindu holy books.[3] Human beings made in God's image are created for fellowship with the personal God revealed in the Bible and through Jesus Christ. We all sense this at some level; yet, in our rebellion from God, we flee his reality. Brooks Alexander insightfully captures the paradox:

> As creatures made in the image of God, we cry endlessly after our Maker. As beings in rebellion against God, we go to almost any lengths to evade his actual presence. The result has been a spiritual schizophrenia. On the one hand, we exhibit a compulsive fascination with things of ultimate reality, good and evil, God and eternity, sin and salvation. We cannot simply dispense with our

religiosity. On the other hand, we experience the self-contradiction that even our seeking is also a flight from God, that our very groping is an effort to struggle loose from his grip. Both our religious urge and our perversions of it seem to be built into our nature.[4]

Our perverse religious urge results in the production of idols, be they of clay, stone, sex, money, "consciousness" or "spirit"—despite the fact that, as Paul reports, we know that God exists and is worthy of worship and thanksgiving (Rom 1:18-22). Calvin rightly noted that apart from the grace of God, "the human mind is, so to speak, a perpetual forge of idols."[5] As Alexander says, "We cannot avoid the reality of our spiritual need, but we search for an answer to that need which avoids the reality of God."[6]

In New Age spirituality, inward meditation replaces prayer. The goal is really monolog—discovery of the Deep Self or Higher Self—not dialog, the interpersonal communication between conscious, interested beings.

The New Age interest in channeling may stem from a spiritual dissatisfaction with the impersonal nature of their world view. New Agers may talk about God, but they can't talk to God—or if they do, there's no one there to listen, let alone answer. Meditation and other "psychotechnologies" may offer powerful personal experiences—just as getting shocked is quite personal!—without an experience of a personal God. Yet channeling (mediumship) offers personal contact with some very personable beings.

For the right price, seekers gain audiences with various exotic "entities" who discourse on the nature of God, humanity and the universe. Specific personal problems may also be addressed. While the New Age God can't provide the personal touch, a 35,000-year-old warrior named Ramtha can and does. A channeler from southern California, Jach Pursel, channels an entity named "Lazarus" who is billed as "the consummate friend."

Whether the channelers are demonized, fraudulent, mentally deranged (or some combination) is secondary to the fact that they are presenting New Age doctrine in an alluring manner. Lies are often psychologically attractive. Paul warned Timothy of those who "suit their own desires" by "gather[ing] around them a great number of teachers to say what their itching ears want to hear" and so turn from truth to myths (2 Tim 4:3-4). For all the New Age's impersonal character and emphasis on self alone, the channeling phenomenon—the promise of contact with personal entities—may indicate the insufficiency of the self as God, despite the fact that the channeled messages herald the same old impersonalism and selfism. This provides existential or psychological evidence against the New Age position It is ultimately unsatisfying for real human needs because it provides no ultimate grounds for worship, adoration, fellowship or obedience in relation to a personal God.[7]

Yet the impersonalism of the New Age is also logically unattractive. New Agers may decry a personal God as but a childish image, a crass anthropomorphism, a God made in the human image. God, they say, is "beyond personality"—which they take to be a "higher" status. If the Christian view of a personal God were exhausted by the image of a heavenly grandfather, the criticism would be telling. But it isn't.

God, as ultimately personal, is not limited to merely human personality, that is, to a finite personality—although without ceasing to be God, the Second Person of the Trinity became a man through the Incarnation (Jn 1:1-2, 14; Phil 2:5-11). God is, rather, infinitely personal. As Walter Martin points out, God performs the acts of a personal being:

> God hears (Exodus 2:24), God sees (Genesis 1:4), God creates (Genesis 1:1), God knows (II Timothy 2:19, Jeremiah 29:11), God has a will (I John 2:17); God is a cognizant reflectable ego, i.e., a personal being, "I AM that I AM" (Exodus 3:14; Genesis 17:1). This is the God of Christianity, an omnipotent, omniscient, and omnipresent Personality, who manifests every attribute of a personality.[8]

Despite New Age semantic smoke screens, I cannot think of God as a "Higher *Consciousness*"—as their literature often puts it—without thinking of some-one being self-conscious, of some-one being there and that some-one having the highest consciousness. An impersonal God cannot logically be said to be conscious: no one is home at all. This is a logical inconsistency of much New Age thinking.

The metaphysical distinction between humans and the God of the Bible is not between the personal and the impersonal. It is rather between the finite and the infinite. Humans are finite (or limited) and personal; God is infinite (or unlimited) and personal.[9] Yet infinite personality does not imply a vague, abstract infinity in which personal attributes dissipate into a mystical mist. God is infinitely personal, not infinitely everything. C. S. Lewis noted:

> We say that God is "infinite." In the sense that His knowledge and power extend not to some things but to all, this is true. But if by using the word "infinite" we encourage ourselves to think of Him as a formless "everything" about whom nothing in particular and everything in general is true, then it would be better to drop that word altogether."[10]

Having explained something of the Christian view of God, the illogic of the New Age God becomes more apparent.

What sense can it make to think of God as both supreme and impersonal? If this were true, God would lack certain human attributes such as mind, will, emotion and morality. He (It) would be less than human, not more. The impersonal, then, would be viewed as somehow higher than the personal. But this is exactly backward, and we do not normally think or live this way. We accord more respect to a professor than to a potato, and for good reason. The professor possesses personal attributes—thought, will, emotion, morality—not dreamt of by even the finest Idaho potato. Likewise, a personal electrician knows how to fix the wiring of your home or office; impersonal electricity knows nothing. A personal plumber can fix your sink; impersonal water is no help at all. We give Academy Awards to actors and actresses, not celluloid.

The following interchange between an East Indian Christian, Vishal Mangalwadi, and a Hindu helps showcase the New Age confusion on this point.

Vishal: Is . . . Universal Consciousness personal or impersonal?

Hindu: It is impersonal and infinite.

V: Is personality higher than impersonality?

H: Of course!

V: Then why do you want to become lower and merge into impersonal consciousness?

H: Well, no. Personality is actually lower than impersonality,

V: Why do you then use the term evolution? You should say that we have devolved out of the impersonal. Then you should really respect this grass on which we are sitting. Being impersonal, it is higher than us, and you should not walk on it.

H: This is confusing.[11]

The confusion stems from deeming the divine both infinite and impersonal. The New Age exalts the person as divine and unlimited at one moment and the next speaks of an impersonal God which would rob humans of any individual significance, value and purpose as real persons!

Yet the Bible avoids such absurdity by affirming that God—who is infinite, personal and the highest Cause of the universe and humanity—made finite humans in his own personal image. This soundly squares with our intuition that a cause must be equal to or greater than its effect(s). Like comes from like. Water does not rise above its source unaided. If human personality is real and not illusory (as most sane people believe), then it makes more sense to believe that a Personal and Intelligent Cause created and sustains human intelligence and personality than it does to pay philosophical tribute to the Impersonal Itness of the It.

The Creator of concrete things (people and the rest of the cosmos) must not be thought of as an amorphous principle, but rather as a concrete, individual Fact himself, or, as C. S. Lewis put it, "the fountain of all facthood."[12] God is not an indefinite thing but a definite, personal being. The idea of an Impersonal Ultimate is as metaphysically impotent as it is conceptually bankrupt (see Acts 17:28-29). It is Christianity that best explains our origin and status as persons; it also gives present meaning, significance and value to us as real, individual persons made in God's image.

The New Age experience of "higher consciousness" is supposed to be a realization of impersonal ultimate reality; yet just *who* would be there to report that his personality was swallowed up by the voracious Impersonal is a bit hard to say. One would be in the odd (actually impossible) position of saying that he experienced a state of impersonal being where he (as a person) ceased to exist! But surely this is self-contradictory since only as a person can one remember![13]

This conundrum of an impersonal God led Hans Küng to ask the rhetorical question, "Are we to say that a God without mind and understanding, freedom and love, is still God? Would such a God be able to explain mind and understanding, freedom and love, in the world and in man? Would the God who gives meaning to persons not himself be personal?"[14]

The psalmist says:

Take heed, you senseless ones among the people;
    you fools, when will you become wise?
Does he who implanted the ear not hear?
    Does he who formed the eye not see?
Does he who disciplines nations not punish?
    Does he who teaches man lack knowledge? (Ps 94:8-10)

The Bible reveals a God who is ultrapersonal, more personal than humans are personal. Further, God is interpersonal within his own being. God is, in a sense, a divine community, a tri-unity of three eternally communing and coequal persons: Father, Son and Spirit. Or, as the Athanasian Creed puts it, "We worship one God in Trinity, and Trinity in Unity."[15] This immeasurably enriches our understanding that "God is love" (1 Jn 4:16). As C. S. Lewis marvelously puts it: "Even within the Holy One Himself, it is not sufficient that the Word should *be* God, it must also be *with* God [John 1:1]. The Father eternally begets the Son and the Holy Spirit proceeds: deity introduces distinctions within itself so that the union of reciprocal love may transcend mere arithmetical unity or self-identity."[16] God is always love—in the profundity of simultaneously being loved, loving and lovable—even before the creation. As Chesterton put it, "For it is not well for God to be alone."[17]

Jesus' prayer for all believers demonstrates God's interpersonal nature when he prays to his Father saying, "Father, glorify me in your presence with the glory I had with you before the world began" (Jn 17:5). He also speaks of "the glory you have given me because you loved me before the creation of the world" (v. 24). For the disciple of Jesus, love has roots in the ultimate reality of the Trinity. The New Age's monism of "ultimate oneness" and impersonal pantheism destroys the very basis of interpersonal love. Frankly, such an "infinite iceberg"[18] leaves me cold and utterly desolate.

In a nutshell, God is personal, interpersonal and also personable—creating us in his own image for fellowship with him and reaching out to lost men and women in the person of Jesus Christ, the God-man. Here alone is the satisfaction for real human need.[19]

Besides choosing between a personal and an impersonal God, the difference between the God of the Bible and the New Age God can also be seen when we explore the issue of justice.

Evil and New Age Relativism

The heartbeat of the gospel is that God sent his "one and only Son" (Jn 3:16) into the world to rescue humanity from evil. But the New Age tends to dismiss the idea of real human evil as heavy-handed moralism. Evil, reports Shirley MacLaine, is just "live" spelled backward—merely a lower form of consciousness.[20]

Christians must articulate the Bible's realism. Since the Fall (Gen

3), we are all infected by a sinful disposition that we indulge when we commit specific sins. The New Ager declares the human problem is ignorance of our true divine potential. Christianity teaches that our essential problem is prideful rebellion against our Superior, God. Sin means breaking God's holy law and offending his holy character. R. C. Sproul dramatically defines *sin* as "cosmic treason . . . against a perfectly pure Sovereign. It is an act of supreme ingratitude toward the One to whom we owe everything, to the One who has given us life itself."[21] Sin is not only universal ("all have sinned," Rom 3:23), it is also omnidirectional: We sin, first, against God; second, against others; and third, against ourselves.[22]

The Christian has no trouble calling incest, holocausts, homosexual practices, Satanism, adultery and everyday selfishness evil. The New Ager cannot consistently do so; and it is here that the New Ager suffers at the hand of moral reality.

In her best-seller *Dancing in the Light,* Shirley MacLaine relates a long conversation with a rather imposing entity named "Higher Self." Higher Self utters the following: "Until mankind realizes that there is, in truth, no good and there is, in truth, no evil, there will be no peace."[23] Anthropologist Wade Davis commented that he hoped the movie version of his book, *The Serpent and the Rainbow,* would "have had a more explicit statement that voodoo is good, that Haiti will teach you that good and evil are one."[24] (Notice that *good* means nothing if "good and evil are one." We could just as correctly say "Voodoo is evil.")

Sadly, such amoral pollutants are not uncommon in New Age atmospheres.[25] New Age thought is riddled with a radical relativism: morality (if we could even call it that) is relative to each individual. There is no standard of morality distinct from one's own consciousness. For the New Ager, the idea of absolute and objective morality evaporates for at least four reasons.

First, if we are gods, we do not stand under a higher ethical authority or law. We are a law unto ourselves. Second, if "all is one" (monism), then clear distinctions between good and evil dissolve into the sea of Being. Third, since New Agers are enthralled by evolutionary optimism, they reject the fixed or static view of morality as "out of date." The evolution of consciousness, they affirm, demands freedom and novelty. Fourth, the teaching of reincarnation often endorses a relativism that says, "Whatever happens is part of my karma. It all fits perfectly into my process of divine discovery. Don't force your views of morality on me."

Yet this New Age morality (or lack thereof) suffers from several sicknesses.

Logically, it is self-defeating to state that there are absolutely no absolutes, to say that everything is "absolutely relative." This statement itself asserts an absolute, namely, that there aren't any absolutes. We should ask the New Ager if she is "absolutely sure there are no absolutes." It is similar to saying or writing that there are no words. It is a statement of denial which cannot be made without using the very thing it denies. Thus it is false.

But the New Ager may qualify the statement by saying there are no moral absolutes, but there are nonmoral absolutes (such as monism and pantheism). But there is a telling objection to this as well because New Agers often say we *should* reject objective ethics and embrace relativism.

When Shirley MacLaine's "Higher Self" says that we *ought* to throw off morality, it seems he is issuing a *moral command* to be rid of morality. But to issue such a command is to assume the morality one is rejecting. This is self-refuting. This is what one of my philosophy professors called a "kamikazi statement." Although New Age kamikazis crash on their own airfield, they inflict no logical damage on the biblical view of morality. A totally consistent amoral relativism can issue no commands binding on anyone else. It's strictly solitaire.

Although many celebrate the death of moral absolutes, existentially it remains quite difficult to live out such a relativism. There often exists a great gap between the lips and the life.

For instance, I often hear New Agers claim that "we all have our own truth," thus appearing tolerant. Yet in the same discussion they say that Christians are "less than fully enlightened" or "less evolved" (especially true for creationists!) and need a few more incarnations to get their metaphysics unmuddled and their self-image adjusted. But by saying this, New Agers are assuming the New Age position is true and right, and that the Christian position is wrong and bad! Who's the absolutist now?

Similarly, the inconsistency of New Age relativism shines brightly when any New Ager is denouncing activities as a violation of "human rights." If they are decrying the injustices of, say, South Africa, we must ask how they can assume any objective and universal human rights when, according to the other side of their mouths, "we all create our own reality"?[26] A consistent relativism can neither praise nor condemn in any morally meaningful sense, and yet because of humanity's God-given conscience (Rom 2:14-15), New Agers act inconsistently with their world view. The Christian's world view, on the other hand, is adequate both to establish real moral categories and to diagnose the New Ager's ethical inconsistencies.[27]

The philosophical finger can also be pointed at other sorts of existential crises. Francis Schaeffer reports a conversation with a Hindu student who held that, in Schaeffer's words, "there is no difference between cruelty and non-cruelty." Another student seized the moment and held a steaming pot of tea above the Hindu's head and repeated, "There is no difference between cruelty and non-cruelty." At this, Schaeffer reports, "The Hindu walked out into the night."[28] In the ethical core of his being the Hindu student knew senseless cruelty was wrong, absolutely wrong. Yet rather than admit the mistake of his amoralism, he walked into the night of meaninglessness. Some, though, when pressed on the results of their relativism will see the darkness of their position and, by God's grace, move toward the light.

Similarly, New Agers speak in excited tones of our "evolutionary journey" into a New Age. To make sense of this optimism it seems that the New Ager must view this "positive future" as ethically superior to the old age from which we are now exiting. Yet the New Age relativism fences them off from this kind of ethical evaluation. If ethics are relative to the person—or the "age"—and not determined by reference to an external, objective, absolute and universal standard, the very idea of progress or regress is impossible. C. S. Lewis explains:

> If "good" or "better" are terms deriving their sole meaning from the ideology of each people [or each person], then of course ideologies themselves cannot be better or worse than one another. Unless the measuring rod is independent of the things measured, we can do no measuring. For the same reason it is useless to compare the moral ideas of one age with those of another: progress and decadence are alike meaningless words.[29]

Or, in Chesterton's words, "If the standard changes, how can there be improvement, which implies a standard?"[30]

The Christian may also point out to the New Ager the universal human experience of guilt and shame as evidence for ethical absolutes rooted in God's existence. Although many New Age teachings try to dynamite any thought of guilt as inherently negative, the holy hound of heaven still hunts unholiness. In fact, the very idea of guilt for wrongdoing makes no sense unless we are in the presence of a person we have wronged. Yet even when no other human knows of our wrongdoing (such as secretly cheating on a test), we feel guilt. Psychologists go so far as to diagnose those who are incapable of guilt as "sociopaths," unfit for human society. The experience of guilt indicates the ethical atmosphere of our moral life, an atmosphere best explained by seeing ourselves as standing before a personal and moral God.[31]

Our sense of "oughtness" indicates that we feel commanded to do some things and not to do others. We have all experienced the common human dilemma of "I know I *should* do it; but I don't *want* to do it." This human drama fits perfectly with the Christian view that

God, as ethical Commander in Chief, gives commands—which he
makes known through conscience and Scripture—to his creatures—
who may obey or disobey them.[32] But New Age amoralism has no
adequate explanation for this moral sense. By asserting that "we
create our own reality/morality," it must instead dismiss this moral
sense as mistaken and unrelated to anyone above and beyond the
self.

A Christian moral standard is based not on opinion, feeling or
intuition, but rather on the character and command of the Moral
Governor of the cosmos. When judged by this standard, all humans
fall pitifully short of moral righteousness. Our guilt, then, is real and
deserved. C. S. Lewis highlights the moral difference between believing in the "Life Force" and a more "troublesome God":

> If . . . you want to do something rather shabby, the Life-Force,
> being only a blind force, with no morals and no mind, will never
> interfere with you like that troublesome God we learned about
> when we were children. The Life-Force is a sort of tame God. You
> can switch it on when you want, but it will not bother you. All the
> thrills of religion and none of the cost. Is the Life-Force the greatest
> achievement of wishful thinking the world has yet seen?[33]

But because we have all done more than our share of "shabby"
things, a provision for moral wrongdoing (sin) must be made not by
the offending party—a bankrupt firm cannot pay its own bills—but
by the offended party, God himself.

The Uniqueness of Jesus Christ

Besides finding that the biblical God is personal, loving and just and
that the New Age God is correspondingly impersonal, indifferent and
amoral, we also need to assess how each perspective deals with the
human situation. For Christians that means an examination of the life
and work of Jesus Christ. The Christian assessment of the human
predicament demands a radical solution—the cross.

But first let us consider some of Christ's credentials that New Agers need to understand.

The New Age patronizes Christ with faint praise, hailing him as a great Master or Teacher or Adept or Guru. Christians can agree with this general attitude of respect, but must move toward accentuating Jesus' uniqueness as God's "one and only son" (Jn 3:16) who claimed to be "the way and the truth and the life" (Jn 14:6), about whom Peter preached that "salvation is found in no one else, for there is no other name under heaven given to men by which we must be saved" (Acts 4:12) and about whom Paul declared "there is one God and one mediator between God and men, the man Christ Jesus" (1 Tim 2:5; see also Rom 5:15-19; 1 Cor 8:5-6; Col 2:9, Phil 2.6). If New Agers say that these verses can be interpreted in other ways, have them read the passages aloud and in context. Then ask them what else they could possibly mean.[34]

As Chesterton underscored, the Incarnation (Jn 1:1-4, 14) is without a competitor: "Omnipotence and impotence, or divinity and infancy, do definitely make a sort of epigram which a million repetitions cannot turn to a platitude. It is not unreasonable to call it unique. Bethlehem is emphatically a place where extremes meet."[35]

Many New Agers are ignorant of the Savior's credentials. Their idea of "the Christ" is dim and dull, based on childhood images, sentimental distortions, occult clichés and misinterpretations of Scripture. Yet Christians have great opportunity to boast in their Lord. Among other things, Christians can highlight these crucial facts about the one and only Christ:[36]

1. *He fullfilled a score of Old Testament prophecies concerning his life, death and resurrection.* These predictions fit only one person, Jesus Christ—as the early church saw so clearly. No other religious leader can rightly claim to fulfill them. Jesus was and is "the Mighty God" of Isaiah 9:6, the personal revelation of God. In view of some New Agers' interest in vague, ancient, pagan prophecies—whether Mayan, Aztec, Hopi or Hindu—they should be willing to consider the reality of specific, fulfilled biblical prophecy concerning Jesus Christ.[37]

Consider the confidence in Christ shown by Pascal, who viewed fulfilled prophecy as a strong reason to believe:

I hold out my arms to my *Redeemer,* who, having been foretold for four thousand years, has come to suffer and die for me on earth, at the time and under all the circumstances foretold. By His grace, I await death in peace, in the hope of being eternally united to Him. Yet I live with joy, whether in the prosperity which it pleases Him to bestow upon me, or in the adversity which He sends for my good, and which He has taught me to bear by His example.[38]

2. *Jesus predicted his own death and resurrection and rose from the dead.* Few others have predicted their resurrection from the dead, let alone actually done it! Christ actually rose again on the third day, thus vindicating his claims (Rom 1:4). The evangelistic vigor of the early church is inexplicable apart from Christ's actual physical resurrection. Without this his disciples would have remained (literally) dispirited. They would have known he predicted his resurrection to no avail. They would have had no gospel to preach. But preach they did—because of the resurrection.[39]

Although the New Age claims we are gods, I know of no New Ager who has died for the karma of the world or has risen from the dead. And none seem forthcoming. (It is said that Swami Yogananda, founder of the Self-Realization Fellowship, decayed quite slowly after his death, but whatever significance that has pales in comparison with the risen Christ.)

3. *Jesus cannot be forced into the New Age mold of just another "enlightened master" if we accept what the Bible says about him.* Either he was who he said he was—uniquely God incarnate—or he wasn't. He never made general claims about the divinity of all people, but singled himself out as *the* Incarnation of God. To some of his detractors he declared, "I tell you the truth . . . before Abraham was born, I am!" (Jn 8:58). At this they tried to stone him because he called himself what God had called himself in the revelation to Moses in the

burning bush (Ex 3:14). Jesus also said to a paralytic he was about to heal, "Son, your sins are forgiven," thus disturbing some of the religious leaders there who thought, "Why does this fellow talk like that? He's blaspheming! Who can forgive sins but God alone?" Jesus didn't shrink back, but knowing their thoughts he revealed that "The Son of Man has authority on earth to forgive sins" (Mk 2:10), after which he demonstrated his divine power by healing a crippled boy (vv. 5-12). Jesus also received the worship of Thomas who—after his doubts about Jesus' resurrection melted in the presence of the risen Christ—cried out, "My Lord and my God" (Jn 20:28). Jesus did not correct him but rather blessed him (v. 29).

If Jesus thought he was uniquely God incarnate but he wasn't, he was far less than "an enlightened master"—he didn't even know who he was! If he knew he was not uniquely God incarnate, but said he was, he was a flaming fraud, and in no sense was he an "enlightened master." Worse yet, he would have been a deceiver, leading a multitude astray. If he thought he was uniquely God incarnate and was— as the record relates—let us throw off this nonsense of placing him in the pantheistic pantheon. Let us worship and serve him instead.[40]

Christians may want to challenge New Agers simply to read through the Gospels themselves, rather than relying on secondhand interpretations given by New Age writers and teachers. Confronted with the uncensured Word of God, they might "believe that Jesus is the Christ, the Son of God, and that by believing . . . have life in his name" (Jn 20:31).

Jesus of Nazareth, as portrayed in the Bible, demands attention and respect for a multitude of reasons which become apparent as we let the story speak for itself. Here are just a few that highlight Jesus' uniqueness.

Christ taught with great authority, certainty and clarity unlike the other religious leaders of the day (Mt 7:28-29). His skills as an orator and teacher were unmatched as he used parables, humor, questions, didactic teaching in ways perfectly suited for his diverse audiences.

His teaching attracted thousands of the open-hearted who hung on his every word, even listening for hours without food. He was the master of his situation and was never successfully tricked by his accusers, but rather often left them befuddled. No one ever outsmarted him. So enraged were his defeated antagonists that they sought to silence him by death.

Christ's ethical teachings are unparalleled. Through his life and instruction Jesus called his hearers to account before his holy Father. The meek will inherit the earth. Love your enemies. The humble are exalted and the haughty humbled. Give and it shall be given to you. Turn the other cheek. These words and so many more words cut to the quick, disturbing and challenging us at the root of our being.

Christ also evidenced miraculous powers unique in history. He healed with a touch or a word, restoring broken bodies and spirits through his compassion: the blind saw, the deaf heard, the crippled walked and the dead rose again. Those who but touched his clothing were physically restored. He commanded even the forces of nature to do his bidding. Calvin notes that although Christ's disciples also performed miracles, Jesus' miracles were unique because they sprung from his own power. The disciples invoked Jesus' name for healing (Acts 3:6), for the power was in him. Concerning his miracles, Calvin notes that sometimes Jesus "used prayer, that he might ascribe glory to the Father, but we see that for the most part his own proper power is displayed. . . . It is not surprising, then, that Christ appealed to his miracles in order to subdue the unbelief of the Jews, inasmuch as these were performed by his own energy, and therefore bore most ample testimony to his divinity."[41] This was no ordinary man. He was a King who had declared the kingdom of God with power.

Sin and the Cross of Christ

But truly to have "life in his name," the New Ager must understand the cross of Christ, for this incomparable figure cannot be understood apart from his death. He who had the power to heal and raise the dead ends up dying on a cross praying for his accusors, "Father, forgive them" (Lk 23:34).

The New Age God is an uninterested Force; the God of the Bible hangs impaled on a criminal's gibbet bearing the sins of the world. This is a divine drama of which New Agers know nothing. For them, the cross and the sin that necessitated it are too "negative." But the Christian knows better, and says with Paul, "May I never boast except in the cross of our Lord Jesus Christ" (Gal 6:14). New Age attitudes to the contrary, whether something is "negative" or "positive" is strictly secondary to whether it is objectively true or false. The fact that my doctor prescribes a heavy, cumbersome cast for my broken leg is quite "negative." Nevertheless, my leg is objectively broken; and only by realizing my true (negative) condition will I take the steps needed for healing. In the same manner, the negativity of human sin is real; and only by taking stock of that fact can the sin be adequately addressed. All the visualizing, affirming, chanting, meditating and resonating in the world will do nothing to negate sin. But how can sin be dealt with?

The justice of a holy God was met when Jesus was crucified for the sins of humanity. Jesus defined his mission this way: "the Son of Man came to seek and to save what was lost" by "[giving] his life as a ransom for many" (Lk 19:10; Mk 10:45). In Jesus the just was sacrificed for the unjust. As Paul says, "God made him who had no sin to be sin for us, so that in him we might become the righteousness of God" (2 Cor 5:21). Martin Luther prayed, "Lord Jesus, you are my righteousness, I am your sin. You took on you what was mine; yet set on me what was yours. You became what you were not, that I might become what I was not."[42]

The apostle John lauds Jesus as the one "who loves us and has freed us from our sins by his blood" (Rev 1:5). This issued forth from an unfathomable love, both the love of the Father to send the Son and the love of the Son to obey the Father to bring glory to the Father and deliverance to his erring creatures. As Richard Lovelace puts it,

"The harmony of God's love and justice is perfectly symbolized by the death of Jesus on the cross. The crucifixion reveals the strictness of God's justice in requiring propitiation for all our sins. But it also shows the depth of his love because he himself offers the required sacrifice."[43] Because Christ suffered on that shameful tree we can live without shame as those freed from the penalty of sin.[44]

The New Age substitutes its monistic idea of "at-one-ment" for the Bible's revelation of Christ's atonement for sin. The New Ager should be shown that the difference spans the gap between heaven and hell.

Ethical Atonement:	Monistic At-one-ment:
1. Assumes sin problem	1. Assumes no sin problem, but ignorance
2. Assumes holy/personal God	2. Assumes impersonal God
3. Evidences love/justice of God	3. Evidences divinity of self
4. Offered freely by God's grace	4. Achieved through mystical techniques
5. Saves from hell	5. Saves from illusionary consciousness
6. Offers heaven	6. Offers self-realization
7. Received by faith in God	7. Experienced through self

Salvation requires faith in Christ and his work. The Christian gospel is only "good news" for those who understand the "bad news" of sin and human depravity. And the "good" part is that the gospel is one of grace, not of human achievement. The New Age sells an experience of self through mystical works wherein we discover our forgotten divinity. (Just how God forgot that God was God—the problem of "metaphysical amnesia"—goes unexplained.)[45] Christianity offers eternal life though faith in the Savior. The New Age promises infinite potential through self-discovery. Christ promises eternal life through self-abandonment. Kurt Koch has said, "We do not need to search deeply into ourselves, but rather into Him who died for us on the cross. We have no need to discover the deep self, but rather to discover our Lord and Savior."[46]

As Pascal declared, Jesus Christ is the source and center of all understanding: "Not only do we know God by Jesus Christ alone, but we know ourselves only by Jesus Christ. We know life and death only through Jesus Christ. Apart from Jesus Christ, we do not know what is our life, nor our death, nor God, nor ourselves."[47]

As we articulate our reasons for our belief in a personal God, supremely revealed in Jesus Christ, and our reasons for holding to biblical morality as opposed to New Age relativism, let us pray that New Agers will be touched by the Holy Spirit to realize their intellectual and moral inadequacies and turn to worship and serve the one true and living God.

Notes

[1]Marilyn Ferguson, *The Aquarian Conspiracy* (Boston: J. P. Tarcher, 1980), p. 382.

[2]Gita Mehta, *Karma Cola: The Marketing of the Mystic East* (New York: Simon and Schuster, 1979), p. 194

[3]Hans Küng, *On Being a Christian* (Garden City, N.Y.: Doubleday, 1976), pp. 301-2.

[4]Brooks Alexander, "Occult Philosophy and Mystical Experience," Audio tape (Berkeley, Calif.: Spiritual Counterfeits Project, 1980).

[5]Calvin *Institutes* 1.11.8.

[6]Alexander, "Occult Philosophy."

[7]On God as a "religious postulate" that must satisfy certain conditions of the soul, see Orr, *Christian View*, pp. 112-15.

[8]Walter Martin, *Kingdom of the Cults* (Minneapolis: Bethany, 1974), p. 284.

[9]See Francis Schaeffer, *The God Who Is There* (Downers Grove, Ill.: InterVarsity, 1976), pp. 92-99.

[10]C. S. Lewis, *Miracles* (New York: Macmillan, 1978), p. 87.

[11]Vishal Mangalwadi, "How to Answer a Hindu," *Cornerstone*, September 1984, pp. 19-20; quoted in Hoyt, *New Age Rage*, p. 214.

[12]Lewis, *Miracles*, p. 88.

[13]Groothuis, *Unmasking*, p. 156. For an example of this ontological oddity see Stephen LaBerg, *Lucid Dreaming* (New York: Ballantine, 1986), pp. 270-71.

[14]Küng, *On Being a Christian*, p. 303.

[15]The entire creed is printed in Phillip Schaff, *The Creeds of Christendom*, 3 vols. (Grand Rapids, Mich.: Baker, 1983), pp. 66-70.

[16]C. S. Lewis, *The Problem of Pain* (New York: Macmillan, 1976), p. 151. See also Evans, *Quest for Faith*, pp. 117-18.

[17]G. K. Chesterton, *Orthodoxy* (Garden City, N.Y.: Image, 1959), p. 135.

[18]The phrase is from Vincent Tymms and quoted in John Stott, *The Cross of Christ* (Downers Grove, Ill.: InterVarsity Press, 1986), p. 331.

[19]See Pascal *Pensées* 7.425.

[20]MacLaine, *Dancing in the Light,* p. 360.

[21]R. C. Sproul, *The Holiness of God* (Wheaton, Ill.: Tyndale, 1985), p. 151. For more on the biblical view of sin see Lovelace, *Dynamics,* pp. 86–89.

[22]For more on the human condition see Groothuis, *Unmasking,* pp. 84–91.

[23]MacLaine, *Dancing in the Light,* p. 357.

[24]Quoted in John Harti, "Movie Rises Beyond Author's Fears, Avoiding Voodoo Stereotype," *Seattle Times,* January 31, 1988.

[25]See Groothuis, *Unmasking,* pp. 152–55.

[26]On the tension between cultural relativism and human rights considerations see Allan Bloom, *The Closing of the American Mind* (New York: Simon and Schuster, 1987), pp. 185–93.

[27]See Schaeffer, *God Who Is There,* pp. 119–30.

[28]Ibid., p. 101.

[29]Lewis, *Christian Reflections,* p. 73.

[30]Chesterton, *Orthodoxy,* p. 35.

[31]See Moreland, *Scaling the Secular City,* p. 123.

[32]God is not arbitrary in his commands. They are based on his unchanging ethical perfection.

[33]C. S. Lewis, *Mere Christianity* (New York: Macmillan, 1976), p. 35.

[34]They may then change ground and say the Bible isn't reliable. But in that case the arguments sketched above can be used.

[35]G. K. Chesterton, *The Everlasting Man* (Garden City, N.Y.: Image, 1955), p. 173.

[36]See also the discussion in Groothuis, *Unmasking,* pp. 151–52.

[37]See McDowell, *Evidence,* pp. 147–84; and Pascal *Pensées* 11.693.736.

[38]Pascal *Pensées* 12.737.

[39]On the historicity of the resurrection see William Lane Craig, *The Son Rises* (Chicago: Moody, 1981); and McDowell, *Evidence,* pp. 185–273.

[40]For a development of this argument see Kreeft, "Most Important Argument"; and Lewis, *Mere Christianity,* pp. 55–56.

[41]Calvin *Institutes* 1.13.13.

[42]Martin Luther, *Letters of Spiritual Counsel,* in Library of Christian Classics, Vol. 17, ed. Theodore G. Tappert (London: SCM, 1955), p. 110; quoted in Stott, *Cross of Christ,* p. 200.

[43]Lovelace, *Renewal as a Way of Life,* p. 26.

[44]For a theologically thorough and devotionally compelling work on the atonement of Christ see Stott, *Cross of Christ.*

[45]See Geisler, *Christian Apologetics,* p. 187.

[46]Koch, *Occult ABC,* p. 146.

[47]Pascal *Pensées* 7.548.

Confronting
the New Age

III

Education
for a
New Age

7

ABRAHAM LINCOLN ONCE SAID THAT "THE PHILOSOPHY OF EDUCATION IN ONE generation will be the philosophy of government in the next." Although much more than formal education contributes to the philosophy of civil government, Lincoln's point still stands; in fact, it can be extended to say that the philosophy of education in one generation will greatly shape not only the philosophy of civil government in coming generations, but the philosophy of the media and the church as well.

Marilyn Ferguson notes that of "the Aquarian Conspirators" she surveyed in her book, *The Aquarian Conspiracy*, "more were involved in education than any other single category of work. They were teachers, administrators, policymakers, educational psychologists."[1] Many complained they could not fully apply their Aquarian agenda, but they have been making progress. The prospect of a New Age seige on education is not at all fanciful, as we will see. But first, a general analysis of the status of the education system is in order.

The Testimony of Texts

The culture-forming power of education is especially noteworthy in light of the United States' system of compulsory education. Tax-supported schools choose curricula through a bureaucracy of vying interests: those of the federal government, school boards, teachers, other interest groups and, often least influential, the parents. The local contributions of parents often are superseded by the official policies, programs and proposals that descend from above. Paul Vitz notes "that in 1931-1932 there were approximately 259,000 separate school districts in the country, by 1980 there were only 1600. This fifteenfold drop has occurred while the number of students has increased by the millions. The result, as countless distressed parents have discovered, is loss of local control."[2]

Local educators have seen their authority overridden by federal and state bureaucracies often out of touch with local educational realities, thus reducing some teachers to little more than helpless administrative drones.[3]

The actual content of public-school textbooks reveals a dreadful dirth of Christian morality and positive references to traditional American religious life. Textbook reviewers Mel and Norma Gabler note that "it is foolish to underestimate the power of textbooks on what students study. Seventy-five percent of students' classroom time and 90 percent of homework time is spent with textbook materials."[4] Even where specific New Age influence is lacking, the moral and spiritual vacuum left in the public schools is an open invitation to New Age infiltration.

Paul Vitz conducted a federally funded, systematic study of the content of public-school textbooks through the National Institute of Education in 1985. He was flabbergasted by the results. His carefully researched conclusion is simply that the textbooks have been censored. "Religion, traditional family values, and conservative political and economic positions have been reliably excluded from the children's textbooks."[5] He found this to be the case at all educational levels from grade one through high school. America's substantial Christian heritage is overwhelmingly edited out. And if the Pilgrims happen to make a rare guest appearance, their Christian orientation is omitted.[6]

Vitz's incisive study demands closer attention than we can give, but I will cite a few of the more conspicuous examples of unfairness. In grade-six-social-studies texts Vitz finds major weaknesses with regard to religion.[7] First, they neglect the formative influence of ancient and modern Jewish history in favor of Greek and Roman. Second, they neglect the life of Jesus of Nazareth. Four major books don't even mention his name, while others spend more time on Muhammad. Third, they neglect the first one thousand years of Christianity. This is routinely skimmed over. Fourth, they neglect Eastern Orthodox Christianity and the Byzantine Empire. Fifth, the sixth-grade textbooks neglect Protestantism. The texts downplay or avoid references to the existence or meaning of the Reformation. One text makes no reference to Luther or Calvin. Sixth, they neglect Christianity in the modern world. Although other cultures' religious concerns are not avoided, Christianity in America is rendered invisible.

Some may believe that editing Christianity from textbooks is of little concern because it is better to say nothing than to say something critical. But consider the piercing words of Sir Walter Moberly:

It is a fallacy to suppose that by omitting a subject you teach nothing about it. On the contrary you teach that it is to be omitted, and that it is therefore a matter of secondary importance. And you teach this not openly and explicitly, which would invite criticism; you simply take it for granted and thereby insinuate it silently, insidiously, and all but irresistibly.[8]

Interestingly, Vitz found more than a few positive references to magic and American Indian spirituality in basal readers (books used to teach reading). Vitz comments that "there are scores of articles about animals, archaeology, fossils, or about magic—but none on religion, much less any about Christianity. In contrast to the serious neglect of Christianity and also Judaism, there is a minor spiritual or occult emphasis in a number of stories about American Indians."[9] He goes on to mention that "there is something of an emphasis on magic in these books. . . . In short, stories referring to the occult, to magic, to Indian and other pagan religions are featured about five times more often than stories which mention anything of a Judeo-Christian nature."[10]

The Muddying of Values Clarification

Vitz's study primarily dealt with the treatment of religion in the texts. Another deeply disturbing trend is "Values Clarification," a method of teaching values that has permeated public education. What was thought to be an attempt to teach right and wrong in a pluralistic age has itself become an ethical system—and a poor one at that.

Pioneered by Louis E. Raths and Sidney B. Simon, the objective of Values Clarification is to coax students to develop their own values free of outside instruction. Students are deemed fit to construct their own personal values—apart from any moral authority and despite not possessing all the pertinent facts. The self is viewed as intrinsically good. The result is an indoctrination into relativism. In the originators' words, the goal of Values Clarification "is to involve students in practical experiences, making them aware of *their own* feelings, *their own* ideas, *their own* beliefs, so that the choices and decisions they make are conscious and deliberate, based on *their own* value systems."[11]

The term "values clarification" itself is instructive. The word *values*—rather than *ethics* or *morals*—carries with it the assumption that right and wrong are something we choose, as we would choose what clothes to wear. The purpose of the process is not to discover an objective system of moral absolutes, but to create a subjective set of values to clarify our value options—in other words, what is right and wrong for me. The clarification of our "sense of values" replaces the quest for true goodness; feeling replaces right; preference replaces virtue. The only thing prohibited by the Values Clarification method is a recognition of and respect for the objective, universal and absolute moral law of God.[12] Immature, subjective impulses can be "clarified," thus obscuring objective verities.

New Age Opportunities

Our culture has given the New Age movement an "in." The New Age often finds fertile soil in an educational context where textbooks are pruned of most all positive Christian references and where teaching methods endorse relativism. "Choosing your own values" can be comfortably translated into the New Age dream of "creating your own reality." In fact, our culture seems to be working with a curious double standard: Christianity is excluded but New Age ambassadors are often welcomed with open arms.

A volume entitled *Child Abuse in the Classroom* documents selected testimonies from witnesses in seven major American cities in regard to the Hatch Amendment, which provides students protection from psychological manipulation. In chronicling their discontent with public education, examples of New Age influence repeatedly appear.

Robert Griggs, for example, testified that "in the fall semester of the school year 1980-1981 in Hocker Grove Junior High in Shawnee Mission public schools, there was a P.E. class that . . . used a mandatory or compulsory course in yoga to teach the kids to meditate." This training included the vocal repetition of unidentified words, most likely Hindu mantras.[13]

Another parent, Joan Lauterbach, from Mexico, Missouri, inquired about the curriculum for the Gifted and Talented Program for grades 3 through 6. She was told that it included "yoga to attain peace, harmony, and self-awareness."[14] Other testimonies object to the presence of the occult, parapsychology and mind-altering practices in the public schools.[15]

In *Growing Up Gifted,* educational theorist Barbara Clark draws heavily on proto-New Ager Teilhard de Chardin and New Age writers such as Marilyn Ferguson and Fritjof Capra in advancing an educational agenda which is fueled by an unabashed New Age orientation:

Lifestyles and belief systems change, dichotomies no longer exist, and time and space have another dimension. Reality is seen as an outward projection of internal thoughts, feelings, and expectations. Energy is the connector, the center, the basis of all matter, and consciousness forms reality. It is this progression we make available as we present opportunities to our students that allow the integration of body and mind. As science continues to validate this interconnected view of reality, Western pragmatists will join Eastern mystics, and all humans will benefit. Human potential, as yet unknown, will have the chance to develop.[16]

She also advocates "integrative education" as a "lifelong way to actualize our transpersonal self." She concludes her work with a breathless endorsement of parapsychology. "Psi research continues to be an area of fascination as it continues to extend the range of human ability and empower each of us beyond the limits by which we believed we were bound."[17] The young and gifted become the experimental subjects in the deification enterprise.

On the college level, many major state universities offer yoga classes, with one northwestern university listing three separate classes in kundalini yoga, the most obviously occult form of yoga. The various experimental colleges connected with many universities—usually created out of the push for "relevance" in the 1960s—also often provide classes on a whole range of New-Age-related phenomena, from aura reading to Wicca (witchcraft) to Zen meditation, usually not for credit but with university assistance, nonetheless.

Neither is New Age indoctrination limited to the public schools. It has even reached the private preschool level. A midwestern preschool founded by the Ananda Marga Yoga Society says in a promotional flyer that it teaches "yoga, meditation, and experiential learning. Nondenominational meditation and centering helps strengthen will power, enhances intuition and imagination, brings calmness, broadens mental vision and awakens a feeling of connectedness with humanity and nature." The flyer also includes a chart on "wholistic education" which views the elements of the self as connected to the "Higher Self." It is pantheism for the babes.

But pantheism for Roman Catholics? Yes. New Age luminary Robert Muller delivered the keynote address at the annual convention of the National Catholic Education Association (NCEA) in St. Louis in April of 1985. Muller, a disciple of Teilhard de Chardin, commented in the NCEA's journal, *Momentum,* that "we know so much we are probably of a divine nature" and that as "cosmic beings, divine beings" we find evolution grants us a cosmos becoming aware of itself as God.[18] Helen Hull Hitchcock, a conservative Catholic observer at the conference, found New Age themes throughout. She says that "dozens of speakers and workshops" advocated the "Utopian 'vision',"[19] and submits that Catholic education is viewed by New Agers as a potentially useful structure in which to inject their religious-sounding ideology.[20]

Global Education
One of the most prevalent and disturbing aspects of New Age thought to penetrate American public education is "global education." Much more than a program for international studies, global education is a method of teaching the humanities and social sciences that often either advocates or assumes a New Age ideology of relativism, religious syncretism and one-worldism. Some materials used in global education are blatantly New Age in emphasis, while others are more subtly so. In its various forms, global education has received the support of influential organizations such as the National Association of Elementary School Principals, the American Association of School Administrators, the American Federation of Teachers, the Council of Chief State School Officers, the National Association of State Boards

of Education, the National Education Association, The Parent-Teacher Association and the National School Board Association.[21]

Western Washington University, for instance, offers a course for educators taught by Philip Vander Velde called "Foundations of Education" which uses Fritjof Capra's *The Turning Point* and the instructor's *The Global Mandate* as texts. The course advances the basic tenets of global education (explained below). *The Global Mandate* declares that "what is needed in a world faced with possible extinction is a new global spirituality."[22] "The faith that was once for all entrusted to the saints" (Jude 3) is now deemed too encrusted with old-age ideas to be entrusted to anyone. A "new" synthesis is called for which actually reduces to that old "perennial philosophy" of Eastern mysticism.[23]

Capra dispenses with Christian theism in favor of an impersonal monistic and evolutionary perspective. Monotheism, he pronounces, will destroy us; monism will deliver us.[24] Vander Velde likewise hails the "universal or cosmic mind" embedded in the All.[25]

Such viewpoints induce visions of global political unity, at the expense, of course, of national sovereignties. "Old creeds" doom "world government"[26] and the "reordering of our traditional values and institutions should be one of the major objectives of our schools."[27] The United Nations or some similar group is seen as the rightful inheritor of global governmental affairs[28] adjudicated by redistributing existing wealth and power according to the centralized wisdom of the state.[29]

Vander Velde, it seems, is using his classsroom to inspire a new world order, with future teachers as his students and global education as the means to that end. And he is not alone. He is leading a charge.

Having glanced at some specific instances of the global vision of Professor Vander Velde, we should consider some salient features of global education in general:

1. *A desire to politicize children.* Many global educators have stated their intention to teach a specific, value-laden world view through

their programs. Their aim is not detached geographical, historical, political or philosophical study, but conversion.[30] Two global educators report that "most educators agree that children should be introduced to global perspectives as early as possible—certainly before the onset of puberty when ethnocentrism and stereotypical thinking tend to increase dramatically."[31]

A curriculum called "peace education"—supported by the National Education Association (NEA) and Educators for Social Responsibility—has been implemented in several states; it shares many basic tenets with global education and could be called a form of global education. One curriculum called *Choices* even utilizes the New Age myth of the "Hundredth Monkey" (see chapter four) to encourage students toward political activism. By pooling our collective consciousness we can paranormally alter the consciousness of the planet and stop nuclear war: "Your awareness is needed in preventing nuclear war. You may be the 100th Monkey."[32]

2. *A very liberal or pacifistic internationalism stressing disarmament as the only approach to conflict.* The peace-through-strength perspective—held by a high percentage of the taxpayers—is seldom, if ever, represented as a plausible option.[33] More representative is the peace-at-any-price perspective, including unilateral disarmament. (Certainly not only New Agers hold to this viewpoint, but it is a common theme in much New Age literature.)

3. *Ethical relativism.* Many global educators endorse Values Clarification,[34] and texts often advocate the "nonjudgmental" approach to studying other cultures—which usually translates as, "Thou shalt absolutely not judge absolutely." For instance, one text asks the leading question, "Do we sometimes have a tendency to define our values and behaviors as 'right' or 'correct' and determine that others' values and behaviors are 'wrong' or 'weird'? Is any one person or culture 'right' or 'wrong'?"[35] The quotation marks say it all. The globalist invokes relativism rather than exercising discernment.

The curriculum guide *Perspectives* tells us that while we provincial

Westerners "tend to see the world in terms of competing interests . . . in Eastern philosophy . . . conflict and paradox (represented by yin and yang) are part of harmonic unity." It then suggests that "the roots of our attraction to conflict" come from the "Western tradition and religious values." It urges teachers to "explore with the students the good guy/bad guy dichotomy that pervades our Western mythology and our texts, or the God and devil imagery that is part of the Christian ethic."[36]

It seems "the Christian ethic" or "Western mythology" is the only "bad guy." The text also approvingly quotes the book *This Is It* by Western mystic, Alan Watts. Watts endorses the relativism of good and evil in the Eastern mindset while noting the "chronic uneasy conscience of the Hebrew–Christian cultures" that wrestles with good and evil rather than wedding them.[37]

4. *Moral equivalence.* The idea that "all nations are morally equal" tends to flow from point three. Yet oftentimes the thesis is revised to mean "all nations are morally equal but the United States is less morally equal than others." This is suggested by the scant attention usually paid in global education to America's unique form of civil government, its history and positive achievements of political liberty and economic opportunity. Even a judicious appreciation of the favorable aspects of America tends to be viewed as "nationalistic" and "ethnocentric." Likewise, an objective treatment of Soviet injustices worldwide—such as Stalin's elimination of millions of dissenters and Soviet global imperialism which includes invasions into Hungary, Czechoslovakia and Afghanistan—is often conspicuously absent.

Global educators would do well to harken to the words of Reinhold Niebuhr:

> It is sheer moral perversity to equate the inconsistencies of a democratic civilization with the brutalities which modern tyrannical states practice. If we cannot make a distinction here, there are no historical distinctions which have any value. All the distinctions upon which the fate of civilization has turned in the history of

mankind have been just such relative distinctions.[38]
Such ethical distinctions are indeed "relative"—not in the sense of
relativ*ism*—because no nation is either perfectly virtuous or perfectly
vile.[39] A legitimate appreciation of foreign cultures need not involve
turning a blind eye to real evils.[40]

The idea of "moral equivalence" also implies "religious equivalence." One text cited by Greg Cunningham has students read the *I
Ching,* a book of Chinese fortune-telling.[41] As was already mentioned,
Vander Velde advocates a synthesized religion. Another text implies
that the American Judeo-Christian heritage is inferior to spiritism
because we are uncomfortable with the idea of visits from the dead.[42]

5. *One-world government.* We have already noted the push toward
global government seen in Professor Vander Velde's text, and it is a
recurring theme in global education. Cunningham notes this "one-
world" ambition.

Using a subliminal but effective technique seen frequently in CTIR
[Center for Teaching International Relations] materials, the *World
Citizen Curriculum* lists a series of seven innocuous progressions,
each comprised of three evolutionary levels, with the seventh predicting the ultimate transcendence of international organizations
over nations. The same document asks students to complete a
"what if" exercise whose scenarios are worded and arranged in a
configuration suggestive of the preferred response. One policy
proposal is the removal of national borders, another is the power
of a world court to impose and enforce the collection of fines.
Further on, disapproval is expressed for "national sovereignty."[43]

A one-world configuration is thought to be necessary because of the
reality of economic and political interdependence and the impending
military and economic perils caused by nationalism. Cooperation
must replace any military or economic competition as we realize that
"we are all one" and need to become "more one" through dissolving
national sovereignties. Although many non-New Agers stump for
world government for a variety of reasons, the idea has particular

appeal to New Age monists who stress the oneness of all things. For them, if all is one metaphysically, all should become one politically.

What is largely lacking from global educational materials is an awareness of the fact that real evil exists and may need to be resisted by military force. "Cooperating" with Hitler meant encouraging genocide; "competing" with him meant opposing genocide. Globalist materials tend to endorse a dangerously utopian mentality that peace is attainable through unilateral good will. The idea is that by merely increasing interdependence we will somehow ennoble human nature, and release its hidden potentialities.

In reality, nations vary greatly in the degree to which they depend on each other, as any study of exports and imports or military assistance will show. Further, increasing interdependence is not an unmixed good, as anyone who has been forced to depend on an organized crime ring's "protection" will attest. Historian Paul Johnson observes that since World War I "splendid isolation was no longer a practicable state policy," because of the "political holism" made possible through international media and travel.[44] Yet while this interrelatedness yielded some positive results, Johnson notes that separation has its benefits: "The Black Death of the mid fourteenth century had migrated over the course of more than fifty years and yet there were some areas it had never reached. The influenza virus of 1918 had enveloped the world in weeks and penetrated almost everywhere. The virus of force, terror, and totalitarianism might prove equally swift and ubiquitous."[45]

Indeed it has: the Soviet Union has an *inter*national sovereignty that exceeds all other powers, and it is unlikely that it would loosen its international stranglehold for the sake of some Superstate created for the purpose of establishing a perfectly egalitarian interdependence.[46] How the benevolence of such a Superstate would be insured or maintained is not addressed; it is merely assumed.

Other disturbing features of global education could be listed— teaching techniques that pry into family concerns, a prevalent anti-

Christian, anti-Western prejudice,[47] and the subtlety by which globalist ideas are injected into the curriculum through semantic facades. For example, a memorandum in the Seattle public-school system warned teachers that in light of current controversy over "global education" a "temporary safe term" is "multicultural/international curriculum development."[48] Global education, though not solely a New Age product, nevertheless is fertile soil for planting the seeds of a New Age world view.

Confronting the New Age Movement in Education

Having witnessed the presence of the New Age in education, we should want to witness against it. But how?

As discussed earlier, we should not adopt a simplistic "quarantine" or "taboo" mentality in critiquing New Age involvement in education. A few elements of global education should be *conserved.* We should recognize that most educators' intentions are good, and some of their proposals are sensible. The aim of global education to acquaint the student with the larger global perspective is not, in itself, objectionable.

Although global education does not consider a biblical perspective, nevertheless, Christians should view themselves as "global Christians," spiritually connected to their Christian brothers and sisters around the globe. Our God is the Creator of the world and and it is out of love for the world that he sent his Son to redeem it (Jn 3:16). Our citizenship in God's kingdom transcends national borders. We should pray and work for the freedom of Christians whose religious and political freedoms are trampled on by oppressive civil governments. We should compassionately share our wealth with the needy worldwide. We can also benefit from learning how Christians from other cultures express their faith.

But the Christian perspective on a person's relationship with the rest of the world differs radically from the perspective of the New Age. When it comes to moral relativism, religious syncretism and monism in its many forms, here we must be *separate*. And it is this basic New Age perspective which is being taught in global education curricula.

Yet making effective objections—which result in concrete change—to New Age material in the public schools is difficult for several reasons, both pragmatic and principled.

We have already discussed the problem of top-down control over schools. The lone Christian citizen or even activist group is grappling against a firmly fortified bureaucracy which is already trying to appease powerful lobbyists: unions, governments, boards and so on. Thus overhauling curricula is a monumental task.

A second pragmatic difficulty is the general secularization of the educational community, which, whether intentionally or not, fosters a non-Christian or antitraditional mindset. Through the considerable influence of the educational philosophy of John Dewey and others, a non-Christian world view has permeated modern public educational thinking. Although openly hostile to the influence of traditional Christian viewpoints, schools may be open to New Age viewpoints posing as nonreligious psychological practices. New Age activist Dick Sutphen makes this general point:

> One of the biggest advantages we have as New Agers is, once the occult, metaphysical and New Age terminology is removed, we have concepts and techniques that are very acceptable to the general public. So we can change the names and demonstrate the power. In so doing, we open the door to millions who normally would not be receptive.[49]

Jack Canfield and Paula Klimek advise their fellow educators how to present 'centering'—a form of Eastern meditation—in the classroom: "Centering can also be extended into work with meditation in the classroom. (Advice: if you're teaching in a public school, don't call it meditation, call it 'centering.' Every school wants children to be relaxed, attentive, and creative, and that is what they will get.)"[50]

Many educators proudly wearing the label of "progressive" greet with open arms *New* Age practices as all the rage, while pushing away "old age" traditions as outmoded relics.

Third, the towering presence of the National Education Association (NEA) darkens hope of substantial educational reform. As the largest union in the country, with a membership of 1.5 million, the NEA is extremely powerful and active. Paul Vitz notes that "the biased content of the textbooks" described in his study "is congruent with the politics of the NEA, and the simplest description of these textbooks is that they are a slightly watered down version of the NEA's own political and ideological stance."[51]

We also find several *principled* problems in reforming public education. First, a tax-funded public education can never, in our pluralistic society, be fully Christian in content or method. In the public schools the testimony of the creation to its Creator is prohibited from being taught. Christians attempting to have the theory of macroevolution and scientific creationism given "equal time" have largely failed. Even if scientific creationism were taught, a theology of creation could scarely be mentioned. If "fear of the Lord is the beginning of wisdom" (Prov 9:10), the public schools would then, in principle, appear to be at the end of the line.

Second, one should question the fairness of a mandatory public educational system that violates the beliefs of so many taxpayers. Christians object to New Age influences in the schools and are concerned that Christianity be fairly presented. Yet so do New Agers object to that which denies their viewpoint. But both New Agers and Christians must pay taxes to support these schools, whether they send their children there or not. How can any curriculum fairly represent and please all the members of a pluralistic society?

Third, some have attempted to answer the question of curriculum fairness by appealing to some "neutral" core of educational materials that would be both educationally appropriate and personally inoffensive. Yet no such neutrality exists. Curricula can vary in terms of fairness and accuracy, but every curriculum is written by human beings whose world views affect their work. As we have seen, excluding Christianity from textbooks is not a neutral presentation of American history. Likewise, presenting all religions as equal is not a neutral presentation because it negates Christ's exclusive claim as Lord. Neutrality is impossible; and, even if possible, it would be undesirable for Christians who seek to have their children raised according to Christian principles and methods (Eph 6:4).

Concerns such as these have led many Christian parents to place their children in private Christian schools or in home schools. Given the availability of such schools and the finances required, or the time, energy and expertise needed to make home schooling work, these seem to be the ideal options for Christians who are concerned about the above considerations and who wish to honor the *separation theme*. Christians need to raise a new generation of Christian students who are taught every subject in terms of the biblical revelation which is relevant to all areas (2 Tim 3:15-16). This, I believe, is a practical impossibility in the public schools.

Transforming the System
Some Christian parents are unable to afford or don't have access to good Christian schools, and sometimes home schooling is a practical impossibility. Other parents who have their children in Christian schools may still want to work toward better education in the public schools. In these cases, the *transformation theme* should be called into action—although, as mentioned above, public education will always be less than ideal for Christians.

Christian parents are responsible to God for the stewardship of their children, which includes their education (Deut 6:7). Schools are not merely a place to drop off the kids for the day. Family support and involvement can help overcome some of the drawbacks of today's public-education system.

The following measures may prove helpful in the effort to transform culture through influencing public schools.

Positive steps have been taken in the area of textbook monitoring and selection. Despite the grim report by Professor Vitz, some textbooks have been either changed or removed because of citizen involvement. Two Davids against the educational Goliath are Mel and Norma Gabler, a husband-and-wife team who have exercised an influence disproportionate to their humble means. They counsel the following:[52]

It is far easier to prevent a particularly objectionable textbook from entering the schools than to eject one already accepted. Citizens interested in participating in textbook selection or rejection should consider six legal rights bearing on their involvement.

1. The Federal Protection of Pupil Rights Act (usually known as the Hatch Amendment) forbids schools—under any federal program—from subjecting students to psychological examination or treatment or from prying into students' personal beliefs regarding family, politics or sexuality without prior written consent of the parent. Predictably, the NEA opposed the act; yet it stands as an important piece of legislation for students rights, although the previously mentioned book *Child Abuse in the Classroom* is chock full of violations of the act. Since many New Age practices involve psychological manipulation and because much of global education/peace education tries to alter children's political beliefs, an appeal to this act may be helpful.

2. Consult state laws that protect parental rights. These laws will vary in each state. The Gablers mention that Oklahoma's Parent's Consent Law has been successfully appealed to in order to stop Values Clarification in schools.

3. Consult any state or school-district guidelines for textbooks. Some states have official guidelines which, if observed, would help improve textbook content. Many school officials either are not aware of these guidelines or are ignoring them. Active citizens can alert textbook adoption/selection committees to these guidelines and hold them to them.

4. Consider the "establishment" clause of the First Amendment to the U.S. Constitution: "Congress shall make no law respecting an

establishment of religion." If a tax-supported public school is actually advocating or establishing a religion—secular humanism, New Age or Christian—it would appear to violate this amendment. Thus in a courageous and thoughtful decision in March of 1987, Justice Brevard Hand, chief justice of the federal court at Mobile, Alabama, ruled in favor of a group of Mobile parents who contended that texts being taught to their children established Secular Humanism as a religion. In an opinion of 111 typewritten pages plus 61 pages of appendices Justice Hand tellingly wrote: "If the court is compelled to purge 'God is great, God is good, we thank Him for our daily food' from the classroom, then this court must also purge from the classroom those things that serve to teach that salvation is through man's self rather than through a deity."[53] Both Secular Humanism and New Age philosophy teach that salvation is through man's self.

Unfortunately, despite his impeccable logic, Judge Hand's decision was eventually overturned by the Eleventh U.S. Circuit Court of Appeals. In a similar case involving Tennessee parents, the Supreme Court ruled in February 1988 that parents could not exempt their children from reading certain books because they taught Secular Humanism. Christian legal experts see these rulings as making further such cases more difficult to win.[54]

Nevertheless, it may sometimes be advantageous to argue against New Age intrusions by claiming they establish a religion. The court cases mentioned argued that Secular Humanism, an *atheistic* perspective, was actually being promoted as a religion. Since New Age influences are *pantheistic,* it might be easier to establish the religious connection, as was done in 1977 when Transcendental Meditation was ruled to be a religion by a New Jersey Court and therefore banned from public schools.

5. Consult the "free exercise" clause of the First Amendment which states "Congress shall make no law . . . denying the free exercise [of religion]." The rights enjoined by this clause may be violated by a one-sided curriculum that excludes Christian perspectives and pro-

hibits Christian practices.

6. Consult the "equal protection" clause of the Fourteenth Amendment which reads, in part, "No State shall make or enforce any law which shall abridge the privileges or immunities of citizens of the United States; nor shall any State deprive any person of life, liberty, or property without due process of law; nor deny to any person within its juristiction the equal protection of law." Texts or school situations that crassly discriminate against Christian citizens could be found in opposition to this amendment.

Christian activists should expect to be caricatured as "censors," "bookburners" and worse, merely for exercising their right to equal participation in educational policy; but a prayerful and well-researched activism can make a difference.[55]

Several other general considerations are important for confronting the New Age in public education.

First, a general knowledge of the New Age counterfeit will help you identify it in its many forms of camouflaged educational infiltration.

Second, this general knowledge is worthless if you are divorced from the actual schooling of your children. Parents should regularly meet with teachers, review textbooks and quiz their children regarding their time in school. A few minutes spent discussing "what happened in school today" is insufficient.

Third, if parents discover some New Age influence—such as a psychic visiting a class—that cannot be totally eliminated, they may suggest that a Christian perspective on the issue be presented for the sake of fairness. Some schools' codes of procedures—which you should be knowledgeable of—may require this of "controversial issues" or "religious issues." This was successfully done in Cupertino, California, in June of 1986 after a psychic was invited to a ninth-grade public-school classroom to discuss the occult, psychic phenomena and how to get in touch with one's "inner self." A Christian presentation was made in response which involved a handout, a short talk, plus the showing of a video on psychic deception.[56]

Fourth, in some cases, occult intrusions may be completely shut down. A teacher concerned about the inclusion of a booth on Tarot cards at a Denver elementary-school fair phoned Rivendell Ministries (an activist/apologetic Christian ministry). Rivendell then prepared a five-page document describing the practice in a factual, nonsensational manner. The teacher passed this on to the principal which resulted in the booth being excluded from the fair. Informed action can make an impact.[57]

The presence of numerous well-informed Christians at school board meetings can serve as "salt and light" as they ask pertinent questions and raise critical issues. This happened at a school board meeting in the Denver area and resulted in New Age materials being dropped.

All forms of media can be skillfully used to stem New Age influence in education and elsewhere. A single call to a radio program or letter to the editor can help mobilize mass support.

Although we have been primarily concerned with public education, private schools may also have a New Age orientation. This is particularly true of the Waldorf schools, designed by the German occultist Rudolf Steiner, and may be true of others. Any private school should be carefully screened.

But Christians with children in Christian schools should not rest assured that their little ones are imbibing nothing but biblical orthodoxy. New Age educational philosophies can easily and subtly find their way into Christian schools, particularly with regard to instruction on self-image (see chapter nine). We must beware of the "chameleon" mentality that absorbs what it should reject or transform.

We should hear Marilyn Ferguson's positive comment on "transpersonal education" as a warning to be vigilant and not adopt the "ostrich" mentality: "Transpersonal education can happen anywhere. It doesn't need schools, but its adherents believe that schools need *it*. Because of its power for social healing and awakening, they conspire to bring the philosophy into the classroom, in every grade, in colleges and universities, for job training and adult education."[58]

Notes

[1]Ferguson, *Aquarian Conspiracy,* p. 280.

[2]Paul Vitz, *Censorship: Evidence of Bias in Our Children's Textbooks* (Ann Arbor, Mich.: Servant, 1986), p. 84.

[3]Ibid., pp. 84–85.

[4]Mel and Norma Gabler, *What Are They Teaching Our Children?* (Wheaton, Ill.: Victor, 1985), p. 22.

[5]Vitz, *Censorship,* p. 1.

[6]Ibid., pp. 18–19.

[7]Ibid., pp. 33–36

[8]Quoted in Richard John Neuhaus, "Belief Is in the Eye of the Beholder," *Religion and Society Report* (August 1986), p. 2.

[9]Vitz, *Censorship,* pp. 65–66.

[10]Ibid., pp. 69–70.

[11]Sidney B. Simon, Leland W. Howe and Howard Kirschenbaum, *Values Clarification* 2nd ed. (New York: Hart, 1978), back cover; see also pp. 18–22; quoted in Paul Vitz, "Ideological Biases in Today's Theories of Moral Education," in *Whose Values?* ed. Carl Horn (Ann Arbor, Mich.: Servant, 1985), p. 114.

[12]Vitz, "Ideological Biases," pp. 113–26.

[13]Schlafly, *Child Abuse in the Classroom,* pp. 209–10.

[14]Ibid., pp. 201–2.

[15]Ibid, see pp. 141–42, 189, 204, 215–16, 282, 365.

[16]Barbara Clark, *Growing Up Gifted: Developing the Potential of Children at Home and at School* (Columbus, Ohio: Charles E. Merrill, 1983), pp. 397–98.

[17]Clark, *Growing Up Gifted,* p. 410.

[18]Quoted in Helen Hull Hitchcock, "Catholic Education Goes Over the Rainbow: The NCEA and the New Age," *Fidelity* (August 1985), pp. 25–26.

[19]Hitchcock, "Catholic Education," p. 26.

[20]Ibid., p. 28.

[21]Gregg L. Cunningham, *Globalism in the Schools: Independence Issue Paper* (Golden, Colo.: Independence Institute, 1986), p. 3.

[22]Philip Vander Velde and Hyuung-Chan Kim, eds., *Global Mandate: Pedagogy for Peace* (Bellingham, Wash.: Bellweather Press, 1985), p. 354; quoted in Eric Buehner, "Terminal Vision," *Education Newsline* (February–March 1987), p. 1.

[23]Vander Velde and Hyuung-Chan, *Global Mandate,* p. 26; quoted in Buehner, "Terminal Vision," p. 2.

[24]See Douglas Groothuis, "Revolutionizing our World View," *The Reformed Journal* (November 1982), pp. 20–23.

[25]Vander Velde and Hyuung-Chan, *Global Mandate,* p. 17; quoted in Buehner, "Terminal Vision," p. 2.

[26]Ibid., p. 25; p. 3.

[27]Ibid., p. 10; p. 3.

[28]Ibid., p. 22; p. 4.

[29]Ibid., p. 23; p. 4.

[30]Cunningham, *Globalism in the Schools*, pp. 4-5.

[31]Jacquelyn Johnson and John Benegar, "Global Issues in the Intermediate School," *Social Education* (February 1983), p. 131.

[32]Quoted in Andre Ryerson, "The Scandal of 'Peace Education,' " *Commentary* (June 1986), p. 40.

[33]Cunningham, *Globalism in the Schools*, pp. 5-6.

[34]Ibid., p. 8.

[35]Ibid.

[36]Quoted in Ryerson, "Scandal of 'Peace Education,' " p. 44

[37]Ibid.

[38]Quoted in Dean C. Curry, "Terrible Weapons, Seductive Illusions," *Eternity* (March 1985), p. 22.

[39]For a detailed analysis of the real differences between the U.S.S.R. and the West see Jean-Francois Revel, *How Democracies Perish* (Garden City, N.Y.: Doubleday, 1983).

[40]Cunningham, *Globalism in the Schools*, pp. 7-9; and Phyllis Schlafly, "What's Wrong with Global Education?" *Daughters of the American Revolution* (May 1986), pp. 450-53.

[41]Cunningham, *Globalism in the Schools*, p. 14.

[42]Ibid., p. 15.

[43]Ibid., pp. 12-13. Footnote references are placed in the original.

[44]Paul Johnson, *Modern Times* (New York: Harper and Row, 1983), p. 102.

[45]Johnson, *Modern Times*, p. 103; see also Thomas Molnar, *Utopia: The Perennial Heresy* (New York: Sheed and Ward, 1967), pp. 48-49.

[46]See Reinhold Niebuhr, "The Illusion of World Government," *Foreign Affairs* (April 1949).

[47]See Cunningham, *Globalism in the Schools*.

[48]Ibid., p. 18.

[49]Dick Sutphen, "Infiltrating the New Age into Society," *What Is* (Summer 1986), p. 14.

[50]Jack Canfield and Paula Klimek, "Education in the New Age," *New Age* (February 1978), p. 28; quoted in Eliot Miller, "Tracking the Aquarian Conspiracy (Part One)," *Forward* (Fall 1986), p. 14.

[51]Vitz, *Censorship*, p. 88. Samuel Blumenfeld has documented the NEA's rise to power and secular philosophy in his revealing book, *NEA: Trojan Horse in American Education* (Boise, Idaho: Paradigm, 1984). The title is regrettably apt.

[52]Gabler, *What Are They Teaching Our Children?* pp. 164-66.

[53]Quoted in Russell Kirk, "Militant Secularism on Trial," *The World and I* (June 1987), p. 121.

[54]Kim A. Lawton, "Striking Down the Textbook Rulings," *Christianity Today* (October 2, 1987), p. 51.

[55]See Gabler, *What Are They Teaching Our Children?* pp. 166-75.

[56]For more information on this episode write: Spiritual Counterfeits Project, Box 4308, Berkeley, CA 97403.

[57]Michael Wiebe, "The Future in the Schools," *Rivendell Times* 1, no. 2 (September 1987), p. 3.
[58]Ferguson, *Aquarian Conspiracy,* p. 288.

New Age
Business

8

T HE HESITANT VOICE ON THE OTHER END OF THE TELEPHONE BETRAYED
both nervousness and deep concern. His family was caught in an
unsuspected crisis, and he was calling me for help. A Christian pastor
was reeling as a result of his twenty-one-year-old daughter's consuming involvement in what to him looked like a cult; and he didn't
know anything about cults. To make matters worse, she was being
enticed to leave home and go to an intensive program to cement her
loyalties further. "It couldn't happen here." But it did.

Erhard Strikes Again

His daughter hadn't renounced her possessions, shaved her hair,
joined a commune, started wearing saffron robes or begun worshiping at an incense-filled oriental shrine. It wasn't that simple. She had
simply attended a business seminar called the Forum, a recent rein-

carnation of est (Erhard Seminars Training).

Est was the premier "consciousness raising" seminar of the 1970s. The founder of est, Werner Erhard (formerly Jack Rosenberg before his "enlightenment"), had captured the psychic market in a big way with est, with approximately half a million people completing the "training" (either by Erhard himself or his trainees). Noted estians included celebrities such as John Denver and elite corporate and professional leaders at august institutions such as MIT, the American Management Association, Harvard Business School and Stanford Business School, all of whom sat at the feet of Mr. Erhard himself.[1]

Erhard's target audience for the Forum is the business world. His strategy may have slightly changed since the days of est, but his world view has not. The Forum is for Erhard the entry point of the New Age into business.

The pastor's daughter, who had made a profession of faith in Christ, had shelled out $525 for the seminar which consisted of two consecutive weekends and one three-hour session. This closely resembles est's sixty-hour ordeal in which people were to get "it": an indescribable spiritual awakening. The Forum now speaks of getting in touch with "being" (only slightly more descriptive than "it"). A promotional booklet says, "The Forum promises to produce an extraordinary advantage in your personal effectiveness and a decisive edge in your ability to achieve." How so? By "being." But what is "being"?

> *Being* is a dimension of ourselves. *Being* is that dimension of ourselves that shapes our actions, our performance and ultimately determines what we accomplish. *Being* limits or expands our creativity, vitality, happiness and satisfaction. Being literally determines *who you are.*[2]

And, as you might have guessed, the Forum ushers you directly into the company of being:

> Your participation in the Forum takes you beyond a mere understanding of *being,* beyond even an occasional, unpredictable experience of *being,* and provides you with direct access to the do-

main of *being* itself. . . . This is the Forum's edge. By providing access to *being* the Forum gives you the key to shaping action, performance and results. Here you find the actual source of ability, competence and productivity. It is like putting your hands directly on the levers and controls of personal effectiveness, creativity, vitality, and satisfaction.[3]

Since the business world craves self-starters and creative instigators, the Forum line has great appeal. To put it more crassly, for the interested business person, *being* begets big bucks. This is especially true for Mr. Erhard (and associates), because seminar attendees are strongly pressured to take expensive follow-up seminars and workshops in the quest for being. The pastor's daughter had pulled away from family and friends in pursuit of *being*.

But this story has a happy ending. After I briefed the pastor on the Forum and spoke with him and his daughter, she eventually began to pull away from the group. Through much prayer on her behalf, time with family members and reading material critical of the Forum, which I had given her, she began to see its incompatibility with Christianity and she further distanced herself from it.

This intensive seminar is administered by one or two charismatic "certified Forum leaders" who skillfully manipulate the audience in a variety of ways. In a critical article, Neil Chesanow describes the leaders of a Forum he attended: "They were forceful, articulate, charismatic leaders, marvelous on stage. They sang. They danced. They told jokes. They persuasively preached the gospel according to Erhard. But, more importantly, they were masters of working an audience. . . . They never lost control of the group."[4]

"The gospel according to Erhard" is a philosophically distilled version of Eastern mysticism and human-potential psychology packaged in a high-pressure group situation. The essence is that we all create our own reality (right and wrong do not objectively exist); we are responsible to no one but ourselves; we become effective not by thinking, but by *being;* and we have limitless potential. This is taught not in a lecture format of critical discussion and evaluation. Trainees are instead jolted by a kind of New Age marathon shock therapy.

Chesanow believes that although "Forum ideas made for interesting intellectual debate," they were presented in a way that conditions people to "stop thinking or make them afraid to think." He believes this is done through bringing them to a state of physical and mental exhaustion, tapping into their fear of public speaking (an integral part of the seminar), and having the forceful leaders humiliate unbelievers "by making them stand and use a microphone to addresss an audience." Chesanow notes that "after long, tedious hours of this exercise, the will begins to erode. The accepters start to outnumber the resisters, not because they really understand and embrace the philosophy . . . but out of exhaustion, fear, eagerness to please the trainer, and a desire to get their money's worth from the experience."[5]

The Forum teaches that salvation is found in the self, not the Savior. Our problem, it preaches, is not sin against a holy God, but disconnectedness from *being*. This problem is supposedly conquered through two weekends worth of what could be called psychic overload. It also preaches an irrationalism that discourages rational reflection in favor of "just being" and an immoralism that severs individuals from any higher moral authority—which in turn gives license for *being* amoral.

Although the Forum's ostentatious approach may alienate some, its basic teaching is also being channeled through another Erhard enterprise, Transformational Technologies, Inc. (TTI), a management-consulting company started in 1984 that has sold intensive (and expensive) seminars to large corporations such as TRW and the City of Chicago, as well as to entrepreneurial companies. Erhard used his well-developed network of est graduates—many of whom sit at elevated positions on the corporate ladder—to establish the venture, setting up in less than two years 47 franchises which are experiencing rapid growth. Each franchise—preferring to be called a "TTI affiliate"—has the right to package Erhardian ideas for various clients in exchange for their initial outlay of $20,000 and 8% of their gross income over their first five years.[6] Yet as Robert Bell notes, the "way the whole things is set up, a corporate client of one of the franchises could buy Erhard's ideas and be totally unaware that Werner had anything to do with it. Erhard is a controversial figure whose notoriety could bar him from many large corporations. But his protégés carry no such baggage."[7]

Putting the New Age to Work

But there is more. New Age ideas are infiltrating the business world on a number of other fronts through a host of organizations large and small. *The New York Times* reported that Ford, Westinghouse and Calvin Klein "are among the scores of major companies that have sent employees for training, according to 'human potential' organizations such as Transformational Technologies, Lifespring, and Actualizations, all of which included techniques modeled to a greater or lesser extent after the techniques started by Werner Erhard."[8]

In the face of declining American automobile and steel industries, unrelenting economic competition from Japan, a massive trade deficit and stressed-out employees, American enterprise is embracing essentially occult endeavors—in the name of increased productivity, creativity and efficiency.

The business manager turned hippie of the late sixties or early seventies would likely, to use Timothy Leary's phrase, "turn on" (to a mystical experience), "tune in" (to the "God within") and "drop out" (of "the establishment"). Today, for many, the reality is more like "turn on, tune in and develop the organization." A look at *New Age Magazine* in the 1970s would reveal few, if any, positive articles on American business. More recently we find in the February 1985 issue of the renamed *New Age Journal* an article called "Transforming the Corporation," which explains the rise of "Organizational Transformation" (OT), a management approach which adds an essentially spiritual dimension to the more established Organizational Development (OD) perspective.

Norman Boucher comments that "the army of transformers is small, though growing. At the first symposium on OT, held in New Hampshire during the summer of 1983, 230 people attended, many of them employees of large corporations. OT practitioners are most often thought of as the maverick 10 percent merging with OD, which in turn makes up about 5 percent of the general field of business consulting."[9]

Boucher cites Linda Ackerman, a consultant in McLean, Virginia, and former member of the Delta Force (a New Age project in the U.S. Army), as an example of OT thinking. Her management views are shaped by physics—most likely a spurious New Age interpretation of quantum physics[10]—and Eastern philosophy, as evidenced by her theory of organizations as "energy fields" generated by various "polarities." A good manager ("a flow state manager"), she thinks, is one who consummately catches the vibes by being intuitively aware of these energy fields, working against energy blocks to keep the energy moving.[11] Exactly what is flowing, where it is flowing and why it should flow is not specified.

Boucher also cites the work of John Adams, the editor of *Transforming Work* (1984) and a leader in the OT movement. Adams's personal pilgrimage includes meditation, yoga, acupuncture treatments, rolfing (a massage technique) and the study of Sufism—all ingested after he realized he was an unhealthy and unhappy tub at age thirty. In the book *Transforming Work* he summarizes the distinctions between OD and OT by cramming just about every New Age catchword into a few sentences:

> A new set of collective beliefs—a new paradigm— . . . is emerging in human consciousness [that] has made me aware that transformations must also be examined at the organizational level, as well as at the global level, in order for us to live our lives more effectively. This new paradigm emphasizes, among other things, *an expanded sense of personal identity and an awareness of the intercon-*

nectedness of people in their organizational cultures to each other in the larger environment.[12]

He also grinds the old New Age saw that "leading edge" scientists are rediscovering ancient views of evolution, spirituality and integrated consciousness.[13] Although some of his ideas may have merit, there can be no doubt as to the essential New Age orientation.

Don Oldenburg, writing in *The Washington Post,* tellingly notes that "the human potential movement is moving into America's board rooms as more and more, corporate climbers set their sights on the key to the cosmos instead of the key to the executive washroom."[14]

New Age themes are interwoven in the best-seller *Reinventing the Corporation* (1985), coauthored by John Naisbitt of *Megatrends* (1982) fame. The book whispers rather than shouts New Age ideas, but it is to the whispers that we listen most carefully. In commenting that intuition is becoming "increasingly valuable in the new information society precisely because there is so much data," Naisbett—who himself meditates, consults a psychic and believes in reincarnation[15]—notes that "in a test at Neward College of Engineering, eleven of twelve company presidents who had doubled sales in the previous four years scored abnormally high in precognition [psychically predicting the future]." He also adds that Peter Senge "notes that successful entrepreneurs score well above average on tests of intuitive ability such as precognition and remote viewing."[16]

Such casual reference to parapsychology assumes its legitimacy and desirability. People who regularly and profitably pursue their "hunches" are one thing, paranormal prognosticators are another.

The effect of the New Age may come through informal associations or mandated business seminars. Concerning the former, *Washington's Business Journal* reports that "in the past couple of years T.M. [Transcendental Meditation] has taken hold in Washington's hard-working and generally conservative business community. About one third of the metropolitan area's 15,000 practitioners are business executives, says Bob Roth, a director with the 600-member Greater

Washington D.C. Association of Professionals Practicing Transcendental Meditation Program." The same story gives the T.M. testimony of Bob LoPinto, a broker with E. F. Hutton who has been faithfully meditating since age sixteen and who credits his success as the top broker in his group to his meditation. He says that T.M. "really does develop your intuition and creativity. Those two things really help you compete against everyone else."[17]

Part of Transcendental Meditation's appeal is its supposed practical, nonmystical approach. In reality, as discussed earlier, the mysticism is simply obscured semantically, a tactic not uncommon as the New Age invades the business world. Pete Sanders, an MIT biomedical chemistry graduate, led consciousness-raising seminars for years before making the connection with business, developing a new division called Success Potentials Unlimited (the name says it all). Sanders explains that he has "streamlined the research and put it into a format that works for the on-the-go professional in terms that relate to their working world." Whereas business people used to reject the psychic dimension as strange and impractical, he believes that stress reduction has been the psychic wedge to get New Age ideas into business. He comments that "now when you talk about psychic attunement and expanded mental states . . . they say 'How can I use that in my business?' "[18]

Michael Ray, professor of marketing and communications at the prestigious Stanford University Graduate School of Business, is teaching students just how to put the New Age to work in business. Since the late seventies Ray and Rochelle Myers have been teaching a course called "Creativity in Business," which advocates dream work, chanting, meditation and the use of Tarot cards (an occult form of divination).[19]

Ray and Myers have launched their ideas into the public through the publication of their book, *Creativity in Business* (1986), which gives detailed instructions on yoga exercises[20] and favorably quotes Swami Muktananda as saying, "Everything is contained in the Self.

The creative power of this entire universe lies inside every one of us. The divine principle that creates and sustains this world pulsates within us as our own Self."[21]

After commenting on his success in teaching the joys of Tarot cards to a class at the IBM Corporate Technical Institute, Ray noted that "the best groups for me to talk to are the hardheaded businessmen from the East Coast" and that he is not surprised when a CEO tells him of mystical experiences: "They whisper, 'I've been meditating for 11 years,' or 'I've been having out-of-the body experiences.' It's like they were almost coming out of the closet. The thing is that some people who are in decision positions now may have been wearing saffron robes 20 years ago . . . whereas the business executive back then would have nothing to do with it."[22]

But just how many business people are coming out of the closet to advocate or even require New Age training for their employees? Hard data from social science seems difficult to come by, but a study by Richard Watring provides some light on the subject. In 1984, Mr. Watring sent questionnaires to 9,000 personnel directors in the United States, 856 of whom responded. Watring asked them to indicate any of the following New Age techniques they thought "particularly effective" in human-resource development: focusing, Silva Mind Control, meditation, hypnosis, est, Dianetics, Transcendental Meditation, biofeedback (see next chapter), centering, imagery and yoga.

One hundred eleven respondents (14%) considered at least one of the eleven techniques to be effective. Biofeedback was the most popular of the techniques, with five per cent of the respondents believing it to be effective. Forty-five per cent had observed the use of one or more of these techniques. Watring concludes that "this illustrates a significant level of acceptance and use of these 'New Age' concepts." Watring also found that those who believe the use of New Age techniques (or "psychotechnologies") are effective for human-resource management have a greater tendency to believe New Age presuppositions than those who do not.[23]

Human-potential seminars sponsored by the Pacific Institute—originally called "New Age Thinking"—"have attracted hundreds of high-paying clients like ABC-TV, NASA, Eastman Kodak, John Fluke Manufacturing, Peoples National Bank, McDonald's Corp., AT&T, IBM, the U.S. Army, General Motors Corp., and most of the nations' top 100 corporate giants—plus many foreign clients."[24] Although the Pacific Institute's seminars are less occult oriented than some, their main emphasis is on self-actualization through visualization and affirmation. Louis Tice, the man behind the highly successful seminars, has drunk deeply from the fount of the human-potential movement as evidenced by the training itself and recommended books mentioned in manuals. In describing Tice's rise to success, John Wolcott comments that Tice's "contagious enthusiasm about his beliefs in the basic intelligence, goodness, and untapped potential in people everywhere soon had people believing in him . . . and then in themselves."[25] Despite Tice's Catholic background, it seems these seminars exalt self more than the Savior and pay more tribute to human-potential writings than to the Bible.

This concern led Steve Hiatt, a car dealer in Tacoma, Washington, to file a suit in February 1987 against a former employer, whom he alleges fired him because of his refusal to participate in a program offered by the Pacific Institute called "New Age Thinking to Increase Dealership Profitability." Mr. Hiatt, a Christian, filed the suit not in revenge—he is seeking neither his job back nor monetary damages over and above his lawyer fees—but to set a precedent against employers' discrimination against their employees' religious viewpoints.[26]

Mr. Hiatt's consternation is not unique. In a similar case, James Baumgartel, an inspector at the Puget Sound Shipyard in Bremerton, Washington, filed a formal Equal Employment Opportunity Class Complaint of Religious Discrimination against the shipyard. His argument is that his First Amendment rights were violated when he was forced to attend training programs using guided visualization, meditation and other techniques that he alleges "can change a person's view of reality and religious beliefs."[27]

Telephoning a New Age

The California Public Utilities Commission was led to investigate the "Leadership Development" training practices by Pacific Bell—the state's largest utility company and the San Francisco Bay Area's biggest employer—because of complaints by employees that the training was based on spiritual philosophies not appropriate in a job setting.[28] The training consists of ten two-day sessions attended quarterly which utilize many of the ideas of Charles Krone, a pioneer in organizational development and a student of the controversial Russian mystic G. I. Gurdjieff (d. 1949). According to *The San Francisco Chronicle*, Krone "has devised an eclectic mixture of common sense, standard organizational development, scientific methodologies and Eastern philosophies."[29]

Pacific Bell has not revealed how much the training cost them, but estimates range from thirty- to one-hundred-million dollars per year. An official publication of Pacific Bell claims that the program has already proven beneficial and that it stimulates workers to be more responsible, intellectually alert and motivated; they disclaim any mystical elements.[30] Yet Dick Gilkeson, a Philadelphia consultant who has interacted with Krone, says that Krone "has adopted a lot of what the cults had done to really turn people on, like creating his own language and being as confusing as he is. Causing people to be interested in reading about Gurdjieff added a mystical transcendence."[31]

An air of mystery surrounded the whole affair because the Leadership Development program is copyrighted, and employees are told not to discuss their training without permission. Although the program was eventually retired, the scope of its influence was significant.

Clearly, something new is brewing in business; and not everyone likes its aroma.

Identifying a New Age Seminar

Space does not permit us to describe all the organizations engaged in New-Age-oriented seminars. Our time is better spent listing a few signposts that signal possible New Age activity. Just because a seminar displays one of these characteristics doesn't necessarily mean that it is New Age in orientation. Nevertheless, it does mean that we should proceed with care, cautiously discerning the assumptions behind what is being taught.

As mentioned in chapter three, we should be wary of two errors in evaluation. The one rejects any new management or personnel strategies in business without considering possible worthwhile features (the quarantine mentality). For example, if a business seminar stresses an affirmative and hopeful attitude toward business and gives some practical helps for achievement, well and good; the whole program need not be rejected. Also, a non-occult concern for developing intuition may be helpful in some areas of business. Legitimate elements should be *conserved.* Yet the opposite error uncritically inhales anything and everything with the scent of success, positiveness and optimism and in so doing becomes asphyxiated by the erroneous (the chameleon mentality).

The first signpost relates to seminars that stress visualization as the key to success: they emphasize the purportedly limitless power of the imagination to "create reality." What is simply a natural function of many people's thinking is absurdly elevated to the status of a magical principle. Seminar participants may be led through long and exotic "guided visualizations" for either relaxation or empowerment. In some cases this may induce a hypnotic trance in which one becomes vulnerable to suggestion. In other cases people may feel the rush of omnipotence, as they measure their abilities by the vividness of their visualizations—much like balancing one's checkbook by figuring out what one wishes were there. (More will be said on visualization in the next chapter.)

Second, seminars that strongly emphasize positive affirmations are suspect. Some seminars sell the science of self-congratulation. They say that our problems are, in large part, based on poor self-esteem. What is the answer? Positive affirmations and self-talk. To be "captains of our own destinies" we need to recapture the helm by praising ourselves mercilessly. Believing in oneself—that is, believing only the good things and stubbornly disbelieving the rest—is the key. Though blind positive thinking is not necessarily the product of the New Age, it is consistent with the world view and often used by its practitioners.

Although it is true that business people can be hindered by an unhealthy self-hate, and that a healthy sense of self-regard should be *conserved,* in many cases self-deception is hailed as self-liberation. Yet when Scripture says "You shall not give false testimony against your neighbor" (Ex 20:16), the principle extends to giving false witness on our own behalf. A lie is a lie whether it be spreading false bad rumors about Jones or equally false good rumors about ourselves. Proverbs charts the course of humility: "Let another praise you, and not your own mouth; someone else, and not your own lips" (Prov 27:2). (More on self-esteem in the next chapter.)

Third, business seminars may include Eastern/occult forms of meditation or other "psychotechnologies" under the guise of "stress reduction" (although all that is labeled stress reduction does not involve meditation). The dangers of these practices have already been discussed in chapters two and four. Some seminars wear away peoples' common sense and rational reflection through long hours of psychic assault, resulting in an artificial and inappropriate change in consciousness.

Fourth, caution is appropriate in evaluating any business seminar that "promises you the world" or guarantees they will "change your life." Although dramatic claims have a long history in salesmanship, extravagant claims in the New Age mode about total personal transformation are nothing less than religious appeals. These usually pander to the pride that desires *self*-actualization as opposed to the humility required to receive salvation from a source entirely foreign to our fallen frame. Some of those who believe they have indeed "gained the world" end up with an inflated sense of power that sets them up for major disappointments.[32]

Fifth, an exorbitant cost for these miracle seminars may tip us off to their dangers. Paying a substantial sum of (nonrefundable) money serves as a good psychological adhesive to insure that people endure the seminars even when their better judgment would normally propel them toward the door at the first few signs of aberration.

Sixth, excessive secrecy about the actual content of these seminars should cause us to wonder if they are hiding something sinister instead of simply protecting a marketable commodity. This may take the form of promoting the charisma of a particular speaker rather than devulging the content of his teaching. A typical tactic of some sects is to conceal their more bizarre teachings—such as Mormon polytheism and "sacred undergarments"—until the recruit is "ready" for them. Some business seminars may mirror this tactic by concealing activities that would initially—and rightly—repulse many.

Seventh, seminars that involve long hours outside of the normal work schedule and/or require the spouse's attendance may have the implicit intention of radically changing one's world view and manner of life to fit the New Age mold.

If these seven points help alert us to New Age tendencies in business seminars, what can be done to confront these practices and construct Christian alternatives?

A Christian Approach to Business

It is crucial that Christians be able properly to identify New Age intrusions into business, despite semantic camouflages. The pastor's daughter referred to earlier was immersed in the Forum experience before she really understood it. Many painful errors can be avoided by a strong dose of prevention.

What should be done if a Christian has identified a recommended or required seminar as New Age in orientation? The ground of all successful Christian action is spiritual awareness and discernment (see chapters two and three). The first issue is spiritual warfare, with prayer wielded as the chief weapon.

With a preparation of prayer, several responses are possible depending on the situation. If a particular seminar is simply being suggested, one can politely demur by explaining the spiritual roots of disagreement. This may even serve as a springboard for evangelism. In addition, reasons that are not specifically based on one's spiritual commitment—for instance, the seminars are ineffective or just too "weird"—can be given with the hope that the use of the seminar will be reconsidered. The Christian employee may also suggest that she attend an alternative seminar or read materials related to job performance that do not conflict with her spiritual views.

If attendance at a seminar is being required and a compromise is rejected, legal recourse is a possibility (as long as the employer is not a Christian; see 1 Cor 6:1-7). Tom Brandon of the Christian Legal Society says: "The employer is prohibited from discriminating against your religious convictions, and if you said, 'I'm sorry, I cannot attend that, it violates my religious principles,' then according to Title Seven they have to make reasonable accommodation for that."[33]

If attendance is being required by any civil governmental agency—such as in the case of Jim Baumgartel cited above—an appeal can be made that the state is violating the First Ammendment by establishing a religion (through state-funded, required programs), in this case the religion of the New Age. Of course, for this allegation to stick, one must reasonably demonstrate that the practices and concepts used are in fact religious in nature. Since many of the seminars are based on monism or pantheism that case can be made.

Given the extent of New Age cultural influence and its targeting of the business community, a few legal cases setting a precedent against coercing people against their religious beliefs might be a boon for religious freedom. Christians need the courage to confront the New Age wherever necessary—even in the courts.

New trends in business indicate that workers, managers and corporations are changing in many ways. To give a few examples: More women are entering the work force; more workers are content with less than full-time employment; and workers seem to be valuing the quality of their work and entire life more highly than simply salary or prestige.

As society changes, some changes in business practices will follow. Some of the emphases of New Age seminars and theory are acceptable and should be *conserved,* such as increased worker ownership and responsibility, a holistic concern for business, the importance of a vision for business ventures beyond mere profit and so on. Yet this does not necessitate a headlong plunge into the pantheistic deep. Some New Agers claim that since Christianity "doesn't work" (for business or anything else), we must embrace the New Age. Yet I side with Chesterton who said that "the Christian ideal has not been tried and found wanting. It has rather been found difficult; and left untried."[34]

Just a brief glance at a few Christian ethical considerations highlights the relevance of Christianity to business and work in general.

1. *A God-ward Orientation.* The biblical prohibition of idols (Ex 20:3-4; Jer 16:20) cautions us not to treat profit, prestige or power as ends in themselves, but as means to serve the Lord in all we do. Thus business ventures should be undertaken for the glory of God in order to contribute to his righteous kingdom. A Christian should never make work itself an idol at the expense of family and church life. A vertical orientation toward God is necessary for an appropriate horizontal relationship on the job (or anywhere else). The Christian's "pursuit of excellence" is a divine calling for a divine purpose, not an exercise in self-seeking.

2. *The Standard of Stewardship.* God is the giver of every good thing; he is the source of all true blessing. We are all debtors to God. Failing to realize this, we become cosmic ingrates. Any gift we enjoy—whether physical, spiritual or material—is delegated to us that

we may use it for him. We are the absolute owners of nothing, save our sin. We are, rather, stewards or caretakers of God's property.

This was so even before our fall into sin. Some have viewed labor itself as the result of sin, as if Adam and Eve were created for perpetual vacationing but somehow fell from leisure into labor. Yet Genesis 1 and 2 teach that Adam and Eve were created in God's image to cultivate the earth according to his commands. Adam named the creatures before the Fall. Upon disobeying God's clear command, our first parents then found work to be weighted by the effects of sin (Gen 3). Still, work is part of our calling as humans; and work, though now done by "the sweat of the brow," can be redeemed through the application of Christian principles. The preacher of Ecclesiastes gives us wisdom: "A man can do nothing better than to eat and drink and find satisfaction in his work. This too, I see, is from the hand of God" (Eccles 2:24).

John Stott gives us a biblical view of work: "Work is the expenditure of energy (manual or mental or both) in the service of others, which brings fulfillment to the worker, benefit to the community, and glory to God."[35]

All work—whether church related or not—when done for God's glory, according to his principles and through his Spirit, is valuable to our Creator. Business people need not feel like second-class citizens because they aren't pastors or foreign missionaries (the so-called full-time Christian workers). The workplace is a full-time mission field and theater of divine drama.

3. _The Value of the Person._ By claiming that humans share the divine image, Christianity values people as responsible moral agents. For business this means not treating people as merely means to a better business, but as valuable in themselves. Yet Christian realism—unlike New Age utopianism—recognizes the reality of human sinfulness and guards against employers having inordinate expectations for employees or vice versa. And although the profit motivation is not intrinsically immoral (the Bible affirms the value of private

property and industry),[36] the Bible condemns a profit domination that sacrifices the value of employees (or consumers) for the sake of greed.

Wayne Alderson, a Christian business consultant, courageously stresses this pivotal principle in his Value of the Person seminars which he has presented to both management and labor across the nation. He asks:

> Is it asking too much for God's people to stand up for the values of love, dignity, and respect in their places of employment? Not at all. . . . As Christians we are commanded by God to take the Biblical principles . . . into the work world to live for God. . . . I believe it is essential that both labor and management exercise their moral obligation and raise the Value of the Person above the Value of the Machine. The unrest that the workplace is experiencing in whatever form, great or small, is just the symptom. The underlying cause is a lack of human dignity.[37]

By God's grace, Alderson has helped management and labor work together harmoniously by using biblical principles. His gripping story of working as a steelworker, manager and consultant is recorded in *Stronger Than Steel* by R. C. Sproul.

Tied to the value of the person is the principle of servanthood. We value what we freely serve. Just as we strive to serve God in our work, Jesus affirms that the measure of our greatness is the measure of our service to others:

> You know that the rulers of the Gentiles lord it over them, and their high officials exercise authority over them. Not so with you. Instead, whoever wants to become great among you must be your servant, and whoever wants to be first must be your slave—just as the Son of Man did not come to be served, but to serve, and to give his life as a ransom for many. (Mt 20:25-28)

Christ's mission of ransom makes possible the revolutionizing of the workplace.

4. *Honesty.* Christian ethics affirms truthfulness as essential to

moral integrity. Honesty isn't the best policy, it's the only (Christian) policy. "Speaking the truth in love" (Eph 4:15) means straight talk to employees, no deception in advertising or merchandising, and no illegalities (in taxes or elsewhere). The Bible repeatedly warns people to use "honest scales and honest weights" (Lev 19:36)—that is, not to shortchange people through deception, as was common in that time since there was no official bureau of weights and measures.

5. *Thrift.* In a credit-happy (or unhappy) society, we should remember that biblical ethics restricts large, long-term debt. Proverbs warns that "the borrower is servant to the lender" (Prov 22:7), and Paul teaches that we should "let no debt remain outstanding, except the continuing debt to love one another" (Rom 13:8). In Old Testament times, loans were to be paid back within seven years (Deut 15:1-6). This all goes to show that the modern convention of massive, long-term debt is less than wise and should be avoided whenever possible. The application of this biblical principle minimizes economic risk and focuses on the gradual development of businesses that grow according to real assets, not according to exorbitant debt liabilities.

These five principles are just an appetizer of a Christian business philosophy. I have not even explored the rich tapestry of leadership examples to be culled from great biblical leaders such as Moses, Nehemiah and Paul. If the Bible is truly "God-breathed and is useful for teaching, rebuking, correcting and training in righteousness, so that the man of God may be thoroughly equipped for every good work" (2 Tim 3:16), it should be mined for principles, strategies and attitudes relevant to the business world.

Consulting the monthly newsletter *Spiritual Fitness in Business* for timely and thoughtful articles related to Christianity and business can be helpful.[38] In the business world—as everywhere else—our strategy should be to *conserve* what is already good, to reject and *separate* from the unredeemable and to *transform* all we can in order to please the Lord. It is not enough to oppose the New Age's insinuation into business—though that is imperative—we must erect alternatives whenever possible. This calls for informed Christian activism at both the theoretical and practical levels, lest the world of business become the captive of mystics in three-piece suits.

Notes

[1]J. Yutaka Amano, "Erhard's Forum," *Spiritual Fitness in Business* (February 1986), p. 2.

[2]Werner Erhard and Associates, *The Forum* (1986), n.p.

[3]Ibid.

[4]Neil Chesanow, "Est Revisited," *New Women* (January 1987), p. 42.

[5]Ibid., p. 46.

[6]Robert Bell, "Est Dressed for Success," *Venture* (March 1987), p. 54.

[7]Bell, "Est."

[8]Robert Lindsey, "Spiritual Concepts Drawing a Different Breed of Adherent," *New York Times,* September 29, 1986, p. 8.

[9]Norman Boucher, "Transforming the Corporation," *New Age Journal* (February 1985), p. 40.

[10]See Groothuis, *Unmasking,* pp. 93-109.

[11]Boucher, "Transforming," p. 40.

[12]John Adams, *Transforming Work* (Alexandria, Va.: Miles River, 1984), p. vi; emphasis mine.

[13]Ibid.

[14]Don Oldenburg, "Zen and the Art of Making Money," *Washington Post,* January 9, 1987.

[15]"Mega-trends Man: John Naisbitt," *Newsweek,* September 23, 1985, pp. 60-61.

[16]John Naisbitt and Patricia Aburdene, *Re-inventing the Corporation* (New York: Warner, 1986), p. 82.

[17]Christie Tierney, "Corporate America Relaxes with Transcendental Meditation," *Washington Business Journal* (January 27, 1986).

[18]Oldenburg, "Zen and the Art."

[19]Lindsey, "Spiritual Concepts," p. 8.

[20]Michael Ray and Rochelle Myers, *Creativity in Business* (Garden City, N.Y.: Doubleday, 1986), pp. 56-61.

[21]Ibid., p. 28.

[22]Oldenburg, "Zen and the Art."

[23]"Religion and the 'New Age,' " *Training* (December 1985).

[24]John Wolcott, "Pacific Institutes' Lou Tice and the Power of Positive Thinking," *The Progress* (September 18, 1986), p. 12.

[25]Ibid., p. 13.

[26]Bill Deitrich, "This Salesman is Motivated—to Sue: Pacific Institute Is Labeled as 'Anti-Christian,' " *Seattle Times,* February 25, 1987.

[27]Robert Lindsey, "Gurus Hired to Motivate Workers Are Raising Fears of Mind Control,"

New York Times, April 17, 1987.

[28]Lindsey, "Gurus Hired."

[29]Kathleen Pender, "Pac Bell's New Way to Think," *San Francisco Chronicle,* March 23, 1987, p. 6.

[30]"Tools to Solve Real Business Problems," *Business Report,* March 30, 1987.

[31]Pender, "Pac Bell's," p. 6.

[32]See Greg Critser, "The Est Factor: Behind the Rise and Fall of Computerland's Bill Millard Was a Corporate Culture that Became a Corporate Cult," *Inc.* (August 1986), pp. 69-76.

[33]Quoted in Miller, "Tracking the 'Aquarian Conspiracy,' " p. 27.

[34]G. K. Chesterton, *Collected Works,* 28 vols. (San Francisco: Ignatius Press, 1987) 4:61; quoted in Gard DeMar and Peter Leithart, *The Reduction of Christianity* (Ft. Worth, Tex.: Dominion Press, 1988), pp. 122-23.

[35]John Stott, *Involvement,* Vol. 2 (Old Tappan, N.J.: Revell, 1985), p. 31.

[36]See Ronald Nash, *Social Justice and the Christian Church* (Milford, Mich.: Mott Media, 1983).

[37]Quoted in "Reconciliation in the Work World," *Tabletalk* 9, no. 1 (February 1985), p. 5.

[38]Available from Probe Ministries, 1900 Firman Dr., Richardson, TX 75081.

Issues in Discernment:
Self-image, Visualization, Biofeedback and New Age Music

9

THE PRESENCE OF THE NEW AGE MOVEMENT IN SO MANY AREAS OF LIFE should deeply challenge Christians to develop a thoroughly Christian mind able to discern the differences between counterfeits and reality. Otherwise we may become like the house of Jacob who was "full of superstitions from the East" and who would "clasp hands with pagans" (Is 2:6; see also Jer 10:2).

Although many New Age ideas and practices are clearly hostile to the Christian world view, some phenomena associated with the New Age movement may resist simplistic analysis. The realization of complexity in some areas need not drive us to despair; rather, it should goad us to develop our discernment skills like those commended as mature in the book of Hebrews: "who . . . have trained themselves to distinguish good from evil" (Heb 5:14).

Steve Scott and Brooks Alexander clearly focus the issue:
The era we inhabit is characterized by the increasing complexity
of life at all levels—economic, material, moral and intellectual. As
the crosscurrents of old and new ideas proliferate, they influence
Christian thought in a variety of ways. Some have more validity
than others; many are unacceptable altogether. We must be prepared to encounter unfamiliar concepts and patiently and prayer-
fully unravel both their sources and their implications. This process may be frustrating and demanding, but its necessity is
increasingly a fact of life.[1]

Lest we fall into the previously mentioned pitfalls of the quarantine,
taboo, paranoid, Chicken Little, chameleon or ostritch mentalities, we
need to scrutinize closely the issues raised by the New Age in order
to develop what Harry Blamires calls a "Christian mind—a mind
trained, informed, equipped to handle the data of secular controversy
within a framework of reference which is constructed of Christian
presuppositions."[2]

We have already addressed several issues in discernment, but in
this chapter we will deal with the issues of self-image, visualization/
imagination, biofeedback and New Age music, viewing them as representative case studies.

Self-Esteem and the Christian

The New Age is preoccupied, above all, with self—Deep Self, Higher
Self, True Self and so on. New Agers in principle reject the very
thought of negative self-image, self-talk or self-esteem; such would
be psychological sacrilege, blasphemy against "the God within." For
the New Age, the love of God is tantamount to self-love. Ramtha, a
supposedly "enlightened" entity channeled through J. Z. Knight, tells
us that since "God is everything," anything we do has "an inner action
of divinity," and that if we remember that, we will learn to love ourselves.[3]

For the New Age, poor self-esteem and an unenlightened self-image are seen as the root cause of all our problems.

But what is a Christian view of self-esteem and self-image?

In an interview, sociologist James Davidson Hunter noted that "conservative Christians historically, and I mean for centuries, always viewed the self with a strong measure of distrust, if not hostility. Today, among evangelicals as among all Americans, the self is more celebrated than held in check."[4] The obvious danger is for Christians to follow the Pied Piper of self-esteem and fall into the trap of the "chameleon mentality."

The problem with the New Age view of self-esteem is that it ignores the fundamental problem of humanity—namely, sin. Sin is rebellion against God, based on and exemplified by *pride*. Pride is the overestimation of ourselves as independent and the underestimation of our dependence on God. Pride says, "I am the Lord my God, and I shall have no other gods besides me," and "I shall love the Lord my Self with all my heart, soul, strength and mind."

To ignore this aspect of ourselves is to significantly skew the picture. Given the reality of the Fall and the sinfulness of the self, the New Age view of self-esteem is loaded with wishful thinking and self-deception—both absent from the psychological realism of Christianity.[5] As Pascal poignantly said, "Truly it is an evil to be full of faults; but it is a still greater evil to be full of them and to be unwilling to recognize them, since that is to add the further fault of voluntary illusion.[6]

Christianity affirms that all humans bear the image of God (Gen 1:26-28). We are not junk. Speaking of humanity the psalmist sings, "You made him a little lower than the heavenly beings and crowned him with glory and honor" (Ps 8:5). We are different from the animal kingdom: "You made him ruler over the works of your hands" (v. 6). But our worth remains grounded in and derived from our Creator who brought forth the universe out of nothing. "Know that the LORD is God. It is he who made us, and we are his" (Ps 100:3).

Our Maker has deigned to descend to earth to redeem us. In our

Redeemer's analysis of what makes a person unclean we find nothing of the idea that a poor self-esteem is the true offender: "What comes out of a man is what makes him 'unclean.' For from within, out of men's hearts, come evil thoughts, sexual immorality, theft, murder, adultery, greed, malice, deceit, lewdness, envy, slander, arrogance and folly. All these evils come from inside and make a man 'unclean' " (Mk 7:20-23). Neither does Paul's assessment of the human problem even suggest that a lack of self-esteem is to blame for our ills (Rom 3:10-18). Rather, it is the sin of pride that is the culprit.

The solution of the cross shows the radical extent of the problem. God provided a way to overcome our sin, based not on human worthiness, but on his mercy. As Titus says, "When the kindness and love of God our Savior appeared, he saved us, not because of righteous things we had done, but because of his mercy" (Tit 3:4). Through God's mercy, anyone can receive forgiveness of sins and life eternal.

Our self-esteem, therefore, needs to be anchored in our gracious God and in what he has provided for us. Paul declares that as Christians we are "a new creation" in Christ Jesus (2 Cor 5:17). Paul describes this new status as being justified by God's grace through faith (Eph 2:8-9). Once we are forgiven and sealed with the Holy Spirit, we can expect to demonstrate the fruit of godliness. In a nutshell, Christians should view themselves—their self-image—as justified by God's grace and freed from the condemnation of sin (Rom 8:1-2).

What the church desperately needs is a better understanding of justification and sanctification, not lessons on self-esteem from New Age psychology.[7] We need more theology and less me-ology. In a superb discussion of justification and sanctification as elements of renewal, Richard Lovelace laments that "few know enough to start each day with a thorough stand upon Luther's platform: *you are accepted,* looking outward in faith and claiming the wholly alien righteousness of Christ as the only ground for acceptance, relaxing in that quality of trust which will produce increasing sanctification as faith is active in love and gratitude."[8]

The differences between justification and sanctification are seen below.

Justification	Sanctification
1. God's work for us	1. God's work in us
2. A once-for-all event	2. A process
3. Complete	3. Incomplete (until death)
4. The root of our position	4. The fruit of our position
5. Declared righteous	5. Demonstrates righteousness
6. By God's grace	6. By God's grace

We cannot justify ourselves by good self-esteem. All the positive self- image, self-talk and self-esteem in the world will not dissolve sin. Nor will any overemphasis on self encourage sanctification. Consider the wise words of St. Augustine in which he contrasts the humanistic earthly city and God's Heavenly City:

We see then that the two great cities were created by two kinds of love: the earthly city was created by self-love reaching the point of contempt for God, the Heavenly City by the love of God carried as far as contempt for self. In fact, the earthly city gloried in itself, the Heavenly City glories in the Lord. The former looks for glory from men, the latter find its highest glory in God, the witness of a good conscience.[9]

When Scripture speaks of self, it usually commends self-denial and self-control and condemns self-worship. Jesus declared, "If anyone would come after me, he must deny himself and take up his cross and follow me. For whoever wants to save his life will lose it, but whoever loses his life for me will find it" (Mt 16:24-25). Paul says that for "those who are self-seeking and who reject the truth and follow evil, there will be wrath and anger" (Rom 2:8) and also warns of those who are "lovers of themselves . . . rather than lovers of God" (2 Tim 3:1-4). The evil comes when love for self rivals and replaces our love for God.

Paul addresses the problem by calling for "sober judgment": "For by the grace given me I say to every one of you: Do not think of yourself more highly than you ought, but rather think of yourself with sober judgment, in accordance with the measure of faith God has given you" (Rom 12:3).

A "sober judgment" of self encompasses a godly self-criticism when we fall short of pleasing God, an honesty that leads to repentance and restoration. This judgment avoids both pride and painful self-hate; it comes from the grace given by God to understand ourselves correctly, based on our justification and in terms of our gifts. If we deny in our negativism that God loves us and has given us gifts in order to serve him, then we think too little of both God and ourselves. If we believe that because of our gifts we deserve acclaim and recognition, we think too highly of ourselves and too little of God. Since our salvation and worth rest in the person and work of Jesus Christ, we are free to see our weaknesses and sins and look to Christ for the grace to overcome them and use our gifts for his glory.

A basic self-regard is natural for all humans (see Eph 5:29) and should not be confused with pride. When Jesus says, "Love your neighbor as yourself" (Mt 22:39), he assumes self-regard. At the same time he does not argue here that we should increase it. Rather, the emphasis in the passage is on loving the neighbor. Paul's emphasis in Romans 12 is not on self-esteem but on accurately understanding how one's gifts can serve the body of Christ.

While New Age psychology tells us to seek first self's kingdom and its psychology, Jesus says, "Seek first his kingdom and his righteousness, and all these things will be given to you as well" (Mt 6:33). Sadly, some Christians have ignored these teachings, shifting attention from God and his kingdom to the kingdom of self.

But lest we *quarantine* the entire idea of self-love, a few distinctions should be drawn. Unconditional self-*acceptance* is certainly unbiblical and psychologically harmful. I cannot unconditionally accept my sinful thoughts and behavior and keep a clear conscience before my Creator. Self-*love* is acceptable and encouraged as long as it is understood within its proper context. First, self-love must never eclipse our love for God. Second, my love for myself is unconditional in the sense that I should not give up on myself as a vessel through which God's glory may come. I don't need to rely on my own strength. God's grace is sufficient for me, despite my weakness. My self-love is based on God's love for me. Third, proper self-love is realistic. I love myself unconditionally (as God loves me), but I do not accept everything about myself unconditionally; rather I am grateful for my gifts, and do not pretend to be able to do what for me is impossible.

Pride can lead to inordinate self-love or to inordinate self-hate. Either direction betrays an improper emphasis. Endless attention to one's faults evidences an ungodly self-preoccupation as does inordinate attention to one's strengths. We were made to look beyond ourselves in order to become better selves.

Paul's view of himself was not unconditional self-acceptance, as is clear from these passages: "For I am the least of the apostles and do not even deserve to be called an apostle, because I persecuted the church of God. But by the grace of God I am what I am, and his grace to me was not without effect" (1 Cor 15:9-10). "Although I am less than the least of all God's people, this grace was given me: to preach to the Gentiles the unsearchable riches of Christ" (Eph 3:8). "Here is a trustworthy saying that deserves full acceptance: Christ Jesus came into the world to save sinners—of whom I am the worst" (1 Tim 1:15). Paul's secret of contentment was Christ and his grace, not Paul. Again he says, "May I never boast except in the cross of our Lord Jesus Christ" (Gal 6:14).

The Bible is full of faithful affirmations centering on God, not self. Listen to Jeremiah:

> This is what the LORD says: "Let not the wise man boast of his wisdom or the strong man boast of his strength or the rich man boast of his riches, but let him who boasts boast about this: that he understands and knows me, that I am the LORD, who exercises kindness, justice and righteousness on earth, for in these I delight,"

declares the LORD. (Jer 9:23-24)

Yet the biblical view of self never precludes joy and appreciation, even of one's own achievements.[10] There are times we can honestly say, "Praise God! He used me to glorify himself and help someone else!" In *The Screwtape Letters*, C. S. Lewis amplifies this from the perspective of a senior devil who is instructing a junior devil.

The Enemy [God] wants to bring the man to a state of mind in which he could design the best cathedral in the world, and know it to be the best, and rejoice in the fact, without being any more (or less) or otherwise glad at having done it than he would be if it had been done by another. The Enemy wants him, in the end, to be so free from any bias in his own favour that he can rejoice in his own talents as frankly and gratefully as in his neighbour's talents—or in a sunrise, an elephant, or a waterfall. . . . He wants to kill their animal self-love as soon as possible, but it is His long-term policy, I fear, to restore to them a new kind of self-love—a clarity and gratitude for all selves, including their own; when they have really learned to love their neighbours as themselves, they will be allowed to love themselves as their neighbours.[11]

Visualization and Imagination

New Age writer Shakti Gawain teaches in *Creative Visualization* that we can bring into existence whatever we visualize, since "we create our own reality" and are not limited by any fixed, objective order of creation. This is the New Age line. We can tap into unlimited potential by visualizing whatever we desire.

Christians have erred in two directions concerning visualization and imagination. One group has uncritically accepted much of the New Age teaching, viewing the imagination as almost unfallen and unlimited. In not taking the New Age poisons seriously, they fall into the chameleon mentality. The other group is so critical of New Age and Christian abuses of the imagination that it rules out the imagination entirely, declaring it to be the devil's playground, thus falling into the quarantine or taboo mentalities. Yet there is a middle course which can be navigated by considering the following points.

The first consideration is that the imagination, like all our mental faculties, is affected by the Fall. Probably the strongest biblical verse on the evil inclinations of our imaginations is Genesis 6:5, which describes the wretchedness of the preflood world: "The LORD saw how great man's wickedness on the earth had become, and that every inclination of the thoughts of his heart was only evil all the time" (see also Gen 8:21). Even if we are being transformed by the renewing of our minds (Rom 12:2), our minds will not be perfected until we see Perfection face to face (1 Cor 13:12; 1 Jn 3:1-3). New Age visualizers deny the Fall wholesale and venture off into the imagination's deep with no sure rudder, compass, map or fixed stars to guide them. They can easily—and tragically—become lost at sea, or even captured by psychic pirates.

Second, visualization and imagination themselves, once demystified, should be seen as natural human faculties which are not intrinsically evil. All people visualize and imagine to varying degrees; some often "think in pictures" while others seldom do so. Jesus himself appealed to the imagination when relating his many parables, fictitious stories aimed at conveying objective truth. But, given some Christians' overemphasis on the importance of detailed visualizations, it is important to note that Jesus used little sensational or detailed imagery. For instance, he tells us nothing very specific about the prodigal son's appearance. The key elements he focuses on are the condition of the prodigal's heart and that of his father's and brother's. Much of biblical literature evokes vivid images; consider, for example, the many images of the book of Revelation. These images do not negate factual content; rather, both rational and imaginative faculties are engaged in this type of biblical writing.

Third, it needs to be clarified that the many *visions* given in the Bible are not the same as *visualizations*. A vision is objectively given by God for a specific purpose: to foretell the future (as with Daniel), to call a prophet (as with Ezekiel), or for some other God-directed reason. Visualization is the subjective activation of the imagination by human will. Visualizing a certain scene is not the same as receiving a vision sent by God. The one is psychologically induced; the other is divinely introduced.

Some have justified quite exotic visualization techniques by blurring this important distinction. Several writers have even advocated visualizing Jesus for the purpose of spiritual growth. This is unwise for several reasons. It neglects the fallen nature of our imagination. Scripture warns us of making and worshiping vain images of God which are really idols (Ex 20:4-5). We may very likely conjure up a Jesus made more in our image than God's. Consider the revelation of Jesus to the apostle John. John was "in the Spirit" on the Lord's Day when granted an incredible vision of the ascended Christ: one "like a son of man" dressed in a long robe with a golden sash, his head and hair white as snow, his eyes like blazing fire, his feet like glowing bronze, his voice like the sound of rushing waters, his face brilliantly shining like the son. He held in his right hand seven stars, and from his mouth came a double-edged sword (Rev 1:12-16). What was John's response? I dare say it was different from the self-styled visualizers of today. He said, "When I saw him I fell at his feet as though dead." Yet Jesus comforted him by saying "Do not be afraid" (v. 17). Visions are certainly possible today (Acts 2:17), but they must be distinguished from visualizations and checked against Scripture.

It seems legitimate sometimes to visualize how Jesus may have looked during a particular Gospel account if this helps to make vivid the event in our minds. For instance, Paul graphically presented Christ in his preaching to the Galatians, before whose "very eyes Jesus Christ was clearly portrayed as crucified," as he put it (3:1). John Stott notes that the Greek word for _portrayed_ probably means to draw or paint. He says that "Paul . . . likens his gospel-preaching either to a huge canvas painting or to a placard publicly exhibiting a notice or advertisement. The subject of his painting or placard was Jesus Christ on the cross. . . . It was so visual, so vivid, in its appeal to their imagination, that the placard was presented 'before your very eyes.' "[12]

Visualizing Jesus on the cross dying on our behalf may indeed stimulate faith, worship, praise and obedience. Yet visualizing Jesus in order to set up a personal counseling session with the Son of God is more than a little presumptuous. Don Matzat puts it well:

> The Christian church has always taught that God reaches down for man, rather than man reaching within for God. Revelation begins with God, and not with man "priming his visualization pump" to talk to Jesus. Biblical Christianity has always directed man outside himself to a God who, by the working of the Holy Spirit through the preaching of the gospel acts upon man in order to bring him to faith and salvation.[13]

We must also realize that the psychological conjuring practice of visualization may, under certain conditions, open one up to counterfeit Christs, "angels of light" (2 Cor 11:14), who are the enemies of God and humanity. An elaborate visualization exercise could induce an altered state of consciousness quite amenable to demonic insurgents. Shakti Gawain, for instance, says that "creative visualization" can easily introduce one to "spirit guides," the likes of which would be thrilled to meet us.[14] Occult visualization has been used for centuries to invoke such blind guides, and if Christians falsely assume that their visualizations will invoke the real Jesus, they could be setting themselves up for deception.

Fourth, although the Bible sometimes uses visually evocative language, we need not vividly visualize Jesus to have faith in him. He himself said to Thomas, "Because you have seen me, you have believed; blessed are those who have not seen and yet have believed" (Jn 20:29). A. W. Tozer was right to distinguish believing from visualizing, saying that believing is moral, while visualizing is mental. "Unwillingness to believe proves that men love darkness rather than light, while inability to visualize indicates no more than lack of imagination, something that will not be held against us at the judgment seat of Christ."[15]

Faith does not depend on our visualizing prowess, but rather on the sure promises of God which we lay hold of by a reasonable faith. Paul's emphasis is that "faith comes from *hearing* the message, and the message is *heard* through the *word* of Christ" (Rom. 10:17; emphasis mine). Paul concentrates on "hearing the word," the propositional content of the gospel, not vivid images (although the imagination can be stimulated through preaching, as mentioned above). Christians shall one day see Christ face to face, but until that great day, "we live by faith, not by sight" (2 Cor 5:7).

Fifth, another problem concerning visualization is the extravagant claims some make on its behalf. "Whatever the mind can conceive, the will can achieve," as the old saying goes. Visualization then becomes a kind of magic, a way of manipulating reality through mind power. New Agers also grant to their imaginations a divine power beyond that of finite creatures. As Rushdoony observes, "In his imagination, the fallen man sees himself as god and creator. In his every dream, he plays god over reality. Magic and witchcraft are products of this fallen imagination. The 'magic words' of witches are 'As my will, so mote it be!' "[16] Or, "As I visualize, so mote it be!"

Some people simply and naturally picture themselves doing a particular act before actually performing it, such as a baseball player visualizing his swing against the pitcher's curve ball. Inasmuch as this mental rehearsal primes him for better performance, it seems harmless. Along the same lines, a positive use of the imagination may encourage physical healing. This natural interaction of mind and body is not to be confused with the New Age claim that we "create our own reality" through "mind over matter."

Similarly, if someone is helped to focus attention in prayer by visualizing the person they are praying for, this seems unobjectionable, so long as no magical power is granted to the act of visualization itself. It is not our minds that answer prayer, but God. The distinction is crucial, lest Christians slip into magical thinking. Colin Brown notes that "the Lord's prayer and other prayers of Jesus have a completely different orientation from magic. The latter is concerned with the control of the supernatural by techniques to further one's own ends. Jesus' concern was to do the will of the Father and to teach men to submit their whole lives to that will."[17]

Imagination and Fantasy

A related point concerns the use of the imagination in fantasy literature, fantasy role-playing games, movies, cartoons or toys. Some Christians, having detected the intrusion of the occult into these genres, have rejected them entirely.

Undoubtedly, New Age ideas have poisoned many a book, game, movie and cartoon. The fantasy tales, for instance, of Ursula LeGuin often resonate with occult themes. Jean M. Auel's tremendously popular *Clan of the Cave Bear* and its sequels portray a supposedly prehistoric culture whose religion is pantheistic/animistic.

The premier fantasy role-playing game, Dungeons and Dragons (not to mention spinoffs), is incorrigibly occult, incorporating actual occult spell-casting (which is spoken), occult symbolism (the magic circle, pentagram and thaumaturgic triangle), hideous violence and a basic amoral, animistic/polytheistic world view.[18] Yet the game has developed a cult following, in addition to being used in many public schools,[19] despite the fact that it has been associated with numerous homicides and suicides.

Various movies such as the *Star Wars* trilogy, *The Karate Kid I* and *II,* and numerous other films either subtly or blatantly sound New Age themes. And even children's cartoons and toys, such as the immensely popular "Masters of the Universe," use occult symbolism and concepts to draw children into their world of error.[20]

In these and many other cases the temptation to overemphasize the separation theme and slip into the "taboo" or "quarantine mentality" is very strong. There is so little wheat among the chaff that the tendency is to throw all of it into the hottest furnace available. That furnace does need to be stoked; and it is regrettable when Christians try, for instance, to "depaganize" Dungeons and Dragons for Christian consumption when the game's controlling world view is occult to the core. Far too many Christians are ignorant of the occult content of many cartoons, toys and movies. J. R. R. Tolkien, himself a noted fantasy author, notes the dangers of fantasy: "Fantasy can, of course, be carried to excess. It can be ill done. It can be put to evil uses. It may even delude the minds out of which it came." But he goes on to point out that people have corrupted every gift of God.[21] The entire fantasy genre itself need not be committed to the flames, but should rather be committed to the discerning mind of the mature believer.

Christian faith in Christ is rooted in fact, not fantasy; it is grounded in reality, not mythology. Peter proclaims, "We did not follow cleverly invented stories when we told you about the power and coming of our Lord Jesus Christ, but we were eyewitnesses of his majesty" (2 Pet 1:16; see also 1 Tim 1:4; 2 Tim 4:4; Tit 1:14).[22] Yet why should fantasy—when recognized as fantasy—be silenced from speaking God's truth? Why should humans made in God's creative image not exercise that creativity through fantasy literature? As J. R. R. Tolkien put it, "Fantasy remains a human right: we make in our measure and in our derivative mode, because we are made: and not only made, but made in the image and likeness of a Maker."[23]

C. S. Lewis's series of books The Chronicles of Narnia is fantasy literature set in a world of his own imagination. Yet that doesn't stop Lewis from saturating the books with distinctly Christian themes. In this sense, Lewis's fantasy may be more real than the supposed realistic novels written by those who deny the biblical world view. Narnia's main character, Aslan the lion, is a kind of Christ figure (although the work is not a strict allegory) who is pictured as good but not tame—a wonderful description of the sovereign goodness of Christ. Lewis's space trilogy—*Out of the Silent Planet, Perelandra,* and *That Hideous Strength*—uses science fiction for the same end. In this sense his apologetic method was two-pronged: he wrote nonfiction works directly defending Christianity from attack, but through his fiction he painted the Christian world view with bright and clear colors such that those who might not read formal apologetics could still catch a glimpse of Truth.[24]

Lewis is just one example among many. Christian themes can also be found in Tolkien, though they may be less obvious.[25] The point to catch is that both writers were creating from an essentially Christian world view which significantly influenced their work. This doesn't exempt Lewis, Tolkien or others from Christian criticism, but it is a clue as to the worth of the fantasy genre.

Here again we see the three themes of cultural response: Although Christians must be *separate* from the evils in the fantasy genre, it should not be rejected entirely. Christians would be wiser to *conserve* the Christian fantasy tradition inherited from Lewis and others and then try to *transform* the present situation to reflect a Christian world view. This can be done by encouraging promising Christian writers, actors, cartoonists and others to bring their Christianity to bear on the arts and so transform them for the glory of God and the good of humanity. If we do not, we will have even more from which to be separate, less to conserve and more to transform. Why abandon it all? Just because the demons dance in the woods is no reason to torch the whole forest.

Biofeedback Therapy

In *Unmasking the New Age* I all too briefly suggested that biofeedback therapy may be appropriate even though it is much heralded in New Age circles as a tool for "enlightenment," even as the "yoga for the west." I now return to this issue of discernment in more depth.

Biofeedback uses technology to monitor and consciously control normally unconscious—or autonomic—bodily processes such as heartbeat, blood pressure and muscle tension. It employs means such as the EEG (electroencephalograph) to test brainwave activity (alpha, beta, theta or delta waves), the EKG (electrocardiograph) to test heartbeat and the EMB (electromyograph) and the GSR (galvanic skin response) for muscle tension.

Someone outfitted with one of these monitoring devices receives feedback concerning his biological state: hence the term "bio-feed-back." They are made aware of a bodily function usually unnoticed and/or uncontrollable. Chronic headaches, muscle spasms, high blood pressure and other maladies may be thus treated. Reports on the medical effectiveness of biofeedback are mixed, but it does seem to be reasonably successful in some cases.

But should a Christian use this modern technology? Several factors need to be considered and carefully weighed.

The first test is medical. Does it work? Is biofeedback a legitimate medical therapy for the specific malady at issue? Here research into biofeedback and the word of a qualified physician is important.

Second, if it is determined to work and to be appropriate for a particular person's malady, is the practice inextricably connected to the occult? Biofeedback's origin is related to the scientific study of non-Christian yogis and Zen masters who could voluntarily—and without outside technology—control their autonomic functions. So the root is in Eastern mysticism. This genetic test is significant, but not necessarily determinative. For instance, the monistic mystic Pythagorus discovered the Pythagorean theorem in mathematics, but this is no reason for Christians to boycott geometry! The genetic test, though, should put us on alert to see if we should be thoroughly *separate* from this practice, or at least separate from certain of its expressions.

Third, we should consider how biofeedback therapists and patients have described their experiences. Some have definitely linked the practice with "altered states of consciousness" at odds with the Christian world view. Some have spoken of spontaneous paranormal and/or mystical experiences. Noted holistic theorist Kenneth Pelletier explains,

Self-healing by means of biofeedback inevitably involves the individual in a process of psychological development and may elicit profound experiences of altered states of consciousness. . . . During the deep relaxation . . . [of biofeedback], the person may experience a unitive sensation in which he merges with the room, chairs, light, or therapist. This process of release appears similar to the profound unitive experiences in meditation and occur when consciousness expands beyond its usual constraints and modes of functioning.[26]

Yet, as Pelletier notes, not all of those involved in biofeedback have these experiences. So the next question is, Does biofeedback *necessarily* open one up to these experiences?

Christians who advocate a wholesale rejection of biofeedback liken it to yoga and hypnosis, claiming that it requires an emptying of the mind conducive to spiritual deception or even demonization. If this is so, biofeedback should be rejected, whatever possible medical benefit. Better sick than demonized!

But it seems that biofeedback can be administered in different ways for different purposes. Christians should reject outright any extravagant claims which are often made on behalf of biofeedback to the effect that it can unleash the unlimited potential of the mind. The Christian's intention for using biofeedback should be medical, not mystical. Christians would also be wise to steer clear of New Age-oriented people administering biofeedback who could administer the therapy in such a way as to lull one into a passive, noncognitive state of mind. But if the biofeedback therapy does not necessarily induce these dangerous states of mind but rather a refocusing of rational concentration on aspects of bodily functioning not normally noticeable and/or controllable, the therapy could be legitimate.[27]

Christian researchers Clifford Wilson and John Weldon caution, though, that those with occult backgrounds—even up to four generations in their past—could find the therapy harmful because of their heightened susceptibility to occult influences.[28] Although it is difficult to know if one's ancestors were involved with the occult, if the biofeedback therapy is not intended to induce negative altered states of consciousness, this danger would seem to be minimized.

Added to these qualifications, though, would be that the biofeed-back therapy be used as a last resort, because of the possible—but not necessary—tie-ins with New Age ideas and experiences. Healing directly from the Lord should be sought first and foremost,[29] but the Lord can also provide other medical means. Yet if the above cautious guidelines are followed, and one has a good conscience before the Lord to consecrate the therapy to him (1 Tim 4:4), biofeedback could be permitted and helpful.

Just as any evaluation of biofeedback has to be *process-specific* (what sort of therapy is it?), so must any evaluation be *person-spe-cific;* that is, you should be convinced biblically, medically and expe-rientially that this is God's will for you. Some Christians will be ame-nable to the practice; others will not. Let us hope and pray that whatever decision is reached is done with prayerful thought and thoughtful prayer. "Each one should be fully convinced in his own mind" (Rom 14:5).

It should be noticed that this response to the biofeedback issue is somewhat involved and nuanced. This goes to show that New Age discernment often takes some concerted effort. Blanket condemna-tions may be inappropriate. Although I find good reasons to be cau-tious concerning biofeedback, I find the "quarantine or taboo men-talities" inadequate; but so is the "ostrich mentality" or "chameleon mentality" that accepts the practice without any of the above con-siderations.

Music for a New Age

During the last several years the music industry has added a new term to its menu: New Age music. The term is extremely broad, covering everything from languid solo guitar or piano pieces to thick-ly textured or minimalist synthesizer music to jazz-rock fusion. The appeal is also extremely broad, with record, tape and disc sales making the new genre an economic force with which to reckon. Artists such as William Ackerman, Steven Halpern, Kitaro, Chaitanya Hari Deuter, Andres Vollenweider, Vangelis, Jean-Michael Jarre, Paul Winter, George Zamfir and Tangerine Dream are some of the bigger names helping to make up the rapidly expanding field. The prestigious Grammy Awards as of 1987 include a category for New Age music. Where I now live (Seattle) there are two FM stations with New Age music formats which can be added to a growing number of stations around the country. One of the station's formats is repeatedly punctuated with advertisements for New Age bookstores, groups and events.

New Age music has been called "Yuppie muzak" because of its claim to soothe the souls of the upwardly mobile. Stephen Hill, director of the weekly half-hour radio program "Hearts of Space," comments that "people with boring jobs usually like exciting music; individuals with exciting jobs and complicated mental lives really need something different. This music generally appeals to people with higher education and mentally complicated jobs."[30] But there is more to it than that.

Some New Age music is intended not just to soothe the soul but to trigger a meditative change in consciousness. This could be called meditative or mystical New Age music. Steven Halpern, an innovator in New Age music with over thirty albums to his credit, has produced many albums that clearly integrate Eastern mystical practices with his music. His "Spectrum Suite" is designed to enable listeners to focus on each of the seven chakras (energy centers) in their body, which he thinks correspond to seven separate colors and sounds. Halpern says, "When the seventh and final selection begins, keynote B, focus your attention at the crown of your head. Visualize a violet color there and welcome the energy of divine consciousness."[31] Halpern's orientation and intent for his music are clear: "The term *spiritual* connotes that which is eternal and that which is most in tune and in harmony with the universal God-force that we know by so many different names. In my work, I seek to align myself with that force, and to uplift the life energies of the performer and listener in order to bring them into closer attunement with their own God-Self."[32]

Kitaro, the popular Japanese New Age performer and composer, has sold more than eight million copies of his seventeen albums. His cover art and song titles reveal the influence of oriental mysticism on his work. Rick Ingrasci comments that Kitaro's *The Light of the Spirit* (1987) album is a means "through which Kitaro says he strives to express the universal ideas about human existence, nature, and the cosmos. . . . Kitaro . . . calls himself a 'musician of the new culture.' He considers his music part of his spiritual path and sees his role as that of a cultural change agent, helping others gain a fresh outlook on the world."[33]

Other artists give away their metaphysical aspirations by their song titles, liner notes or advertisements. Consider the following description of the tape *The Eternal Om:*

The OM is all sound and silence throughout time. . . . It invokes the ALL that is otherwise inexpressible, and it is the highest spiritual sound on the earth. And now, using the latest in electronic technology, we have synthesized various pitches from human voices, and all intoning the OM together at the prescribed vibrations. In the background is an almost subliminal sounding choir.[34]

It's a choir I don't care to hear.

Another tape by Robert Slap is called *Ascension to All That Is.* A promotional blurb says that it is "a musical interpretation of ascending up through the astral planes to the seventh level—the Godhead, the Universal Mind . . . the All That Is."[35] A tape with similar ethereal aspirations is *Journey Out of the Body* by David Naegles; it claims to bring the performer's own paranormal proclivities to bear on the music which is said to induce out-of-body experiences.[36]

The above meditative/mystical tapes are called examples of "inner harmony New Age music," according to an explanatory advertisement by the Valley of the Sun New Age label (which is owned by the prominent New Age seminar leader and lecture tape distributer Dick Sutphen). Such music is described as "gentle, flowing, sustained environmental music without tension or resolve" which has been (supposedly) "scientifically proven to produce dramatic changes of consciousness" and is "ideal for altered-state-of-consciousness work." Some of these tapes also contain subliminal messages thought to break into the unconscious mind to alter one's thoughts and entire life.

This sort of music is differentiated from what Sutphen calls "progressive New Age music" which is "mellow, but high energy music that usually combines acoustical and electronic instruments" for a "stimulating, but not distracting effect." Vangelis's *Chariots of Fire* soundtrack, he says, fits this category.[37] Much of modern jazz-rock fusion might also fit this classification, music which may or not be composed and performed by people with a New Age world view.

Another category of New Age music besides progressive and meditative/mystical New Age is "Christian New Age music." The term need not necessarily frighten us, though. In the last few years several Christian record labels have released mostly instrumental albums that somewhat resemble non-Christian New Age music but with a different twist. These albums do not seem to be hypnotically repetitive, and if they are composed, performed and produced by Christians, are certainly not oriented toward inducing New Age mystical experiences. They are, rather, a combination of light jazz, folk, rock and classical music. Some pieces are even variations on standard hymns or popular choruses. Some of this material has crossed over to non-Christian New Age stations. The liner notes for guitarist/ songwriter/singer Phil Keaggy's album *The Wind and the Wheat* speak of the spiritual reflection behind each of the pieces. Although the phrase "Christian New Age music" may sometimes be used, the words themselves—although a bit incautious given the connotations—are not sufficient grounds to condemn the music. The term in this case refers to a musical style rather than to an unbiblical world view.[38]

What, then, should Christians do? Should they burn their *Chariots of Fire* album which brings back so many good memories from a film emphasizing some solid Christian virtues?

To reject categorically all music labeled "New Age" would be to once again fall prey to the taboo and quarantine mentalities. I have seen an album by Christian performer John Michael Talbot placed in the "New Age Music" section of a record store and a record catalog. This doesn't mean he is a crypto-pantheist. Much of what gets labeled as "New Age" is in the category of "progressive" New Age music—for the most part relaxing, instrumental music written and performed by people who do not necessarily have a New Age world view. This style of music could be acceptable for Christians if they find it aesthetically pleasing and edifying. It doesn't seem to pose the spiritual threat that the meditative/mystical New Age music does.

Yet to accept categorically all music labeled "New Age" would be to fall prey to the ostrich or chameleon mentalities. Much of New Age music is inspired by a pantheistic, monistic and spiritistic world view which is revealed in the music both instrumentally and vocally. Many New Age musicians and writers see their genre as a tool to advance the New Age agenda. *Newsweek* described the New Age Windham Hill artists as being tied together by "a vaguely mystical world view and a striving toward a relaxing musical mood."[39] Stephen Hill, director of the New Age radio program "Hearts of Space," heard on 220 stations, comments that "many of the artists are very sincerely and fully committed to New Age ideas and way of life."[40]

The question becomes, to what extent and in what ways will a given piece of New Age music affect the listener? A perusal of any given album, tape or compact disc can reveal clues as to whether the composer and/or performer has a mystical agenda for the music (although listening to an unidentified piece on the radio may leave this unknown). Information on specific artists gleaned from books and magazine articles can also fill in the picture. The apostle Paul says to set our minds on that which is true, noble, right, pure, lovely, excellent, or admirable (Phil 4:8). We should evaluate the music to discern whether its New Age intent and message pollutes what beauty may be present.

Paul grounds us squarely on truly spiritual music: "Let the word of Christ dwell in you richly as you teach and admonish one another with all wisdom, and as you sing psalms, hymns and spiritual songs with gratitude in your hearts to God" (Col 3:16). Music intended to flip us into a mystical state of mind doesn't seem to fit these qualifications.

If a Christian should inadvertently listen to New Age music intended to induce a mystical experience, it is not necessarily the case that the music will have this effect. Just as someone cannot be hypnotized against her will, I don't think it likely that someone can be psychically coerced into having a counterfeit mystical experience through listening to New Age music, especially if that person is indwelt by the Holy Spirit and does not seek such an experience.

We need to recognize that God can use non-Christians to create beautiful music that edifies as well as delights. Also, music may affect different people differently and we should allow for these differences in our practices. At the same time, some matters are clear. No Christian, for example, should listen to New Age music such as *The Eternal OM* (mentioned above), because to do so would be similar to entering into pagan religious practice (see 1 Cor 10:18-22); and all the meditative/mystically oriented New Age music should be viewed with suspicion.

There is a certain sphere of behavior—not condemned by Scripture—where Christians may legitimately differ on what is acceptable for them and what isn't. After a thoughtful and prayerful evaluation, people should decide what they do or don't find edifying, being careful not to cause someone else to stumble (see Rom 14).

If one is unsure, one might want to ask: What would you rather risk? Would you rather risk missing out on some potentially harmless and pleasant music out of concern for being adversely affected by a non-Christian musical influence? Or would you rather risk being adversely affected by New Age music in order not to miss out on a potentially pleasant and harmless musical experience? In other words, when in doubt, it is better to play it safe.

Careful discernment is called for in all of the areas discussed—self-image, visualization, fantasy literature, biofeedback, New Age music. We could increase the list substantially, but these examples are offered as representative test cases that help sharpen discernment skills. Particularly in the areas of biofeedback and New Age music, I do not claim to have given the final word. But I hope I have given a helpful word that will inspire others critically to evaluate these and many other areas.

The modern world presents us with a host of issues demanding Christian assessment, many of which require more than a quick, black or white judgment. To admit this is not to plead for a terminal tentativeness that never arrives at conclusions. Far from it.

Biblically oriented Christians may disagree in some areas of discernment because of various factors such as ignorance, immaturity, poor reasoning, a difference of conscience or, in some cases, outright sin. The means for dealing with disagreement should be to "speak . . . the truth in love" (Eph 4:15). Disagreements over matters such as the ones mentioned should result in discussions, not denunciations. In some matters, we must "agree to disagree agreeably."[41] One's views on New Age music are important, but not as crucial as one's views on the person of Christ or salvation. But in all things the goal should be to "take captive every thought to make it obedient to Christ" (2 Cor 10:5). Only then can Christians confront the issues raised by the New Age with truly Christian discernment.

Notes

[1]Steve Scott and Brooks Alexander, "Inner Healing," _Spiritual Counterfeits Journal_

(April 1980), p. 13.
[2]Harry Blamires, *The Christian Mind* (Ann Arbor, Mich.: Servant, 1978), p. 43.
[3]Ramtha and Douglas J. Mahr, *Voyage to the New World* (New York: Fawcett, 1987), p. 37.
[4]James Davidson Hunter, "Orthodoxy and the Challenge of Modernity," *Public Eye* 1, no. 2 (August 1987), p. 2.
[5]See William Kirk Kilpatrick, *Psychological Seduction* (Nashville: Nelson, 1983), pp. 36–88.
[6]Pascal *Pensées* 2.100.
[7]On psychological self-esteem teachings, see Jay Adams, *The Biblical View of Self-Esteem, Self-Love, Self-Image* (Eugene, Oreg.: Harvest House, 1986).
[8]Lovelace, *Dynamics,* p. 101.
[9]Augustine *City of God* 14.28.
[10]For an excellent biblical assessment of self-affirmation and self-denial see John Stott, *Cross of Christ,* pp. 274–94.
[11]Lewis, *Screwtape Letters,* pp. 74–75.
[12]Stott, *Cross of Christ,* p. 343.
[13]Don Matzat, *Inner Healing: Deliverance or Deception* (Eugene, Oreg.: Harvest House, 1987), p. 118; see also pp. 156–57. This is an excellent critique of the inner healing method.
[14]Shakti Gawain, *Creative Visualization* (New York: Bantam, 1985), pp. 70–72.
[15]A. W. Tozer, *That Incredible Christian* (Harrisburg, Pa.: Christian Publications, 1964), p. 68.
[16]Rousas John Rushdoony, *Revolt Against Maturity* (Fairfax, Va.: Thoburn, 1977), p. 84.
[17]Colin Brown, "Magic," in *The New International Dictionary of New Testament Theology,* Vol. 2, ed. Colin Brown (Grand Rapids, Mich.: Zondervan, 1976), p. 561.
[18]See John Weldon and James Bjornstad, *Playing with Fire* (Chicago, Ill.: Moody, 1984).
[19]See Schlafly, *Child Abuse in the Classroom,* pp. 69, 210.
[20]Phil Phillips, *Turmoil in the Toybox* (Lancaster, Pa.: Starburst, 1986).
[21]J. R. R. Tolkien, *The Tolkien Reader* (New York: Ballantine, 1966), p. 55; quoted in Richard Purtill, *Lord of the Elves and Eldils* (Grand Rapids, Mich.: Zondervan, 1974), p. 19.
[22]See also Henry, *God, Revelation, and Authority,* 1:44–69.
[23]Tolkien, *Tolkien Reader,* p. 55; quoted in Purtill, *Lord of the Elves,* p. 19.
[24]This does not suggest that his fiction was preachy or only apologetic in emphasis or intent. See Purtill, *Lord of the Elves,* for an elaboration of Lewis's fantasy.
[25]See Clyde S. Kilby, "Mythic and Christian Elements in Tolkien," in John Warwick Montgomery, ed., *Myth, Allegory, and Gospel* (Minneapolis: Bethany, 1974), pp. 119–43.
[26]Kenneth R. Pelletier, *Mind as Healer, Mind as Slayer* (New York: Dell, 1977), pp. 297–98.
[27]Paul Reisser, M.D., agrees with my basic assessment. See his "Holistic Health: Marcus Welby Enters the New Age," in Hoyt, *New Age Rage,* pp. 71–73.
[28]Wilson and Weldon, *Occult Shock,* pp. 224–25.
[29]See Wimber with Springer, *Power Healing.*

[30]Quoted in Richard Dinwiddie, "New Age Music: Understanding the Enigma of the New Wave in Sound," _Gloria_ 1, no. 2 (February 1987), p. 1.

[31]Steven Halpern and Louis Savary, _Sound Health_ (San Francisco: Harper and Row, 1985), p. 186.

[32]Stephen Halpern, "A Spiritual Context for Music," _The American Theosophist_ (Fall 1986), p. 311; quoted in Richard Dinwiddie, "New Age Music Theology," _Gloria_ 1, no. 3 (September 1987), p. 3.

[33]Rick Ingrasci, "A Little Light Music," _New Age Journal_ (November/December 1987), p. 71.

[34]Quoted in _Master of Life_, Issue 35, p. 38.

[35]Ibid., p. 2.

[36]Ibid., p. 39.

[37]Ibid., p. 38.

[38]On Christian New Age music see Steve Rabey, "Christian Music Enters the New Age," _Christianity Today_, February 6, 1987, pp. 52-53. Rabey, though, does not seem to take the non-Christian intention of the meditative, mystical New Age music seriously enough.

[39]Bill Barol, "Muzak for a New Age," _Newsweek_, May 13, 1985, p. 68.

[40]Quoted in Dinwiddie, "New Age Music," p. 2.

[41]For a helpful discussion of the issue of Christian freedom under Christ see Gary Friesen, _Decision Making and the Will of God_ (Portland, Oreg.: Multnomah, 1980), pp. 377-426. I do not, though, endorse everything he says on guidance.

The Future
of the
New Age

10

HAVING BROUGHT SCRIPTURE, LOGIC AND EVIDENCE TO BEAR AGAINST THE
New Age world view and having employed them in favor of biblical
Christianity, we need to consider the New Age movement's possible
future in relation to the Christian witness.

Assessing the actual cultural clout of the New Age movement is
difficult for several reasons. First, the "movement" itself is quite diverse and loosely structured organizationally, despite its fundamental
philosophical unity. Hard-and-fast analysis of its effectiveness is
problematic because there are no centralized progress reports. Rather, a general analysis of a wide variety of groups, individuals and
events must be taken into consideration.

Second, because many New Agers overstate their numbers and
effectiveness—following the imperative to be positive at all costs—
one cannot always trust their own reports of success. In an article in

The Wall Street Journal, Anthony Downs notes the tendency of three New Age-oriented books—*Megatrends* by John Naisbitt, *The Third Wave* by Alvin Toffler and *The Aquarian Conspiracy* by Marilyn Ferguson—to "mega-hype the pseudo-facts" through several methods. These "exagger-books" often make their case by these methods:

Proof by Assertion. Simplified generalizations replace factual arguments.

Proof by Anecdote or Global Gossip-Gathering. A few examples of a supposedly sweeping phenomenon are cited from around the world without probing their statistical significance.

Hyper-Extended Novelty or Exagger-trend. A barely noticeable development is prophesied to "dominate society at some unspecified later date." This is especially evident in "futurism," which vaunts speculation—if not esoteric extrapolation—as a science.[1]

Pseudo-Data. The display of distorted statistics. If John Naisbitt says that something happens in "as many as 80%" of the cases, this could mean anything from 1% to 80%.

Presumptive But Plausible Inter-relatedness. Positing an underlying, growing current of societal change at the expense of more detailed and careful analysis. Talk of "quantum leaps" and "paradigm shifts" may sometimes be more a result of wishful thinking than sound social research.[2]

Similarly, the New Age intoxication with a mystically endowed evolutionary process is inferred from insufficient data. The many problems with macro-evolutionary theory—such as the dearth of fossil evidence for transitional forms, the stasis (relative unchangeableness) of species and the radical discontinuity between humans and animals (concerning abstract thought, speech and culture formation)[3]—is conveniently ignored in favor of evolution as the engine of enlightenment, with an impersonal God somehow at the helm.

Furthermore, the idea that cultural evolution is steadily improving our lot ignores the fact that the twentieth century, despite its material and technological improvements, has been the bloodiest century in human history concerning those killed in wars and through political terror. Gil Elliot estimates that the number of human-caused deaths from 1900 through 1969 to be 110 million; he believes the twentieth century to be "incomparably . . . more violent" than previous eras. And these numbers do not include the millions killed by abortion throughout the world.[4] Evolution seems to be something of an underachiever.

The presence of New Age "exagger-books" and inaccurate views of science and history does not negate the evidence offered throughout this book that the New Age is a deep cultural trend and not a passing fad. Consider, for instance, the increasing number of New Age titles appearing in mainstream stores. In the last decade, the leading paperback publisher, Bantam books, has increased its number of New Age books by ten times and reports that they are their "fastest growing line of nonfiction books."[5] The B. Dalton Booksellers chain reported that sales on occult-related topics increased by 95% the week of the Shirley MacLaine miniseries *Out on a Limb* and continue to increase.[6] The Waldenbooks chain of stores reported a similar explosion of occult interest.[7] The phenomenon of New Age book-publishing is substantial enough for *Publishers Weekly* (Sept. 25, 1987) to dedicate an entire issue to assess it. This is no flash in the pantheistic pan. But we do need to take New Age hype with a few grains of sociological salt.

Some critics, though, have dumped whole truckloads of sociological salt over the tangible evidence of pervasive and substantial New Age influence. Some do this by seeing the decline of flamboyant guru-cults as indicative of the decline of Eastern mystical and occult ideas at large.[8] Others may have lost some faith in the New Age because it failed to win the world on time. William Irwin Thompson comments:

> In the seventies, the New Age movement expected a millenarian revelation. Looking back on the seventies, it seems as if humanity had voted overwhelmingly for a postponement of the revela-

tion. . . . The new age movement ended with Reagan and not Zen Governor Brown as the Californian President, and the spirit of the age made itself felt at every level of the culture by replacing "Star Trek" and "Kung Fu" with "Dynasty" and "Dallas," Joni Mitchell with Madonna, and "Close Encounters" with "Rambo."[9]

If the New Age movement is, above all else, a pervasive world view shift, the decline of specific cult groups and the loss of a few cultural figures does not, in itself, drastically diminish the New Age's appeal or potential. Although it is undoubtedly true that America's Judeo-Christian history and tradition is much deeper and broader than the New Age philosophy—America was founded by Christians, not Hindus or Druids—the New Age movement's cultural successes have been substantial and do tap into a pantheistic/spiritistic subculture of American life which first noticeably surfaced with Transcendentalism, Theosophy and Mind Sciences of the middle to later nineteenth century— a century before the counterculture.[10]

The New Age's cultural staying power seems largely tied to its ability to insinuate itself into the general culture by providing a unified world view and way of life for its adherents. This would involve the development of New Age organizations and even churches which would rival or surpass traditional church organizations in drawing power, cohesiveness and retention of membership. It would also involve the successful infiltration of Christian churches with New Age theology.

Noted historian Christopher Lasch sees the New Age as lacking the religious backbone to pull this off: "The indiscriminate eclecticism of these [New Age] movements provides an important clue to their lack of staying power. The mix of ingredients is too unstable to hold together, to provide a coherent explanation of things or even a coherent answer to the personal difficulties that attract adherents in the first place."[11] He adds that New Age teachings also lack a "submission to a body of teachings that has to be accepted even when it conflicts with immediate interests or inclinations and cannot constantly be redesigned to individual specifications." He thinks that the "it's true if you believe it" standard of truth is "appealing in the short run; but in the long run it works no wonders."[12]

We can only hope he is correct in his analysis that the New Age will not pan out to be a lasting social force. Yet illusion has its own appeal, and eclecticism can be unified around the old lie of self-deification. Abraham Kuyper saw the deep allure of pantheism at the turn of the century, noting that

> Pantheistic ferment is deeply seated in our sinful desires. The waters of pantheism are sweet, their religious flavor is particularly pleasant. There is spiritual intoxication in this cup, and once inebriated the soul has lost its desire for the sober clearness of the divine Word. To escape from the witchery of these pantheistic charms, one needs to be aroused by bitter experience. And once awakened, the soul is alarmed at the fearful danger to which this siren had exposed it.[13]

Further, it seems that a recent New Age strategy has been to present itself as "the true Christianity," thus adding attractiveness to those only nominally Christian or unrooted in the Bible. The occult heart of the New Age is veiled when apostates appear as apostles wearing the robes of religion.

The Devil's Due

However we weigh the above cultural factors, a major error of analysis is to incorporate pagan prophecies and propaganda into one's theology. Although we sometimes must "give the devil his due," we should never give him the pen with which to rewrite our theology. Some Christian critiques of the New Age movement—innocently enough, I'm sure—accord the hellish heralds with almost as much authority as holy writ. They do this by taking various New Age predictions, boasts or plans as definitive. But it is the Bible, not the boast of New Agers, that is fully authoritative. Brooks Alexander puts this point well: "If Alice Bailey's 'plan' is truly the blueprint for our future, it amounts to saying that demonic revelations can flesh out our understanding of divine revelation. It is giving the devil more than his due."[14]

This is not to negate the influence of the voluminous Bailey writings, but we must remember that Satan is a liar, and his "revelations" should never edge out the truth revealed in the Bible by the God who never lies (Heb 6:18). God's revealed plan is more important than Satan's rebellious one. Various occult prophecies have electrified both New Ager and (misguided) Christian alike, only to be added to the metaphysical scrap heap of falsified fancy. Witness Edgar Cayce's prognostication that Atlantis would rise again in 1968 or 69, not to mention a score of other not-so-near misses.[15] The words of Scripture still apply: "If what a prophet proclaims in the name of the LORD does not take place or come true, that is a message the LORD has not spoken. That prophet has spoken presumptuously. Do not be afraid of him" (Deut 18:22).

New Age Apocalypse Now?
Many New Agers—and purported channeled entities—prophesy an apocalyptic prelude to the New Age. Yes, the New Age of peace, light and love awaits us, but . . . we must first experience a "cleansing" or purgation of planetary problem spots. These blots on the biosphere are typically described as those "less evolved" souls who do not see "all as one" or "all as God," and who cling to "old age" notions such as sin, human finitude, the uniqueness of Jesus Christ and the need for external redemption. These sorts, New Agers sometimes claim, are hindering world peace by their separatistic emphasis. Although divine in their essence, the "underevolved" are not divine in their expression; all are God (pantheism), but seemingly some are more God—or more God-realized—than others. The God-realized ones will form the occult elite, truly fit to lead us through the apocalypse and into the New Age.[16]

These kinds of predictions have led some Christians to believe that

New Agers have a secret plan to eradicate Christians and other obstinate monotheists. The idea of the coming "cleansing" means different things to different New Agers. Some may see it as a natural process of planetary re-education for the metaphysically retarded. Others have a more violent viewpoint, but do not envision actively silencing, neutralizing or terminating the Christians. Ruth Montgomery, a pioneer New Age writer well-tutored by her (spirit) "Guides," expects a radical shifting of the earth's position sometime around the turn of the century causing a global catastrophe which "will cleanse the earth of pollution and evil people and will usher in the long-awaited New Age of a thousand years of peace."[17]

Those rare New Agers who allude to doing in—or "removing"—Christians justify these actions as being in the highest service of evolution. Several factors could contribute to this notion. First, since the New Age teaches that death is unreal, rationalizations could justify murder by viewing it as a vehicle for "re-education" in another life. Second, the idea of collective bad karma could be used against Christians who are thought to have brought it all on themselves. Moira Timms even invokes the book of Revelation by saying that "the plagues of Revelation are special packages of karma visited upon the obstinate that they might awaken to their wrong attitudes."[18] The "wrong attitudes" constitute Christian orthodoxy. Granted, this is mostly speculation on my part, but the foundational beliefs for this kind of thinking are in place.

In all this we should consider Rebecca Boren's important distinction:

> There is a material difference between expecting some kind of apocalypse—from which only those who have achieved higher consciousness will emerge unscathed—and planning to commit the apocalypse yourself. The former is a major theme of New Age thinking, the latter only appears in carefully selected extracts.

Despite her qualifications, she wisely goes on to point out, "When you combine that expectation of world destruction with reliance on direct revelation from spirit guides, and add a philosophy that embraces 'do your own thing' as a guiding principle, you are asking for trouble."[19]

She is right: the mixing of messianic and millennial enthusiasm, apocalyptic expectation, ethical relativism and occult intrigue makes for a combustible compound. There is every possibility that if the people of God do not rise up in the Spirit's power and the New Age movement does not disillusion its followers with its superstition, unfulfilled promises and exotic irrationality, it will assume an increasingly potent and sinister form marked by hostility toward its opponents and more openly demonic forms of spiritual experience such as Lucifer/serpent worship and black magic.[20]

Inasmuch as New Age thinking is based on supposedly "creating your own reality," it is, in principle, a form of occult magic or witchcraft. This fact should bring us back to the scriptural assessment of pagan magic. Rushdoony highlights this:

> Because Scripture recognizes the deadly consequences of witchcraft, it strikes at it sharply as a murderous force (Ex. 22:18; Lev. 19:26, 31; 20:6, 27; Deut. 18:10; Micah 5:12; Mal 3:5; Gal. 5:20; Rev. 21:8; 22:15). Witchcraft murders both individuals and cultures and is a deadly and anti-social force. The so-called "primitive" societies are rather degenerate societies in which envy and witchcraft have triumphed. The triumph of these evils in any culture will mark its decline into barbarism.[21]

The Kingdom of God and Eschatology

Some Christians see certain developments in modern Christianity itself as indicative of New Age influence. Scripture warns us of the acids of apostasy (1 Pet 2; Jude 4-16) and directs us toward doctrinal maturity (1 Tim 1:10; 2 Tim 3:15-17; Tit 1:9). We dealt with several "issues in discernment" in the last chapter, but here we will consider the issue of the kingdom of God and eschatology (the doctrine of things to come).

Several Christian critics have faulted other Christians for adopting a supposed "New Age" mentality toward the future which emphasizes the present-day power of God for social transformation combined with a long-term optimism. There has been much discussion of "dominion" or "kingdom theology" in this regard. Lest we slip into the quarantine, taboo, paranoid or Chicken Little mentalities, several important distinctions need to be drawn.

The New Age strives for global transformation. New Agers are long-term optimists, despite their apocalyptic tendencies. But their method of transformation is rooted in falsehood.

Simply because many Christians are now emphasizing the comprehensive nature of God's kingdom, the total lordship of Christ as it relates to all of life, and the relevance of the Bible to social, cultural and political issues, this, in itself, does absolutely nothing to identify them with the New Age. Many Christians are beginning to crawl out from their cultural cocoons and shine their light before the world, not being content to hand the world over to Satan and his minions by default. I have tried to make a case for this in chapter three. Christians are called to *transform* their culture for the glory of God. The method of transformation for the Christian is rooted in the biblical doctrine of the lordship of Christ.

Some who have not adequately recognized this transformation theme have sharply criticized Christians who seek to bring heaven to bear on earth in all walks of life.

Some of these critics have highlighted the heretical teachings of "the manifest sons of God," an aberrant Pentecostal movement which emphasizes the deification of humanity,[22] exalts purported "new revelations" over Scripture, and holds unorthodox views of Christ. People influenced by this approach have deviated from any biblical notion of transformation and deserve loving criticism based on biblical truth. But simply because these "manifest sons"—and New Agers—sound the theme of transformation doesn't mean that everyone motivated to "have dominion" (Gen 1:26-28) or to proclaim the kingdom for their King Jesus (Rev 1:5-6) is similarly infected with false doctrine.

Critics of the transformation theme have sometimes also wrongly interpreted the aims and actions of those Christians who have a burning desire to make known "the crown rights of Jesus Christ," as the Puritans powerfully put it. The critics see any effort toward cultural transformation as "worldly" attempts to usher in the kingdom through human effort, and they see this as dangerously close to New Age thinking.

But a concern to be good stewards of the creation God entrusted to us and to see his kingdom brought to bear universally is emphatically not "worldly"; it is, rather, applied spirituality. "Worldliness" is based on mere human wisdom (Col 2:8), which is opposed to God's wisdom (1 Cor 1—2; Jas 3:14-16). When he was being tried before Pilate, Jesus said, "My kingdom is not of this world" (Jn 18:36); yet this does not mean that his kingdom had nothing to do with his creation, or that it would have no success before the Second Coming. Rather, Jesus meant that the kingdom of God is not *derived* from this world; it is not based on human opinion and the traditions of men (Mt 15:1-9), but on the power and wisdom of God. If it had been based on mere human wisdom, Jesus declared, "My servants would fight to prevent my arrest by the Jews. But now my kingdom is *from* another place" (Jn 18:36). The kingdom's "mission control center" is not earth, but heaven—although the kingdom centers on earth as its mission.

Robert Culver clarifies this often misunderstood verse:

The words "of this world" translate *ek tou kosmou toutou* that is, out of this world. Source rather than realm is the sense. . . . The future consummation of the kingdom of Christ cannot be rightly said to be beyond history. No indeed! It will occur in history and is history's goal. . . . So Jesus very clearly is making no comment on either the nature of His kingdom or His realm, rather on the power and source of its establishment.[23]

After Jesus stated the source of his kingdom, he owned up to his kingship, saying to the inquiring Pilate, "You are right in saying that

I am a king. In fact, for this reason I was born, and for this I came into the world, to testify to the truth. Everyone on the side of truth listens to me" (Jn 18:37). John identifies the ascended Jesus as "the ruler of the kings of the earth" (Rev 1:5). Even from heaven, he is Lord of the earth (Mt 28:18-20).

Although those active in transforming culture for the glory of their King Jesus may occasionally lapse into fleshly self-effort, they should never believe that they are bringing in the kingdom through *human effort.* We are but instruments of God who alone has the power to declare and demonstrate his kingdom. As Paul said, "But we have this treasure in jars of clay to show that this all-surpassing power is from God and not from us" (2 Cor 4:7). Unless we abide in Christ we can do nothing of lasting value (Jn 15:1-10). We must be truly heavenly minded in order to do any earthly good.

Some critics also accuse transformation-oriented Christians of denying evangelism for the sake of social action, as if the two were mutually exclusive. Yet a balanced view of the kingdom involves both personal transformation through Christ and social transformation led by those zealous to proclaim Christ's rule. The latter flows from the former. Making people ready for heaven does not exclude encouraging them to do good works here on earth.

Tragically, some Christians think they are honoring God by condemning social action as "worldly" and by concerning themselves exclusively with evangelism. But by doing this they are really giving the devil more than his due by creating a social vacuum for him to occupy. Citizens of the kingdom are to displace the demonic, not encourage its occupation.

The chart on the following page summarizes the crucial differences between biblical and New Age views of social transformation.

The Purpose of Prophecy

Those who have overemphasized the *separation* theme view a transformation emphasis with suspicion and may lapse into the Chicken

Views of Social Transformation: Biblical and New Age

Biblical	New Age
1. For God's glory	1. For human glory
2. Authority: the Bible	2. Authority: self and spirits
3. Heavenly inspired and directed	3. Occultically inspired and directed
4. Results in God's hands	4. Results in our hands
5. Nonutopian: realistic and optimistic	5. Utopian: unrealistic and optimistic
6. Final hope: the Second Coming	6. Final hope: self-realized humanity

Little mentality, which proclaims the nearness of The End rather than working to see all people make Christ their end in all things. They may expend more effort trying to correlate biblical prophecy to the New Age movement than they do searching the Scriptures in order to present a comprehensive alternative world view adequate to confront the New Age (Rom 12:1–2). However, it is pivotal to remember that biblical prophecy is not primarily concerned with predicting the future, but with summoning people to obey the Lord.

Vernon Grounds comments that the assumption that "God's prophets were merely foretellers" is wrong.

They certainly did foretell the future, often with a specificity that can be attributed to nothing except omniscience. This is strikingly and undeniably evidenced in the messianic prediction of the Old Testament. Yet the primary responsibility of a prophet was not to function as a superior Nostradamus, foretelling what would be happening sooner or later in space-time. Primarily it was to tell-forth . . . God's truth, His ethical demands, His promises, His judgment on sinful nations including Israel, His compassion and grace. . . . As God's forthteller, the prophet's compassionate concern was to stimulate the faith, obedience, and morality of his contemporaries.[24]

Grounds laments over the "eschatologists" who tend "to reduce the magnificent phenomena of biblical prophecy to a kind of precognition which is sadly devoid of spiritual and moral impact."[25] If speculations concerning the future take the place of seriously considering the ethical demands of prophecy, much is lost. And, sadly, if we do not bring Scripture to bear on all of modern life, we leave a cultural vacuum that the New Age is only too happy to fill. Richard Mouw likewise rejects this "scorecard approach to matters of Bible prophecy, whereby the Christian seems to be little more than a passive observer checking off event after event in what he views as the prophetic scenario." He rightly sees the church as "equipped with prophetic visions in order to act responsibly *in* the present, in the confidence that God has promised the ultimate triumph of justice and righteousness."[26]

Noted Old Testament scholar Walter Kaiser emphasizes the ethical nature of prophecy by revealing that "repeatedly, the law turns up in the prophetical writings."[27] Consider just one example of ethical urgency in Isaiah: "Learn to do right! Seek justice, encourage the oppressed. Defend the cause of the fatherless, plead the case of the widow" (Is 1:17).[28] Philip Edgcumbe Hughes says that "the prophetic teaching of the New Testament is consistently presented with a strong *ethical* emphasis. It is intended, not as pabulum for mystery-mongers and puzzle-solvers, but as incentive to godly living."[29] The upshot is that biblical prophecy is chock-full of applicable ethical instruction which we ignore to our own shame, folly and peril.

Regrettably, some Christian eschatologically oriented critics of the New Age have overemphasized an apologetic against the New Age movement that looks something like this:

1. Whatever fulfills end-time biblical prophecy about forces that oppose God and his people is bad.

2. The New Age movement fulfills these end-time biblical prophecies.

3. Therefore, the New Age movement is bad.

The obvious weakness in this argument is that it rests on whether modern-day events really fulfill or confirm end-time biblical prophecy. Some have gone so far as to confidently *define* the New Age movement as the religious error that will usher in the final cataclysm. But this is incautious, and it may set up the eschatological apologist for a fall.

Martin Luther, great Reformer and student of Scripture that he was, believed that the Roman Catholic Church was the Antichrist soon to wreak havoc on earth. He identified the Turks as the devilish people of Gog and Magog, as indicated by Ezekiel. Although he didn't set dates, he thought the end was imminent. He was wrong, and so have countless others been wrong in nominating various candidates for Antichrist and in setting dates for the Second Coming.[30]

Without minimizing either the harmful effects of the New Age and its massive appeal or the veracity of biblical prophecy (properly interpreted), we should take the New Age movement with a few grains of eschatological salt as well as sociological salt, lest we be left with apocalyptic egg on our face. After surveying several centuries of false prophecies, historian Mark Noll concludes:

> The verdict of history seems clear. Great spiritual gain comes from living under the expectation of Christ's return. But wisdom and restraint are also in order. At the very least, it would be well for those in our age who predict details and dates for the End to remember how many before them have misread the signs of the times.[31]

Agreement on the Essentials

Some critics of the New Age have cast suspicion on fellow Christians who deviate from their particular interpretation of eschatology, which is usually dispensational premillennialism. This is not the place to give a detailed explanation of eschatology, but a major point should avert false accusations. The historic creeds of the Christian church have been necessarily detailed and specific on key matters such as the authority of the Bible, the nature of Christ and the doctrine of salvation, but they have never articulated a specific eschatology, besides the general belief that Jesus will "come again to judge the living and the dead," as the Apostle's Creed states.[32]

The fact that Jesus Christ will bodily and visibly descend from heaven is nonnegotiable (Acts 1:11). *That* Christ is coming is more important than *when* he is coming, and orthodox Christians throughout history have held a variety of eschatological viewpoints as to when Christ is coming. Kenneth Kantzer wisely comments,

> Too often . . . Christians have allowed eschatology to divide them. Rather than attack each others' views, we believe it would be far better to engage in a solid exegesis of the relevant scriptural passages. Honest study of the Word as it relates to each millennial view will help us understand and appreciate our own convictions as well as the beliefs of those who disagree with us.[33]

Certainly, conflicting eschatologies cannot all be correct and we should strive for maximum fidelity to what Scripture teaches; yet there is room for disagreement concerning views of the end times.[34] Nevertheless, some zealous premillennialists have charged that postmillennialism (the teaching that Christ will return to a substantially Christianized world) is somehow oriented toward the New Age or leads to collusion with New Age causes. Although any given postmillennialist could be unorthodox in aspects of his theology, the postmillennial position itself need not entail anything even remotely New Age—as can be seen by the impressive list of orthodox postmillennialists such as John Owen, Jonathan Edwards, George Whitefield, Matthew Henry, Charles Hodge, B. B. Warfield and other notable non-New Agers. Some evangelicals' ignorance of history keeps them from realizing that postmillennialism has been a major conservative theological viewpoint for centuries.[35] These considerations don't settle the matter, but they should restrain us from rashly judging other brothers and sisters in Christ.

All Christian critics of the New Age need to unite in facing a common challenge and remember that one's views of Christ are more important than one's views of the timing of Antichrist. Evangelizing the Soviet Union is more important than determining if Gog and

Magog refer to the Soviet Union. And most importantly for our concerns, unmasking and confronting the New Age is more pressing than proffering predictions.

When the disciples last saw Jesus just before his ascension into heaven, they pressed him for an eschatological detail. They asked, "Lord, are you at this time going to restore the kingdom to Israel?" Yet Jesus shifted their attention from eschatological questions to their earthly mission. He said, "It is not for you to know the times or dates the Father has set by his own authority. But you will receive power when the Holy Spirit comes on you; and you will be my witnesses in Jerusalem, and in all Judea and Samaria, and to the ends of the earth" (Acts 1:7). That same power for world-changing witness is available to Jesus' disciples today through the Holy Spirit. We dare not quench the Spirit through fruitless speculations or arguments.

Whither the New Age?
The immediate future of the New Age movement is uncertain. On the one hand, we should view its own claims to fame and fortune with some suspicion. Bragging comes naturally to those who think they can "create their own reality" irrespective of hard, stubborn, objective facts. Also, the movement itself may lack the organizational dynamics to capture the age. On the other hand, some of their bragging is tragically true; a broad-based, loosely structured but intensely visionary coalition of activists and academics, mystical adepts and marketing agents, all yearn for and strive toward a New Age. They have had their successes and aren't about to give up.

For the Christian with a passion for the Lord and the lost, there is work to be done. A balanced assessment of the New Age movement and Spirit-led thinking and activism are required to confront this spiritual counterfeit effectively. This book is offered as a tool to help motivate and mobilize Christians to that end, and to challenge the thinking of New Agers who have ears to hear and eyes to see.

Notes

[1]For a critique of futurology see Robert Nisbet, *Prejudices* (Cambridge: Harvard University Press, 1982), pp. 131-35.

[2]Anthony Down, "They Sell Sizzle, But Their Predictions Fizzle," *Wall Street Journal,* April 6, 1983.

[3]On the logic of biblical creationism see Norman Geisler and J. Kerby Anderson, *Origin Science: A Proposal for the Creation-Evolution Controversy* (Grand Rapids, Mich.: Baker, 1987).

[4]Gil Elliot, *Twentieth Century Book of the Dead* (New York: Scribners, 1972), p. 1; quoted in Gary North, *Moses and Pharaoh* (Tyler, Tex.: Institute for Christian Economics, 1985), p. 360.

[5]"Mystics on Main Street," *U.S. News & World Report,* February 9, 1987, p. 68.

[6]J. A. Trachtenberg and Edward Giltenan, "Mainstream Metaphysics," *Forbes,* June 1987, pp. 157-58.

[7]David Tuller, "New Age: An Old Subject Surges in the 80s," *Publishers Weekly,* September 25, 1987, p. 30.

[8]Richard John Neuhaus, *The Naked Public Square* (Grand Rapids, Mich.: Eerdmans, 1984), pp. 145-46.

[9]William Irwin Thompson, "A Gaian Politics," *Whole Earth Review* (Winter 1986), p. 4.

[10]On historical trends leading to the New Age movement, see Robert Burrows, "The Coming of the New Age," in Hoyt, *New Age Rage,* pp. 17-32.

[11]Christopher Lasch, "Soul of a New Age," *Omni,* October 1987, p. 80.

[12]Ibid., p. 82.

[13]Abraham Kuyper, *The Work of the Holy Spirit* (Grand Rapids, Mich.: Eerdmans, 1975), p. 328.

[14]Brooks Alexander, "The Final Threat: Apocalypse, Conspiracy, and Biblical Faith," *Spiritual Counterfeits Newsletter* (January-February 1984), p. 8.

[15]For extensive documentation see Neher, *The Psychology of Transcendence,* pp. 159-61.

[16]Texe Marrs documents these kinds of claims in his book *Dark Secrets of the New Age* (Westchester, Ill.: Crossway, 1987), pp. 136-65.

[17]Ruth Montgomery with Joanne Garland, *Ruth Montgomery: Herald of a New Age* (New York: Doubleday/Dolphin, 1986), p. 237.

[18]Moira Timms, *Prophecies and Predictions: Everyone's Guide to the Coming Changes,* pp. 57-58; quoted in Marrs, *Dark Secrets,* p. 144.

[19]Rebecca Boren, "Don't Give Me That New Age Religion," *The Seattle Weekly,* January 7-13, 1987, p. 22.

[20]See Carl A. Raschke, "Satanism and the Devolution of the 'New Religions,' " *Spiritual Counterfeits Journal* (Fall 1985), pp. 23-29.

[21]Rousas John Rushdoony, *Law and Society* (Vallecito, Calif.: Ross House, 1982), pp. 94-95.

[22]On self-deification teachings in general, see Robert M. Bowman, " 'Ye Are Gods': Orthodox and Heretical Views on the Deification of Man," *Christian Research Journal* (Winter/Spring 1987), pp. 18-22.

[23]Robert Culver, *Toward a Biblical View of Civil Government* (Chicago: Moody, 1974),

p. 195.
[24]Vernon Grounds, "The Purpose of Prophecy," *ESA Parley* 4, no. 3 (July 1987), p. 5.
[25]Ibid.
[26]Richard J. Mouw, *Politics and the Biblical Drama* (Grand Rapids, Mich.: Eerdmans, 1976), pp. 121-22.
[27]Kaiser, *Toward Old Testament Ethics*, p. 43.
[28]On the ethics of the Old Testament prophets see Heschel, *Prophets*, pp. 195-220.
[29]Philip Edgcumbe Hughes, *Interpreting Prophecy* (Grand Rapids, Mich.: Eerdmans, 1976), p. 30.
[30]See Dwight Wilson, *Armageddon Now!: The Premillenarian Response to Russia and Israel Since 1917* (Grand Rapids, Mich.: Baker, 1977).
[31]Mark Noll, "Misreading the Signs of the Times," *Christianity Today*, February 6, 1987, p. 10-I.
[32]See Harold O. J. Brown, *Heresies* (Garden City, N.Y.: Doubleday, 1984), p. 447.
[33]Kenneth S. Kantzer, "Agreement Is Not Required," *Christianity Today*, February 6, 1987, p. 13-I.
[34]For some interesting observations on the relationship of eschatology to social renewal, see Lovelace, *Dynamics*, pp. 401-35.
[35]For an introduction to postmillennialism, see John Jefferson Davis, *Christ's Victorious Kingdom* (Grand Rapids, Mich.: Baker, 1987).

Event-Specific
Evangelism

Appendix

EVENT-SPECIFIC EVANGELISM IS A KIND OF "STREET EVANGELISM" WHERE THE Christian brings the gospel directly to the non-Christian in a public manner. It is event-specific in that those evangelizing are equipped to give a Christian response to a particular event, such as a lecture or film. It applies the Word to the world in a specific way. Although it may lead to friendship evangelism, it is more of a one-time encounter.

Event-specific evangelism is not limited to reaching those in the New Age movement because it can be applied to any situation. I have participated in several New Age efforts and will try to distill some strategic points.

1. *The Materials Distributed.* Your literature should be relatively short in length, very clearly written, tactful, nonsensational and neatly produced. Slipshod tracts should be avoided. Given our litigious so-

ciety, it may be appropriate to have a lawyer look over the tract to clean up any actionable language. The content should be directly related to the event in question. If you are leafletting a lecture by a noteworthy New Ager, you should produce a tract dealing with his or her ideas or at least with New Age ideas in general. The gospel would be simply presented. A phone number should be included for comments or questions. When Scriptures are quoted or cited, a good policy is to note the chapter and verse of the text by indicating "ch." for chapter and "v." for verse. The standard reference of the chapter number followed by a colon which is followed by a number (for instance, John 3:16) may be unfamiliar to the millions of biblically illiterate people. (The text of the tract referred to in chapter one is reproduced below.)

With modern computer technology, one can produce an attractive tract without too much difficulty. For some events, previously produced materials can be used or incorporated into a new tract. The following ministries have a wide variety of tracts and materials suitable for making tracts:

Christian Research Institute, PO Box 500, San Juan Capistrano, CA 92693-0500.

Jesus People USA, 4707 N. Malden, Chicago, IL 60640.

Spiritual Counterfeits Project, P.O. Box 4308, Berkeley, CA 94704.

Watchman Fellowship: A Personal Freedom Outreach, P.O. Box 26062, St. Louis, MO 63136.

2. *Recruitment of People.* Those recruited should be somewhat knowledgeable about the issue addressed and have a concern for the lost. For eager but inexperienced evangelists, a short teaching session before the event would be helpful. Those Christians who cannot brook disagreement and controversy without agitation are not good recruits. Shouting matches make for bad evangelism.

Recruitment can be done through church bulletins and announcements, radio programs and general word of mouth. This should be done as early as possible in order to consolidate and prepare all who will be involved.

3. *Distribution Strategies.* Before leafletting any event, local laws regarding handbills should be consulted. It is not unusual for the police to be summoned during the leafletting. By mastering the relevant laws and working within them, friction can be reduced. For instance, when my group was leafletting the World Peace Event outside the Seattle Kingdome, we were told by police to back off the actual Kingdome property. Although we didn't think this was legally required, after some discussion, we complied without any loss in efficiency. Since people may try to intimidate leafletters with false information about the illegality of their efforts, it is important to know the facts and stand your ground! Once while leafletting a lecture by a noteworthy guru, I was told to leave four separate times. Each time I stood my ground by simply and calmly saying I had a legal right to do what I was doing. All the tracts were distributed.

The tracts should be distributed in a pleasant, noncoercive manner, with people preferably operating in pairs. Tracts should never be forced on anyone. Hostile responses should be taken in stride. The gospel is an offense to those who reject it, but this is no excuse for Christians being offensive. Whether the distribution of tracts should be done before or after (or at both times) an event depends on the nature of the event itself. Some event-sponsors may object to people leaving your tracts at their event; in this case leafletting would be more appropriate after the event. But the rush of people leaving an event may be too heavy to permit each person being handed a leaflet. Discretion is needed for each situation.

4. *Media Attention.* Leafletting a larger event may attract radio, television and newspaper coverage, as it did with the World Peace Event outreach. If possible, the more articulate and experienced members of the leafletting team should make statements. If this is not possible, statements should be as clear, concise and unambiguous as possible.

5. *Spiritual Warfare.* Event-specific evangelism puts you on the

frontlines of spiritual combat. Those without the full armor of God (Eph 6:10–18) are ill-equipped for the challenge. Those that are equipped can do great things for the Lord and receive great encouragement in their faith. But leafletting shouldn't even be considered without a substantial backing of prayer, both by those participating and by those enlisted to pray before, during and after the event. Several prayer warriors may choose to attend the event solely for the purpose of on-the-spot prayer.

A short time of group prayer, praise and worship before the outreach is advisable.

Event-specific evangelism is not for everyone; neither is it the best method of evangelism (because of its somewhat impersonal nature); but it can be used by the Holy Spirit to reach those who might not hear otherwise, to plant seeds and even to convert people on the spot! It is a helpful way to confront the New Age—on its own territory.

The following is the tract we used at the World Peace Event:

Peace for Planet Earth?

True peace only comes through a change of heart. Yet false paths to peace abound, leading well-intentioned souls away from the Source of true peace.

What Kind of Peace Event?

The World Peace Event is known by various names around the nation and the world and is supported by millions. It was proposed in John Randolph Price's book, *The Planetary Commission* (1984), in which he says that "the salvation of the world *does* depend on you!" (p. 31). How are we to be saved? Price envisioned global events on December 31, 1986, during which at least 50,000,000 people would harmonize their thoughts on peace and catapult the world into a New Age.

In his "World Healing Meditation," which he believes we all should affirm, he says: "I am a living Soul and the Spirit of God dwells in me, as me. I and the Father are one, and all that the Father has is mine. In Truth, I am the Christ of God" (p. 157).

Price labels as "anti-Christ" the denial of "the divinity of man" (p. 163). He believes the global event will help dissolve such errors. He also claims to be in touch with a "spirit guide" named Asher who warns him that "Nature will soon enter her cleansing cycle" in which individuals with "lower vibratory rates" will be removed from the planet *(Practical Spirituality,* pp. 18-19).

Although the World Peace Event is hailed as inter-faith and ecumenical, its mastermind, John R. Price, is anti-Christian. For him, biblical Christians are "anti-Christ" because they deny the divinity of all men. They are to be "removed" because of their "lower vibratory rate."

Most of the groups supporting the event are also New Age or New Thought or Metaphysical in orientation. In the December 10 issue of *The Daily,* the University of Washington-Seattle newspaper, René Hillis, media coordinator for the Seattle event, refers to Price's *The Planetary Commission* as inspiring the "peace" events worldwide. The Seeden Institute, the main organizer of the Seattle event, uses Price's logo (for the Quartus Foundation) on its materials. Some involved in the event may not know about Price—but they should.

The Way to True Peace

Many people believe we can save ourselves and our planet by looking within and finding our own divinity. But they are looking in the wrong place. The world needs peace, but the world itself can't give the peace it needs.

The historical record reveals that Jesus Christ diagnosed our *sickness,* not our cure, as proceeding from within! He said:

> For from within, out of men's hearts, come evil thoughts, sexual immorality, theft, murder, adultery, greed, malice, deceit, lewdness, envy, slander, arrogance and folly—Gospel of Mark, ch. 7, vv. 21-22.

The human condition cannot be solved by humans themselves, only by God—*and we are not God.* Those so deceived are but tragic impostors of deity. The prophet Ezekiel's prophecy against an ancient king makes this clear:

> In the pride of your heart you say, "I am a god; I sit on the throne of a god." . . . But you are a man and not a god, though you think you are as wise as a god—Ezekiel, ch. 28, v. 2. (See also Isaiah, ch. 14, vv. 13-15; and Romans, ch. 1, vv. 18-32).

We are made in God's image, but we are not God. The creature is not the Creator. Jesus, God made flesh, taught that all people need to come to him to be spiritually healed, for they cannot heal themselves. He said:

> It is not the healthy who need a doctor, but the sick. . . . For I have not

come to call the righteous, but sinners—Gospel of Matthew, ch. 9, vv. 12–13.

We sin whenever we disobey God's moral law summarized in the Ten Commandments. Sin is lawlessness.

But Jesus has good news. He said:

For God so loved the world that he gave his one and only Son, that whoever believes in him shall not perish but have eternal life. . . . *But whoever does not believe stands condemned already*—Gospel of John, ch. 3, vv. 16, 18.

John R. Price to the contrary, you are not "the Christ of God." Rather, we all need the one and only Christ of God to forgive us of our sins and give us life and peace. Jesus said:

I am the way and the truth and the life. No one comes to the Father except through me—Gospel of John, ch. 14, v. 6.

We all want peace. Yet the greatest counterfeit peace-broker is the human self pretending to be God. We pray you will consider the peace offered by the only "Prince of Peace" and that you will come to him by faith. Jesus said to his disciples:

Peace I leave with you; my peace I give you. I do not give to you as the world gives. Do not let your hearts be troubled and do not be afraid—Gospel of John, ch. 14, v. 27.

Produced and distributed by Probe Center Northwest and the Colossian Fellowship, Seattle, Washington.

Related Reading

All of these books are written from a Christian perspective, but I do not agree with everything presented by the authors. But on balance I believe each book is worth considering and will help increase one's understanding of the New Age movement and how to respond to it intelligently. For books related to other aspects of the New Age not treated in depth here, please see the bibliography in *Unmasking the New Age*.

General Christian Critiques of the New Age

Dave Breese. *Know the Marks of Cults*. Wheaton, Ill.: Victor Books, 1986. Although not specifically about the New Age, this short, readable book lists "the twelve basic errors of false religion."

Gary DeMar and Peter Leithart. *The Reduction of Christianity*. Ft. Worth, Tex.: Dominion Press, 1988. A lengthy and thorough response to Dave Hunt's *Seduction of Christianity*. Develops a positive, Christian view of culture.

Ronald Enroth. *The Lure of the Cults and New Religions*. Downers Grove, Ill.: InterVarsity Press, 1987. Excellent introduction to cult beliefs and techniques, many of which relate to the New Age movement.

Ronald Enroth, ed. *A Guide to Cults and New Religions*. Downers Grove, Ill.: InterVarsity Press, 1983. Chapters by various authors on traditional and

224

new religious groups such as Transcendental Meditation, est, Rajneesh and others.

Ajith Fernando. *The Christian's Attitude toward World Religions.* Wheaton, Ill.: Tyndale, 1987. Although not specifically about the New Age, it takes Paul's Mars Hill sermon as a guide for encountering those in non-Christian religions.

Douglas R. Groothuis. *Unmasking the New Age.* Downers Grove, Ill.: InterVarsity Press, 1986. Shows New Age influences in many aspects of culture and offers a biblical response. See also the booklet *The New Age Movement* (IVP) for a condensed treatment.

Irving Hexham and Karla Poewe. *Understanding Cults and New Religions.* Grand Rapids, Mich.: Eerdmans, 1986. Good, scholarly overview of the theological, psychological and sociological dynamics of new religious movements.

Dave Hunt and T. A. McMahon. *The Seduction of Christianity.* Eugene, Oreg.: Harvest House, 1985. Shows New Age infiltration into the church, but is a mixed effort. Sometimes on target in spotting heresy; sometimes a bit too heavy-handed. See DeMar's *Reduction.*

Karen Hoyt, ed. *The New Age Rage.* Old Tappan, N.J.: Revell, 1987. Contains two excellent introductory chapters plus a collection of thoughtful essays on New Age themes such as holistic health, politics and psychology. Highly recommended.

Gary North. *Unholy Spirits.* Ft. Worth, Tex.: Dominion Press, 1986. A large, in-depth analysis of the New Age phenomenon. An updated and expanded version of *None Dare Call It Witchcraft* (1976).

Paul C. Reisser, Teri K. Reisser and John Weldon. *New Age Medicine.* Downers Grove, Ill.: InterVarsity Press, 1987. An excellent critique of holistic health practices and their roots.

James W. Sire. *The Universe Next Door.* 2d ed. Downers Grove, Ill.: InterVarsity Press, 1988. Compares the Christian world view with others including Eastern pantheistic monism and the New Consciousness. Very helpful.

James W. Sire. *Scripture Twisting.* Downers Grove, Ill.: InterVarsity Press, 1980. Carefully examines twenty ways non-Christian religious groups misinterpret the Bible.

F. LaGard Smith. *Out on a Broken Limb.* Eugene, Oreg.: Harvest House, 1986. A popularly written critique of Shirley MacLaine's New Age viewpoints.

Clifford Wilson and John Weldon. *Occult Shock and Psychic Forces.* San Diego, Calif.: Master Books, 1980. Encyclopedic treatment of many aspects of occult and New Age thinking and practices.

Spiritual Discernment and Warfare

Mark Bubeck. *Overcoming the Adversary.* Chicago: Moody Press, 1984. Born of practical experience and biblical investigation, Bubeck gives sound advice on defeating the demonic through putting on the full armor of God.

Kurt Koch. *Occult ABC.* Grand Rapids, Mich.: Literature Mission Aglasterhausen, 1983. Koch, a long-time counselor and writer on occult subjects, critiques a host of occult practices, ideas, and movements. Also deals with deliverance.

Kurt Koch. *Christian Counseling and Occultism.* Grand Rapids, Mich.: Kregel, 1981. A thorough and scholarly investigation of the occult and paranormal.

Andre Kole. *Miracles or Magic?* Eugene, Oreg: Harvest House, 1987. A Christian illusionist looks at the paranormal claims of the New Age and finds more magic than miracle.

Danny Korem and Paul Meier. *The Fakers.* Grand Rapids, Mich.: Baker, 1980. A Christian illusionist and psychologist argue that many paranormal claims are not truly miraculous.

C. S. Lewis. *The Screwtape Letters.* Old Tappan, N.J.: Revell, 1976. Classic literary treatment of the dynamics of demonic deception.

Don Matzat. *Inner Healing.* Eugene, Oreg.: Harvest House, 1987. A careful and critical look at inner healing.

Eric Pement. *The 1988 Directory of Cult Research Organizations.* Available from Cornerstone Press, 4707 N. Malden St., Chicago, IL 60640. A unique resource for locating cult-research organizations both nationally and internationally. Updated yearly.

"Spiritism: the Medium and the Message." *Spiritual Counterfeits Project Journal* 7, no. 1, 1987. An excellent, in-depth analysis of the pseudo-Christian, New Age document *A Course in Miracles* which is claimed to be channeled writing.

John Weldon and James Bjornstad. *Playing with Fire.* Chicago: Moody, 1984. A critical investigation of occult-oriented fantasy role-playing games such as Dungeons and Dragons.

John Wimber with Kevin Springer. *Power Healing.* San Francisco: Harper and Row, 1987. Develops a sane theology for healing and spiritual warfare wedded to a practical emphasis. I disagree somewhat, though, with the chapter on inner healing.

Christianity and Culture
Gary DeMar. *God and Government.* 3 vols. Atlanta: American Vision, 1982–86. A broad-ranging application of biblical principles to many aspects of culture. Workbook format.

Os Guinness. *The Gravedigger File.* Downers Grove, Ill.: InterVarsity Press, 1983. An insightful look at the social realities of modern society and the

Christian's response to them. Distills and creatively applies a wealth of sociological material.

Richard J. Mouw. *When the Kings Come Marching In.* Grand Rapids, Mich.: Eerdmans, 1983. A short, provocative, biblical and theological study of common grace in culture. Emphasizes the conservation and transformation themes.

Herbert Schlossberg and Marvin Olasky. *Turning Point: A Christian Worldview Declaration.* Westchester, Ill.: Crossway, 1987. Calls Christians to develop a Christian world view and practical responses to modern culture. Gives encouraging examples to emulate.

Henry R. Van Til. *The Calvinist Concept of Culture.* Grand Rapids, Mich.: Baker, 1959. Classic survey of the views of Calvin, Kuyper and others.

Robert Webber. *The Secular Saint.* Grand Rapids, Mich.: Zondervan, 1979. Surveys various Christian views of culture.

Reliability of the Bible

F. F. Bruce. *The New Testament Documents: Are They Reliable?* 5th ed. Downers Grove, Ill.: InterVarsity Press, 1960. The answer is yes. A standard introductory work by a noted scholar.

J. Edgar Goodspeed. *Modern Apocrypha.* Boston: Beacon Press, 1956. Debunks nonbiblical "other gospels," some of which New Agers appeal to as authentic.

Gary R. Habermas. *Ancient Evidence for the Life of Jesus.* Nashville: Nelson, 1984. Examines extrabiblical material that helps corroborate the New Testament. Refutes some of the nonbiblical views of Jesus often cited by New Agers.

R. Laird Harris. *The Inspiration and Canonicity of the Bible.* Grand Rapids, Mich.: Zondervan, 1975. A substantial, scholarly treatment.

John Warwick Montgomery. *History and Christianity.* Downers Grove, Ill.: InterVarsity Press, 1972. Short work with compelling reasons to trust the New Testament.

Reincarnation

Mark Albrecht. *Reincarnation: A Christian Critique of a New Age Doctrine.* Downers Grove, Ill.: InterVarsity Press, 1987. An excellent critique, especially helpful in exploding the myth that the Bible teaches or at one time taught reincarnation.

Norman L. Geisler and J. Yutaka Amano. *The Reincarnation Sensation.* Wheaton, Ill.: Tyndale, 1986. Thorough biblical and logical refutation. Covers a variety of reincarnational models.

Robert A. Morey. *Reincarnation and Christianity.* Minneapolis: Bethany

House, 1980. A helpful pamphlet.

John Snyder. *Reincarnation vs. Resurrection.* Chicago: Moody, 1984. A short, but carefully argued analysis.

The Uniqueness of Jesus Christ

Jon Buell and Quentin Hyder. *Jesus: Ghost, God, or Guru.* Grand Rapids, Mich.: Zondervan/Probe, 1978. Short, but convincing argument for the unique deity of Christ.

John Stott. *The Authentic Jesus.* Downers Grove, Ill.: InterVarsity Press, 1985. A short but tightly argued book that defends the biblical view of Jesus.

John Stott. *The Cross of Christ.* Downers Grove, Ill.: InterVarsity Press, 1986. A masterpiece on the atoning work of Jesus Christ.

Education

Samuel L. Blumenfeld. *NEA: Trojan Horse in American Education.* Boise, Idaho: Paradigm, 1984. Chronicles the history and influence of the NEA.

Mel and Norma Gabler. *What Are They Teaching Our Children?* Wheaton, Ill.: Victor Books, 1985. Information and advice from two of America's leading textbook critics.

Rousas J. Rushdoony. *The Messianic Character of American Education.* Nutley, N.J.: Craig Press, 1963. Documents anti-Christian elements in American state education.

Phyllis Schlafly, ed. *Child Abuse in the Classroom.* Westchester, Ill.: Crossway, 1984. Testimonies of harmful influences in state schools. Contains suggestions on dealing with the problem.

Paul C. Vitz. *Censorship.* Ann Arbor, Mich.: Servant, 1986. Documents the evidence of bias in state textbooks.

Business

Spiritual Fitness in Business Newsletter. A monthly publication applying Christian principles to the business world. Available from Probe Ministries, 1900 Firman Drive, Suite 100, Richardson, TX 75081.

R. C. Sproul. *Stronger than Steel: The Wayne Alderson Story.* San Francisco: Harper and Row, 1980. The inspiring story of a courageous Christian activist in business.

Index